ANIMATED FILM AND DISABILITY

ANIMATED FILM AND DISABILITY

Cripping Spectatorship

SLAVA GREENBERG

INDIANA UNIVERSITY PRESS

This book is a publication of

Indiana University Press
Office of Scholarly Publishing
Herman B Wells Library 350
1320 East 10th Street
Bloomington, Indiana 47405 USA

iupress.org

© 2022 by Slava Greenberg

All rights reserved
No part of this book may be reproduced or utilized in any form or by any means, electronic or mechanical, including photocopying and recording, or by any information storage and retrieval system, without permission in writing from the publisher. The paper used in this publication meets the minimum requirements of the American National Standard for Information Sciences—Permanence of Paper for Printed Library Materials, ANSI Z39.48–1992.

Manufactured in the United States of America

First printing 2022

Cataloging is available from the Library of Congress.

ISBN 978-0-253-06449-3 (hardback)
ISBN 978-0-253-06450-9 (paperback)
ISBN 978-0-253-06451-6 (e-book)

© Elizabeth Swados, *My Depression: The Up and Down and Up of It* 2014

CONTENTS

Preface: Call Me Trans Crip vii

Acknowledgments xiii

Introduction: Animation, Disability, and Spectatorship   1

1. Resisting the Ableist Gaze: Between Mainstream and Experimental Forms   30
2. Embodying Spectatorship: Intersubjective Ways of Being-in-the-World   68
3. Blinding the Spectator: Non-Vision-Centric Pleasures   97
4. Deafening the Spectator: Rethinking Sonic Pleasures and Audism   125
5. Toward Accessible Spectatorships   159

Bibliography 173

Filmography 187

Index 191

PREFACE: CALL ME TRANS CRIP

[TW: Please note that this text contains a mention of a suicide attempt and discussion of psychiatric violence. Discretion is advised.]

WHEN I WAS IN HIGH school, one of my closest friends was coping with depression and swallowed some pills. After getting her stomach pumped at the ER, she accepted being voluntary committed to a psychiatric hospital. This commitment turned from voluntary to involuntary, and it took her longer than expected to get out. During her time there, she was forced to endure humiliating and dehumanizing practices—policing of nonheteronormative desires, solitary confinement as punishment for disobedience, prevention of visitations, and more. Seeking an external perspective, as well as a desire to share what was going on behind closed doors with the rest of the world, she asked me to make a film about the violence of institutionalization.[1]

I pretended to be her cousin—as visitations were only granted to family members—and came to visit with a camcorder hidden in my backpack. While we were sitting alone on her hospital bed, with the door closed, she asked me to document our conversation. I had been warned by people in white robes not to take any photos and was scared of getting caught. My unrealistic fear was that the punishment would be getting locked up there too. I ended up making a short film out of a single late-night conversation we had during one of her visits home. It was a grainy, green, night vision sequence juxtaposed with digitally manipulated breaking glass objects in slow motion or played in rewind. At her request, it was never publicly screened. This was the moment where I first discovered my desire to find nonindexical, realist, or objective ways of showing and telling without taking the privilege of visibility for granted.

At the same time and on a different level, the panic I experienced in that hospital was not quite tangible to me at the time and lingered on for years. I had already been diagnosed with ADHD and dyscalculia and experienced anxiety, and it could also be the gender dysphoria I did not have the language to articulate, but the irrational fear of being omitted seems more generational or communal rather than my own trauma.

Fifteen years later, I found myself at a psychiatrist's hospital office, being interrogated as part of my gender-affirmation process, or rather attempting to get my insurance to pay for top surgery. I had contacted the Gender Reassignment Committee at Tel Hashomer Sheba Medical Center to seek funding for my top surgery. After a phone conversation with the committee's secretary, I received a letter stating: "1. The above-mentioned patient has been/is under diagnosis in the psychiatric clinic at Tel Hashomer Sheba Hospital. 2. He/she has been diagnosed as suffering from the following diagnosis according to ICD-10 [International Statistical Classification of Diseases and Related Health Problems]: F-64." This code stands for "gender identity disorder," a condition removed from the *Diagnostic and Statistical Manual (DSM)* in 2013.[2] At my meeting with the psychiatrist, I was mostly preoccupied with the diagnostic process—how did my mere self-identification as trans classified me as having a personality and behavior disorder? Not only was I diagnosed over the phone, but it was based on an outdated version of the *DSM* because it had already been renamed "gender dysphoria" in *DSM-V*. After this encounter, I began thinking about the necessity of coalitions between the trans and disability rights movements. The trans community could greatly benefit from learning more about the significant knowledge and experience the Mad Pride movement had already gained over years of activism. After all, we face similar histories and presents of stigmatization. We depend on the same oppressive psychiatric diagnostic process to be able to access treatment, often being gaslighted in the process, while also taking the risk of being marginalized or becoming outcast by that same psychiatric label.

However, I believe it is not only the Mad Pride movement that trans advocates need to pay attention to but also the overall disability rights movement. One specific case might illustrate what I mean here. Some five years ago, two colleagues of mine managed to get gender-neutral restrooms approved in their buildings on campus. Using this precedent, I then wrote the dean with the same request for the building I worked in. Shortly after, a new sign appeared on the door of the only accessible single-stall restroom in the building: the feminine and masculine figures, next to a figure in a wheelchair.

At the time, the sign seemed revolutionary to me, like the symbol for crip, trans, gender-nonconforming solidarity; here we were, trans, gender-nonconforming people and people with disabilities occupying the same space. Enthusiastic about the new sign, I took a selfie with it and posted it on my social media account. However, I did not even consider the possible consequences. A filmmaker with a disability, commented on the photo: "I cannot believe YOU of all people would do that." For her, I should have known better than to turn the only accessible stall in the building into an even busier one. During our conversation, I was angry about the exclusion from the Americans with Disabilities Act (ADA) that would have made clear the similar needs of our communities in access to restrooms as well as other accommodations. I was dreaming of a future where all stalls are accessible and gender-neutral and she was thinking of the worsening of conditions in the present. I was not able to change her mind because the accessible restroom is still a relatively fresh victory and there is no guarantee it will be permanent. However, another reason for her justified anger is that our struggles have been segregated for so long, and we have internalized that when public spaces accommodate our needs, it is not a rule but rather an exception and thus something fragile that may be easily taken away and cannot be shared. A recent visit to a Palm Springs restaurant's restroom shed a new light on a surprising mutual necessity for an accessible stall. As I approached the bathrooms, I saw two doors; the one right in front of me had a brown rectangle sign with only the word *MEN* in white bold letters, and the one on the left had a brown triangle with a masculine symbol, and the disability symbol on top, and a the word *MEN* below. I was in a hurry to go in and only noticed that there was an accessible bathroom on the left and walked into the one right in front of me. When I opened the door and found a rather large stall with a single urinal and a sink, I had no choice but to use what was apparently the wheelchair- and trans-accessible men's stall.

In her thought-provoking *Feminist Queer Crip*, Alison Kafer uses "the toilet" as both a physical space and a potential political meeting point between disability and trans research and activism: "Recognizing bathroom access as a site for coalition building can potentially move us beyond the physical space of bathrooms, turning our critical attention to acts of elimination that occur beyond the socially sanctioned space of the toilet, public or private." However, trans people were explicitly excluded from coverage under the ADA. This is despite the potential for coalitions and solidarities between trans people and people with disabilities and despite the fact that gender dysphoria is still classified in the latest *DSM 5 Revisions* of March 2022. Thus, "attending to the space of the toilet not only makes room for coalitions between trans and disability concerns, it continues the crip theory move of keeping the meanings and parameters of disability, access."[3] The toilet is an example of a political sphere binding the body to space and forcing a shift in perception.

The year Kafer published these words, "gender identity disorder" was finally removed from the *DSM*. At the same time, debates about bathroom use became a bone of public contention between US Democrats and Republicans. Approaching the terrain of disability studies without marking that closeness,[4] Jack Halberstam also refers to the bathroom debate. He describes it as part of the denial of "trans* access to public facilities" and, in a way, reads the addition of "gender dysphoria" to *DSM-V* as part of the social model of disability.[5] He writes: "As with past definitions of LGT identities, there is no accounting here for the fact that a person's distress over their gender identity may be the result of social exclusion, family violence, or reduced employment opportunities rather than of struggle with gender identification."[6] It seems that the trans and gender-nonconforming movement and research can no longer overlook the disability rights movements and crip theory.

Here I briefly cover some phenomenological experiences that trans people and people with disabilities share both physically and mentally. These occur not only because we face very similar types of marginalization. We also share chronic pain (before/after/regardless of gender-affirming medical procedures), the use of prosthetics, sensations of phantom limbs, and dependence on medical and psychiatric diagnosis to access treatment.[7] Unveiling these connections is the focus of my next book centering on Gender Dysphoria; however, the relations between trans and disability experiences that I was aware of at the time were what drew me to investigate the transformative opportunities provided by animation.

After two decades of activism from the margins—participating in "old-fashioned" demonstrations and writing op-eds, as well as more creative forms of social change—I have reached a burned-out, pessimistic conclusion that "changing someone's mind," even if desirable, is impossible. However, providing a glimpse into another point of view can force people into self-reflection. I was so emotionally engaged in a screening of the tearjerker *CODA* (Siân Heder, 2021), laughing and crying through my mask, but this was quite effectively disrupted by a single moment reflecting (or rather echoing) my hearing privilege back at me. A film about a child of deaf adults who is passionate about singing luring hearing audience members through audio pleasures risks using deafness as means to intensify the melodramatic conflict; however, *CODA* makes an exception and for a moment provides the audio perspective—or audibility, as termed by Pooja Rangan—of the deaf parents (played by Marlee Matlin and Troy Kotsur) and brother (Daniel Durant) on the same emotionally loaded singing performance scene.[8] This audition at its best may ruin the audist and ableist pleasures of the film.

Altering spectators' perception of the world—forcing a new perspective, offering estrangement—has long been the main agenda of avant-garde cinema. Filmmakers like Sergei Eisenstein and Dziga Vertov have experimented and debated the various ways images can touch bodies, attack senses, bypass intellectual constructs, and move audiences. I agree with Halberstam that "in the contemporary climate of crude literalism even social satire seems risky" but even more so his contention that "it is *only* in the realm of animation that we actually find the alternative hiding."[9] Indeed, current revolutionary activity has been taken up by animators, especially those stretching the boundaries of conventional spectatorship.

Film theoretician Vivian Sobchack offers an "intimate laboratory" through which she theorizes the phenomenological autobiography of being-in-the-world with a disability. Her body's transformations and shifting intentionalities position the disabled body closer to the renewed awareness that phenomenological philosophy strives to achieve. Sharing her vocabulary, perception, and articulation of disabled embodiment, even without stating it as such, she provided film and disability studies scholars with a philosophical methodology that stretches disciplinary boundaries.[10] Perhaps this is because gender-nonconforming and crip people do not have the privilege of overlooking the phenomenology of our bodies; it has been argued that embodied awareness is forced on us. In turn, this heighted sense of an external limit evokes an embodied spectatorship in which we cannot simply "watch" and "listen" without involving all parts and senses of our bodies. My analysis is mainly inspired by Sobchack's theory and is based in the ways animation speaks to my body and all its senses, phantom parts, scars, and pains, being attentive to the particular body doing this reading.

"Watching" *Animated Minds* (Andy Glynne, 2003–2018), *Orgesticulanismus* (Mathieu Labaye, 2008), or *Rocks in My Pockets* (Signe Baumane, 2014) for the first time repositioned my body in space and shifted my sense of being-in-the-world. Crip animation redefined my notions of filmic "spectatorship," rendering the words *viewing* and *listening* as too narrow. Such animated films force an embodied shift in perception by distancing us from former cinematic conventions and structures, *DSMs* and *ADAs*. By immersing viewers in a temporary alternative for some and affirming for others bodily experience, this emergent cinematography introduces an entirely new spectatorship in film history.

Animation, much like speculative media—a broad umbrella category that includes any nonrealist representation such as science fiction, fantasy, magical realism, ghost stories, horror, futuristic tales, and alternative histories—as read by Sami Schalk includes infinite possibilities and allows "both desirable and frightening ones—in order to comment upon, challenge or critique contemporary realist concerns." The imagining of alternative worlds is an important practice for those who have been marginalized and oppressed historically and contemporarily, as groups and individuals. Despite an increasing number of writers from marginalized groups producing new speculative media, many of whom have similarly increased the number of disabled and racial minority characters in speculative literature, film, and television, producers of these alternate worlds are still steeped in the many social systems of oppression currently operating in the world.[11] This form of spectatorship has a transformative potential not only for films about disabilities but also for mainstream cinema. *Animated Film and Disability* argues that crip animation promotes the development of artistic styles that seek to disrupt the traditional forms of the medium, evoking disorientation in spectators. It does so by focusing on representations of inner states of bodyminds and subjective perspectives of disability.[12] The book interrogates the possibilities of spectatorship—immersion in films that shudder the senses and disorient their physical comfort—in reflexively evoking our awareness of our bodies.

ACKNOWLEDGMENTS

THIS BOOK IS THE RESULT of my search for the meanings of what I first experienced during a screening of *Animated Minds* in Michael Renov's avant-garde documentary course in 2012. Renov's focus on the documentary subject, as well as his generous guidance and support, inspired this project, and for this I am grateful.

Thank you to my colleagues and friends at the Steve Tisch School at Tel Aviv University. Their comradery, advice, and encouragement during the years of my PhD allowed me to write this book. Thank you to Anat Zanger, Boaz Hagin, Raz Yosef, Dan Chyutin, Ohad Landesman, Yaara Ozery, Nir Ferber, Yael Levy, Ori Levin, Itay Harlap, and Pablo Utin. I am especially grateful to Iris Rachamimov for her continuous support, encouragement, and friendship.

The excitement and curiosity of the students in my "Critically Crip: Film and Disability," "Global Disability Media," and "Embodiment, Disability, Gender" courses over the years were an energizing force much needed to sustain the project.

The time spent researching for this project was afforded to me through the kind support of several bodies. Thank you to the David and Yolanda Katz Faculty of the Arts, the Sara and Dr. David Orgler Humanities and Arts Doctoral Scholarship for excellent PhD students in the Humanities at Tel Aviv University, and the Steve Tisch School of Film and Television Scholarship Committee for the grant.

The conversations I have had over the years at conferences, through cowriting, over coffee and cocktails, and in writing groups (both in person and over Zoom) have greatly shaped my thinking about this book. In particular, I am grateful for dialogues with disability studies scholars, artists, activists, and friends nili Broyer, Mariela Yabo, Rona Soffer, Doron Dorfman, Carrie Sandahl, Jim LeBrecht, Eunjung Kim, Octavian Robinson, Akemi Nishida, Tanya Titchkosky, Eliza Chandler, Jay Dolmage, and Alison Kafer.

Thanks to the labor of the organizers of unique disability film and media conferences, I was able to think through the opportunities that intersections between disability studies and film may offer. Thank you to the organizers of the Documentary and (Dis)Ability Conference at the University of Surrey in September 2013 (organized by Catalin Brylla and Helen Hughes), the Rethinking Disability on Screen Symposium at York University (May 2015), and the Crip Futurities: The Then and There of Disability Studies Conference at the University of Michigan, Ann Arbor (February 2016).

My ongoing conversations with colleagues, in inspired and informed panels at film and media studies conferences, continue to enrich and challenge my thought processes and writing. I am grateful to Catalin Brylla, Phoebe Hart, and Linnéa Hussein for our exchange through the Visible Evidence panel Documentary and Disability (August 2017); to Laura U. Marks, Allison R. Ross, and Kathleen McHugh in our Society for Cinema and Media Studies (SCMS) annual 2018 conference (titled "Cripping Film and Theory: What Can We Learn about Spectatorship from Disability Studies"); to Chris Straayer, Erica Rand, and Phoebe Hart through our panel discussion (titled "Trans Queer Crip: Explorations of Cinematic Transformations") at SCMS 2019 and for their overall support and friendship over the years; to Bill Kirkpatrick, Octavian Robinson, and Frank Vito Mondelli through our panel ("Transforming Bodies: Film, Disability, and Embodiment") at SCMS 2021; and to Neta Alexander, Pooja Rangan, and Jonathan Sterne through our panel (titled "From 'Disemediation' to 'Unmediation': Cripping Spectatorship and Listenership") at SCMS 2022.

I am grateful for the sponsorship of the Queer and Trans SCMS Caucus in both these latter years and for the ongoing support of its board and members. In particular, I am grateful to Kyle Stevens for his mentorship Chris Holmlund, Eliza Steinbock, Rox Samer, Cáel M. Keegan, and Victor Fan for their support. I am thankful to nili Broyer, Ilana Szobel, and Osnat Yehezkel-Lahat's rigorous study of the dramatic possibilities of the hospital. In particular, I was much assisted by our conversation through the "Anticlimax of the Hospital Drama: Gender, Reproduction, and Sexuality" panel at the Society for Disability Studies' annual conference (April 2021) and "Accessing Disability Media" (April 2022).

I am also grateful to others (too many to mention) who have made comments and suggestions and exposed me to new work. In particular, my thanks go to Annabelle Honess Roe for introducing me to Shira Avni's films at the Approaching Animation: Critical Enquiries into Art, Artists, and Industry Conference at St. Andrews University (April 2014).

I am thankful to my partners in the University of Southern California School of Cinematic Arts Disability Caucus initiated by Howard Emanuel and collaboratively led by Evan Hughes Beverley Neufeld, and myself. The caucus aims to create a taskforce for improving accessibility in our community, providing resources, and making crip experience valuable in a school that trains a significant portion of the film and television industries.

I am grateful to Shiri Eisner, who has done an incredible translation and editing job on this book and skillfully improved my communication with readers in various stages of this project. I am also grateful for the support of Laura Horak and her writing accountability group. I owe particular thanks to Jennifer Tyburczy, Dale Spencer, Erica Rand, and Kester Dyer, who cushioned my revisions process. I am also thankful to Indiana University Press editor Allison Blair Chaplin for her open communication and advocacy for this project.

I am grateful to the animators whose works are discussed in this book for providing their permission to include images from their works. In particular, I thank Signe Baumane, Shira Avni, Petra Tolley and her family, Mathieu Labaye, Samantha Moore, Yoav Brill, Dan Monceaux, Rosalind Lichter on behalf of Elizabeth Swados, and many others who have not been included but continue to create anti-ableist transformative animated films. I also thank the institutions and individuals who funded these works, such as the National Film Board of Canada, for their permission to use their images in this book.

I dedicate this book to my love, Revital Kishinevsky (and our Sasha), without whose endless support, critique, advice, and care this book could not have been written.

NOTES

1. For more on subject of disability and institutionalization, see Liat Ben-Moshe's work and, in particular, her most recent book, *Decarcerating Disability: Deinstitutionalization and Prison Abolition* (Minneapolis: Minnesota University Press, 2020).

2. The *Diagnostic and Statistical Manual of Mental Disorders* is compiled by the American Psychiatric Association. Shifts in diagnostic categories are most apparent in LGBTQ identities. While "homosexuality" was removed in 1987, it was not until 2013 that "gender identity disorder" was changed to "gender dysphoria" (applying to both trans and intersex identities). Please see chapter 2.

3. Alison Kafer, *Feminist, Queer, Crip* (Bloomington: Indiana University Press, 2013), 157.

4. As pointed out by Alison Kafer and Ellen Samuels.

5. For an elaboration about the social model of disability, please see the introduction.

6. J. Jack Halberstam, *Trans*: A Quick and Quirky Account of Gender Variability* (Oakland: University of California Press, 2018), 46–47.

7. See Alexandre Baril and Jake Pyne in the introduction to this book. Also, in two recent articles, Chris Straayer introduces transmasculine phenomenological experiences with what was previously considered an exclusively disabled perception. See: "Trans Men's Stealth Aesthetics: Navigating Penile Prosthetics and 'Gender Fraud,'" *Journal of Visual Culture* 19, no. 2 (2020): 254–271, and "Phantom Penis: Extrapolating Neuroscience and Employing Imagination for Trans Male Sexual Embodiment," *Studies in Gender and Sexuality* 21, no. 4 (2020): 251–279.

8. Pooja Rangan, "Audibilities: Voice and Listening in the Penumbra of Documentary—An Introduction," *Discourse* 39, no. 3 (2017): 279–291.

9. J. Jack Halberstam, *The Queer Art of Failure* (Durham, NC: Duke University Press, 2011), 22–23.

10. For an elaboration on Sobchack's contribution to disability studies, please see Slava Greenberg, "Stories Our Bodies Tell: The Phenomenology of Anecdotes, Comings Out, and Embodied Autoethnographies," *Review of Disability Studies: International Journal* 14, no. 4 (2018): 1–16.

11. Sami Schalk, "Resisting Erasure: Reading (Dis)Ability and Race in Speculative Media," in *The Routledge Companion to Disability Studies*, ed. Katie Ellis, Gerard Goggin, Beth Haller, and Rosemary Curtis (New York: Routledge, 2020), 143–144.

12. Margaret Price first coined the term "bodymind"—a combination that acknowledges that mental and physical processes tend to act as one—in her groundbreaking *Mad at School: Rhetorics of Mental Disability and Academic Life* (Ann Arbor: University of Michigan Press, 2011) and further developed it in "The Bodymind Problem and the Possibilities of Pain," *Hypatia* 30, no. 1 (2015): 268–284. Sami Schalk expanded the term to explain the psychic stress of oppression that has lasting mental and physical manifestations of people of color and people with disabilities in her *Bodyminds Reimagined: (Dis)ability, Race, and Gender in Black Women's Speculative Fiction* (Durham, NC: Duke University Press, 2018).

ANIMATED FILM
AND DISABILITY

INTRODUCTION

Animation, Disability, and Spectatorship

THE SHORT ANIMATED FILM *ORGESTICULANISMUS* (2008) was directed by Mathieu Labaye about his father. This film offers animation not just as a means of expression for the inner world of a person with a disability but also as a tool for stretching the boundaries of our perceptions about bodies and movement. This film gradually transitions from the stifling monotony of indexical or realistic representations of the body to the endless possibilities of animation. This emphasis placed on mundane physical experiences, out of the subjectivity that experienced them, is characteristic of Labaye's work.[1]

This animated documentary is divided into three parts, containing three sound tracks with the voice of the director's father, Benoît Labaye. Benoît began using a wheelchair following a series of strokes and continued to do so until his death. The first part of the animation relies on a series of indexical still photos of Benoît. The second part emphasizes phenomenological experiences of daily movements while exposing the mechanical aspects of producing motion in animation. The third part transgresses the cinematic conventions of representations of the physical body, offering the movement allowed through the imagination as realized in animation. *Orgesticulanismus* suggests that the indexical or realistic representation of the body, in and of itself, limits the possibilities of movement allowed through imagination and animation. This reflexive treatment of the process of animation creation, and the ways it creates alternative worlds, is characteristic of animation in general—and, in particular, of animation relying on the subjectivity of people with disabilities.

Animated films illustrating subjectivities that cannot be shown through live action have come into being thanks to cinematic, political, technological, and philosophical changes that have taken place over the last two decades and continue today.² According to Annabelle Honess Roe, this phenomenon began in 2003 with the production of the animated documentary series *Animated Minds*.³ The series revolves around the experiences of people who identify as mad and people living with a mental disability. "Mental Disability," a combination of "psychiatric disability, mental illness, cognitive disability, intellectual disability, mental service user (or consumer), neurodiversity, neurotypical, psychiatric system survivor, crazy, and mad," was articulated by Margaret Price in her thought-provoking and nuanced investigation of the construction of "madness" in US higher education.⁴ Another example of the change taking place in this field is the geographical expansion of ReelAbilities, the disability film festival, from New York to over thirteen cities across the United States and one in Canada.⁵ Politically, the disability rights movement in the US has gained both institutional and social successes since the beginning of the 1990s.⁶ Simultaneously, the development of computer technologies has made the production, distribution, and consumption of animation more widely accessible. Therefore, the circle of artists choosing to create animated films is also expanding.⁷

One interesting example in this context involves the animated films uploaded to YouTube by autistic and neurodivergent people. Most of these creators use animation in order to represent the experience of sensory overload for other neurodivergent and neurotypical audience members.⁸

In addition, posthumanistic perceptions also receive broad attention within the philosophical field in general and the humanities in particular. Various fields of study deconstruct normative perceptions about the body by analyzing animated films, as well as other nonrealistic genres.⁹ These changes have contributed to the increasing popularity of avant-garde or experimental animated films that challenge the ableist point of view by rejecting classical cinematic norms and focusing on the subjectivity of disability throughout and not merely as glimpses, as evident in many recent popular live-action films.

From the outset of cinema until today, many films have been produced about people with physical or mental disabilities and their relationships with the world around them—starting with *The Near-Sighted Cyclist* (1907), *The Cabinet of Dr. Caligari* (Robert Wiene, 1920) and *Freaks* (Tod Browning, 1932) through *The Elephant Man* (David Lynch, 1980), *Mask* (Peter Bogdanovich, 1985), and *Crash* (David Cronenberg, 1996) and ending with *A Beautiful Mind* (Ron Howard, 2001), *Shutter Island* (Martin Scorsese, 2010), and *Wonderstruck* (Todd Haynes, 2017).

However, despite the popularity of these films among audiences as well as film critics, critical disability studies scholars have argued that such films are created from an ableist point of view, which perceives people with disabilities as having less value.[10] This means that cultural representations of disability characterize it as an expression of traits carrying negative social value, such as evil, victimhood, lack or excess, hypersexuality or asexuality, aggressiveness, or self-pity.[11]

As of today, the study of disability in film and television has centered on questions of representation and inclusion (of participants and creators). Two of the most recent "Hollywood Shaming Documentaries"—that is, films contesting Hollywood's alignment of its protagonists and overall heroism with whiteness, masculinity, heterosexuality, cisgenderness, and able-bodiedness—have considered their own community members as possible viewers. *Disclosure* (Sam Feder, 2020) looks at the depiction of trans people and *Code of the Freaks* (Salome Chasnoff, 2020) is concerned with the portrayal of people with disability. In her account of making *Code of the Freaks* eloquently entitled "It's All the Same Movie," Carrie Sandahl emphasized the ways disabled spectators were considered in the production of the film: "Our interviewees not only school the audience on their own perspectives and experiences of the movies; they also include detail that speaks directly to other disabled people by using cultural references and insider language, which is often politically incorrect. Unlike Hollywood, then, we assume our 'general audience' includes people with disabilities."[12] This new addition is what the "Hollywood Shaming Documentaries" lacked all along. As this genre exposes, if you are not "the general audience," you have been consuming degrading images about yourself and were probably watching them alone.

Code of the Freaks uses Tod Browning's *Freaks* from 1932 both as a prologue and an epilogue; in the beginning it uses the film to argue it was the worst of times in representation and in the end to imply that it may have been the best of times for disabled actors. One of the most effective tools of *Code of the Freaks* is this circular narrative, which shows that change is never linear or chronological and that improvement or intersectionality in some contemporary films does not necessarily mean progress. The Farrelly brothers, like Tod Browning in his time, employ more disabled actors than any other contemporary Hollywood directors. At the same time, their films, like *Freaks*, contain degrading representations of people with disabilities alongside some of the most daring and subversive ones. *Code of the Freaks* reminds us that change is not linear but also allows us to watch together, because even the same movie is not the same when you watch it with your own community.

In light of this, *Animated Film and Disability* illuminates new methods of accommodating spectatorship for diverse bodyminds. It then describes the innovative aesthetic forms that they create. The book uses animation—a popular and accessible cinematic format—to explore alternative bodily spectatorships in a developing cinematic expression ("crip animation"). Crip animation relies on "disabled subjectivities," both in form and in content, and allows for a fresh outlook on the world from the margins. By immersing viewers in a temporary alternative bodily experience, this emergent form of cinematography introduces an entirely new type of spectatorship in film history. This has transformative potential not only for films about disability but also for mainstream cinema. While examining the alternative sensory spectatorship experience offered by crip animation, I use Merleau-Pontian phenomenology and its interpretations and uses in film theory. Though we perceive the world through our senses, these are often transparent to many of us. Phenomenological art and philosophy help us "remember" their existence and notice them.[13]

I use the term *crip* as articulated by Carrie Sandahl, Robert McRuer, Alison Kafer, Ellen Samuels, and others, who suggested is more confrontational than disability. Kafer adds a phenomenological articulation of the term that aligns the crip with a "desire to make people wince" and suggests it urges people to jolt out of their everyday understanding of bodies and minds, of normalcy and deviance. Most relevant to the analysis of crip spectatorship, Kafer weaves the stare/gaze into the core definition of the term: "It recognizes the common response of nondisabled people to disabled people, of the normative to the deviant—furtive yet relentless staring, aggressive questioning, and/or turning away from difference, a refusal to see."[14]

Using a crip animation analysis, I examine the role of the senses in forms of spectatorship that challenge their natural status. The study of this new subgenre raises a number of questions: How do bodily senses participate in spectatorship experiences that emphasize the sensory? What intersubjective and intercorporeal relationships are evoked while watching animated images and listening to the voices of people with lived experiences of disabilities? How do diversely sensible bodies come into contact with these indexical voices and symbolic images?[15] Might they evoke the feeling of being-in-the-world (*in-der-Welt-sein*) with a particular disability for the spectators who experience the same disability differently or may not otherwise have been exposed to it?[16] What kind of bodily excess is depicted in these films?[17] Can these sensations cause the able-bodied/able-minded or cis spectators to feel uncomfortable with the privilege of having their bodyminds accommodated?[18] Can animation construct new and omnipotent bodies, thus making us forget our "corporeal" lived experiences?[19] Can these films give way to physical experiences that change the boundaries of our skins?[20] And finally, what can crip animation teach us about film and media spectatorship more broadly?

Crip animation, which this book explores, challenges the ableist gaze on the level of cinematic representations of people with disabilities, yet it also challenges the way this gaze assumes an "abled" spectator and "ableist" spectatorship.[21] The first chapter discusses the ableist gaze as constructed in mainstream cinema by what Carrie Sandahl identified as an "all the same movie" confinement. The chapters that follow examine the ways some animated films challenge this gaze by evoking the spectators' and listeners' bodyminds and senses. They demonstrate the potential of crip animation to challenge the sensory hierarchy by emphasizing the primacy of vision in conventional film spectatorship experiences.[22] By centering the senses, this type of animation attempts to challenge the imaginary unity of both the represented human body and the spectator's and listener's bodymind. At the same time, it seeks to expose the illusion of unity in cinematic production, which obfuscates the gaps and differences between individual cinematic units.[23]

ANIMATING THE SPECTATOR

The first comprehensive anthology, *A Reader in Animation Studies*, was published in 1997 and introduced by its editor, Jane Pilling, apologetically explaining how the field has shifted from children's animation (cartoons) to more artistic forms, as well as its recent acceptance within film studies. When I first started researching and teaching animated film and disability in 2013, her compelling argument equipped me with counterarguments in facing an imaginary film scholar disregarding the field. Now, only twenty years forward, the field of animation studies has evolved into "A legitimate field of academic enquiry in its own right.... The pejorative perception of animation as 'just' children's entertainment or funny cartoons, and therefore not worthy of intellectual enquiry, has, we hope, long been surpassed."[24]

During this time, scholars of old and new cinema, and media have taken on the task of exploring animation. They engaged with its themes, techniques, subgenres, and auteurs, with its history and possible futures. At the same time, prominent and intriguing theoreticians like Alan Cholodenko Lev Manovich, and Gertrud Koch, who focus on the form and apparatus, have argued that film is, in fact, a form of animation, rather than the other way around.[25] Such arguments have certainly helped legitimize the study of animation within film theory and have made room to redefine both cinema and animation. As suggested by Paul Wells, "it is necessary to properly define animation as an intrinsically 'modern' art that facilitates 'difference' and 'otherness' in the creative enterprise."[26]

Now that scholars and practitioners no longer have to justify animation as an artistic form, they are free to discuss it as a unique form that communicates differently with its spectators. In her articulation of film as an experiment in animation, Gertrud Koch offered an explanation of animation's process of "bringing to life" as a twofold process: "(1) through the technological setting-into-motion of individual pictures, the film itself is animated in a general sense, which exceeds the strict definition of the genre 'animation film' and constitutes animation as a moving image that suggests the quality of vitality, and (2) the spectator is animated by the animation and displaced in a specific way into the state of vitality."[27] Thus, the assumption, focus, and agenda of this book are animation's otherness and the ways it may go even further than live action in abandoning physical laws, realist conventions, and perhaps some of the embedded biases in the cinematic apparatus. Animation does so not only by distancing itself from the social restrictions and limitations of "objective reality" but also, and mostly, by animating its spectators—that is, moving them and bringing them to life.

The possible effects of animation on its spectators have been a concern for many social sciences and humanities theoreticians, starting from Walter Benjamin and Sergey Eisenstein and ending with the contemporary works of Vivian Sobchack, Paul Wells, and Jack Halberstam. Susan Buchan suggests, however, that prior to discussing alternative spectatorships, we must first understand animation's unique conditions.

Animation presents graphic and plastic worlds and impossible spaces, and it has the potential to transcend the physical laws dominating our experiences.[28] Contemporary animation scholarship emphasizes these conditions in its analyses of content. However, investigations of spectatorial experiences are still rare, and almost none of these studies address emotions, affect theory, or phenomenology. Buchan explains this relative lacuna by arguing that animation creates its own visual culture, obeying different rules than live-action cinema. Theories ignoring animation overlook its subversion of the physical laws dictating cinematic representation and its reuse of cultural codes and images for creating "worlds" and characters that offer an experience for spectators. Buchan mentions Joanna Bouldin, Vivian Sobchack, and Laura U. Marks as the most notable exceptions to this scholarly oversight.

According to Sobchack, the growing interest in animation as an idea and as a cinematic style is not only related to the expansion of computer graphics but also the humanities' focus on the posthuman. Sobchack argues that the *post-* articulates a primary shift in cultural consciousness from the mechanical to the electronic, between future and past, between the promise of life in animation and the lack of animation and death.²⁹

It is therefore unsurprising that Benjamin, who studied the spectatorship experience, showed a special interest in this cinematic form. According to Jack Halberstam, in an early version of "The Work of Art in the Age of Mechanical Reproduction," Benjamin reserved a special place for the new animation art of Walt Disney. According to him, Disney's animation conveyed a kind of magical consciousness to audiences, conjuring new utopic spaces and worlds. Benjamin focused on studying the utopian possibilities of presenting the colorful worlds of Mickey Mouse and friends.³⁰

Halberstam further argues that despite animation's subversive potential, only a few mainstream films have the audacity to tread on the dangerous territory of revolutionary activity. In a world of romantic comedies and action films, few films offer any alternative; however, animation is where we might find it: "Nonanimated films that trade in the mise-en-scène of revolution and transformation, films like *V for Vendetta* and *The X Men* [sic], are based on comic books and animated graphic novels. What is the relationship between new forms of animation and alternative politics today? Can animation sustain a utopic project now, whereas, as Benjamin mourned, it could not in the past?"³¹ According to Halberstam, while animation tends to be read only as form or as content, as message or as image, it is, in fact, a mix of science, math, biology, alchemy, engineering, and puppetry. Therefore, "the reduction of the animated image into pure symbol and the simplification of animated narratives into pure allegory do an injustice to the complexity of the ... surrealism that we find in animated cinema."³²

The subversive nature of animation has served as an inspiration for many animators, who wished to represent their subjective lived experiences, particularly of disability, and communicate them to other community members as well as nondisabled people for educational purposes.

Disability is present in all animated subgenres and fulfills different functions depending on its assumed spectators. Animated films targeting children rely on didactic neoliberal narratives of "accepting the other" as a personal rather than a systemic problem of racism, ableism, or cissexism/transphobia and simultaneously contain differing and othering elements. Televised animated series targeting millennials focus on identity searching, self-doubt, and self-realization. Avant-garde animation is aimed at cinephiles and thus seeks to deconstruct conventional spectatorship and normative (cinematic) points of view.

Children still make up animation's largest and most significant audience. Many feature-length animated films for children use disability as a means of exploring (or educating for) the inclusion of different species, bodies, and minds, within neoliberal constraints. Some even replace romantic narratives with tales of collaboration and codependence, thus resonating with children's desires of collectivity, as Halberstam shows.

Animated feature films produced by large studios (e.g., Disney, Pixar, DreamWorks, and Blue Sky) are included in the screening programs of commercial cinema theaters and streaming networks year-round, and their popularity peaks during the summer. Though they adopt various techniques, from cel stop-motions to computer-generated images, these films tend to sustain a unified style throughout, with minor instances of mixing between different styles. Because of their target audience, these films' narratives revolve around child or animal protagonists and typically involve becoming part of a group or fitting in. Some films assume a liberal audience (parents) and thus conclude with a moral of individuality, integration, and assimilation (e.g., *Frozen* [Disney] and *Ferdinand* [Blue Sky]). Others, on the other hand, rely on the child-spectator's desire for codependence and belonging to a group[33] (e.g., *Frozen* 2013; *Ferdinand* 2017; *Chicken Run* 2000; *Finding Nemo* 2003; *Finding Dory* 2016).

From a disability studies perspective, the first type affirms the individual model, in which difference is to be erased in order to participate in society. The second type, however, derives from the social model, seeking to challenge the construction of ableism. Animals are thus used for explaining desired human social behavior. Furthermore, animals are also used to investigate different embodiments and their surroundings.[34] While Pixar's animal heroes Nemo (mainly his father) and Dory have been praised for their queerness by Halberstam,[35] they are both disabled fish—Nemo has a shorter fin and Dory a memory-loss issue—who navigate the ocean only to return to their community and renegotiate the ways it can hold space for them. Most recently, Pixar has gone even further in their recent *Loop* (Erica Milsom, 2020), a short that explicitly features the point of view of an autistic nonverbal girl on a canoe trip with a neurotypical boy.[36]

Young adults are the second most prominent animation audience. This group is currently expanding, as more television networks and streaming services are beginning to broadcast animated series. These shows use disability as a means of challenging neoliberal conventions of political correctness and address millennial concerns about identity and physical and metaphoric accessibility.

Contemporary animated television series for adults exist on most large networks and streaming services.[37] Older and more established series, like *The Simpsons* and *South Park*, have become the flagship programs at Fox and

Comedy Central. Consequently, they led to the rise of *Futurama*, *Family Guy*, *American Dad*, and *Rick and Morty*.[38] Both these older series set the tone for addressing disability as well as issues of gender nonconformity. These series animate their critique of the way film and television have represented people with disabilities. The "Homer's Triple Bypass" episode of *The Simpsons* includes an animated critique of the "freak show" and the spectacular representation of the bodyminds of people with disabilities within contemporary talk shows.[39] Simultaneously, the creators of *South Park*, who engage with disability in the context of US-specific debates over political correctness and "cancel culture," mock the ableism in liberal discourses—a social phenomenon that leads to the exclusion and oppression of many diverse groups. Thus, for example, the episode "Conjoined Fetus Lady" includes an apparent physical difference through the portrayal of a character who has a dead fetus attached to her head.[40] This difference, which does not bother this character at all, raises ableist responses under the cover of liberal acceptance. One such response is the declaration of a "Conjoined Twin Myslexia Week." The episode is concluded with the understanding that the "Conjoined Twin Myslexia Week" was only meant to ease the conscience of the townspeople, who never asked the lady what she truly wanted.[41] Among other things, the popularity of these two animated series is rooted in their use of grotesque imagery to subvert cultural hierarchies, as well as traditional narratives and means of expression.[42]

Thanks to this growing popularity, Netflix was required to keep up and thus released *Bojack Horseman* and *Big Mouth*. However, as with animation for children, the visual style is unified within each series, with only rare changes in individual scenes or episodes.[43] These series tend to be more reflexive about their production processes and the possible spectatorships they might invoke. In the fifth season of *Bojack Horseman*, the leading character is acting in a television series called *Philbert*. This show is insinuated to also be on Netflix, and it bears ironic resemblance to Bojack's own life. Thematically and ideologically, the series critiques television's portrayals of socially oppressed groups. As in the case of *Zootopia* (2016), Bojack Horseman's life in Los Angeles investigates the situating of a humanized animal in a big city. This premise is also a means of exploring perceptions of disability and accessibility, targeting millennials.

The smallest audience group is the "film buffs"—the art house audience members and film festival visitors. This group seeks avant-garde, independent, and experimental films that evoke their senses unconventionally. The cinephiles, like the general population, include disabled and nondisabled spectators. These types of film are at the center of my analysis in the following chapters. They rely on the subjectivities of people with disabilities as a means of undermining conventional, and often ableist, spectatorships through sensual disorientation.

The audience for avant-garde and experimental animation is relatively smaller. These films are usually animated by independent filmmakers, including film students funded by national funds (e.g., The National Film Board of Canada, The British Film Institute). As I discuss in the third section of the first chapter, only rarely do animation studios (for example, Aardman) also experiment with feature animation for adults aimed for the big screen. As with more mainstream animation, these films vary in length and technique. However, they do tend to mix these up, thereby creating a hybrid style composed of clay animation and film noir, musical and animated documentary, or animation and live action.

Increasingly, experimental and independent animators have focused on the experiences of people with disabilities, often relying on their own points of view, and occasionally those of loved family members or friends, on being-in-the-world. While the animated films have a certain educational aspect to them because they are addressing spectators and listeners who may not share the experience, they can be received beyond the abled/disabled binary. For example, a deaf viewer may enjoy an animated musical about depression while a neurotypical spectator could be drawn to an animated documentary aimed at neurodivergent audience members. Two of the most prominent animators who have illuminated experiences of disability are Signe Baumann (*Rocks in My Pockets*, 2014) and Adam Elliot (*Mary and Max*, 2009). Alongside feature films such as these are short experimental films about disability produced by dozens of independent animators.[44]

The subversiveness of animated films about disability relies on the ways they challenge not only physical but also political reality—through both their content and form. In addition to content that criticizes the ableist gaze, the formal alternative of this type of animation gives way to expressing the disavowal of ableist cinematic conventions and providing a peek into a world that operates on other terms. This alternative offers its spectators a sensory experience that forces them to reflexively observe their world and the social rules by which it works. Contemporary animated television series make use of a grotesque type of expression to convey social critiques about the ableist viewpoint. However, independent animation in general and short experimental animation in particular add a sensory spectatorship experience to this criticism, which exposes social hierarchies and privileges. Animated films that engage with the experiences of people with disabilities demonstrate how this type of animation constitutes an alternative to cinematic forms that construct an ableist point of view and a coherent spectatorship experience.

CRIPPING THE SCREEN

Critical disability studies are an interdisciplinary academic field that investigates the complex relationships between society and people with disabilities. The field was largely inspired by work in women's, gender, and sexuality studies, ethnic studies, and LGBTQ studies, similar to the way the disability rights movement was inspired by the feminist, civil rights, and gay rights movements, as suggested by Sami Schalk. When scholars combine theories and methods from disability studies and theories of gender and sexuality, Schalk explains, the work is typically referred to as feminist disability studies (Rosemarie Garland-Thomson) or crip theory (Robert McRuer 2006). Feminist disability studies as defined by Alison Kafer:

> explores the relationship between gender and disability, particularly through lived experiences and cultural representation, as well as how feminist movements and scholarship have either perpetuated or resisted ableism within their work. Crip theory, on the other hand, takes its inspiration from queer theory and moves away from disability identity politics (as queer theory moves from gay and lesbian identity politics) to critique and understand the creation of the stigmatized category itself. Crip theory, therefore, pushes the edges of disability studies to include more engagement with chronic illnesses and diseases, including psychiatric ones, which were often marginalized or ignored in early disability studies that focused more on physical and sensory disabilities (Kafer 2013, 36, 18).[45]

This book is written in the spirit of crip theory and relies on the works of scholars such as Alison Kafer, Janet Price and Margrit Shildrick, Ellen Samuels, Margaret Price, Carrie Sandahl, Sami Schalk, Robert McRuer, David Mitchell, Sharon L. Snyder, Rosemarie Garland-Thompson, Georgina Kleege, and many others. These scholars aim to make use of deconstructionist and anti-ableist writing while integrating the phenomenological principals, emphasizing corporeal physicality, connected to the experience of being-in-the-world.[46] Starting from the 1980s, two main writing models have developed in the field of disability studies: the individual/medical model and the social model. The first locates the "problem" of disability and the reason for it within the disabled person's functional or physiological impairments. Thus, the individual/medical model forms the narrative of a personal tragedy, the solution for which is individual/medical/rehabilitative or relies on professional care. The social model, on the other hand, rejects this reasoning and argues that disability does not constitute an individual impairment. Instead, it reflects a social failure to provide adequate accommodations for the needs of people with disabilities. It is not an individual problem, since people with disabilities experience the impact of this failure as institutionalized social discrimination.[47]

About a decade after they were formed, these oppositional models began being criticized for creating an oppositional binary between impairment, perceived as personal and physical, and disability, defined as a social issue. Contemporary disability studies scholars now argue that in order to continue subverting the binary of disability/impairment, these models should be left behind. Instead, research should focus on the physicality of disability and disability as an identity and offer a physical ontology as a new starting point for disability studies.[48]

It is the relatively simple dualism of the social model distinguishing between impairment and disability that had become the most dominant model of disability, as Nick Watson and Simo Vehmas argue in their opening chapter to the second edition of the *Routledge Handbook of Disability Studies* in 2020. They reflect on the new ideas and concepts disability studies faced back in 2013 that were discussed in their introduction to the first volume, including disabled feminist perspectives, ethnicity, sexuality, and social class, and conclude that these challenges and critiques have continued and become stronger. Scholars from disability studies have been unpacking "disability through a variety of different approaches including ableism ([Goodley] 2014), normalcy (Thomas and Sakellariou 2018), and embodiment (Stephens et al. 2015), which explores representations and constructions of disability through discourse analysis (Grue 2016)." Current approaches focus on "the cultural and ideological underpinnings of disablement and ableism."[49]

The cultural model of disability has been suggested in opposition to the narrowed possibilities of the social model for its disavowal of the disability impairment divide and considers "impairment, disability *and* normality as effects generated by academic knowledge, mass media, and everyday discourses."[50] Focusing on the center rather than the margin of society, this model proposes to change disability studies into dis/ability studies; the slash is meant to show that "one should no longer problematize just the category of disability, but rather interplay between 'normality' and 'disability.'"[51] Finally, the use of dis/ability is explained by Anna Waldschmidt as a "contingent, always 'embodied' type of difference relating to the realm of health, functioning, achievement and beauty (and their negative poles), [dis/ability offers] essential knowledge about the legacies, trajectories, turning points, and transformations of contemporary society and culture."[52]

Animated Film and Disability follows a composite model of disability as offered by trans and disability studies scholar Alexandre Baril, one that combines the social restrictions and othering with the phenomenological experiences of disability, not only because it complicates ableist notions of embodied spectatorship but also because it opens up a space to explain "transition-related subjective realities, affects and potential suffering for some trans people in terms of debility."[53] By adopting a feminist, queer, trans, activist, anti-ableist perspective, as well as applying an intersectional framework and employing an autoethnographic methodology based on his own experiences as a trans, disabled man who is coping with nonapparent disabilities, Baril introduces the possibilities of the model to trans studies. Baril presents four compelling arguments to include transness under the definition of disability: First, gender dysphoria, the psychological/mental perspective that included trans experiences in the *DSM* are not considered as a disability under the ADA; however, the distress caused by dysphoria could be qualified as debilitating or as a disability. Second, the dysfunction or absence of organs, body parts, or physical characteristics resulting from transitioning could be considered a disability. Third, being trans interferes with several aspects of life (professional, financial, legal, social, interpersonal, and sexual) and spheres of activity before, during, and after transitioning. And fourth, trans people, like other disabled people, face forms of violence and discrimination based on their identity and body/mind configurations. Baril asks why the experience of transness is excluded from the disability category.

Jasbir Puar explains the trajectory of this exclusion from the ADA (1990s) to the present moment (2014) "of trans hailing by the US state, that merits rethinking in ways that reassemble difference and highlight shared debt to more generalizable material processes" as part of the socio-juridical segregation between trans and disability.[54] The inclusion of gender identity disorder (GID) in *DSM-III* (1980) after depathologizing homosexuality explains the specific focus on childhood behavior as a compensatory maneuver for the deletion of homosexuality, "thus instating surveillance mechanisms that would perhaps *prevent* homosexuality."[55] Moreover, the emphasis on the exclusion of GID as a disability in the ADA because it does not result from physical impairment, "couched in an exclusionary clause that includes transvestism, transsexuals, pedophilia, exhibitionism, voyeurism, and 'other sexual disorders' as well as completely arbitrary 'conditions' such as compulsive gambling, kleptomania, pyromania, and use of illegal drugs—was largely understood, unlike the specific exclusion of homosexuality, as a commitment to the entrenchment of pathologizing GID." Finally, Puar quotes Kevin M. Barry, who concludes this exclusion in moral terms: "The ADA is a moral code, and people with GID its moral castaways."[56]

Most recently scholarly work in the field of transfeminist disability studies has been claiming its rightful place within the filed. In her piece "The Ramblings of a Chronically Ill Mad Trans Femme," Madeline Stump draws attention to the absence of disabled trans and femmes in feminist, trans, and disability studies and writes about the conditions that most frequently disable trans femmes as a combination of capitalism and transmisogyny: "transfeminine people, particularly Black and Indigenous transfeminine people, are systematically denied basic necessities through capitalism for our genders. This interplay manifests in many different ways: a disproportionate amount of transfeminine people are homeless/housing insecure, without insurance/underinsured, unemployed/underemployed, fearful of transmisogynist medical practitioners, etc. . . . Among many other challenges, this results in potentially smaller/shorter-term illnesses/complications compounding over time into larger/longer-term disabilities. Because we can't afford, can't access, and/or don't trust medical practitioners."[57] Opening with an analysis of Black trans activist and filmmaker Tourmaline's *Salacia* (2019), Niamh Timmons has also taken up the task of investigating the integration of transfeminism and trans women within feminist disability studies and disability justice. Timmons suggests transforming feminist disability studies and further argues that trans women's oppression and activism are integral to feminist disability studies: "By doing so, the subfield will benefit from engaging the intrinsic patriarchal structures, racism, and ableism that are all at play in transmisogyny."[58]

Animated Film and Disability is positioned in the intersection between cinema studies and disability studies theories of spectatorship, embodiment, and lived experience in the analysis of anti-ableist animated films. Yet recent exciting work in media studies, and, in particular, disability media studies, may offer the required tools to unpack the mediation of these films through technology. In the foreword to the *Routledge Companion to Disability and Media* (2020), Faye Ginsburg[59] details the wide-ranging writing in what Elizabeth Ellcessor and Bill Kirkpatrick dubbed "disability media studies,"[60] most prominently produced and edited by Gerard Goggin, Katie Ellis, and Beth Haller. Ginsburg particularly mentions Gerard Goggin and Chris Newell's *Digital Disability: The Social Construction of Disability in New Media* (2003), Beth Haller's *Representing Disability in an Ableist World: Essays on Mass Media* (2010), Katie Ellis and Mike Kent's *Disability and New Media* (2013), Katie Ellis and Gerard Goggin's

Disability and Social Media: Global Perspectives (2017), and Elizabeth Ellcessor's *Restricted Access: Media, Disability and the Politics of Participation* (2016).

Specifically, Ginsburg situates this expansive and timely companion as answering the call for dismediation issued by media scholars Jonathan Sterne and Mara Mills in their afterword to the aforementioned *Disability Media Studies* volume.[61] The dismediation proposed "appropriates media technologies and takes some measure of impairment to be a given, rather an incontrovertible obstacle of revolution."[62] Contemporary dismediations attending to "the intersections of disability and media both on-screen and off-screen conditions that 'crip the media' through the affordances that enable those with sensory impairments access to print, television, film, and other popular forms: those include (but are not limited to) closed captioning for d/Deaf audiences, audio description for those with low vision or who are blind, accommodations increasingly mandated by law in some locations, while embraced by disabled artists as an incitement to creativity."[63] *Animated Film and Disability*'s focus on spectatorship from avant-garde cinematic theories and phenomenological writing in film theory nevertheless coincides with the spirit of dismediation in its goal to think through experiences of people with disabilities on- and off-screen, at times cripping ableist spectatorship.

The link between critical disability studies, or crip theory, and film, television, and media studies began developing as early as the outset of the disability studies corpus. The intersection between these two fields of scholarship had gone through three main phases.[64] The first phase, which took place in the 1980s, focused on the formulation of a methodology for exposing the negative representation of people with disabilities in film and television. The pioneer of this endeavor was scholar and activist Paul K. Longmore, who introduced the fundaments for analyzing stereotypes in cinema and television.[65]

The second phase, which took place in the 1990s, consisted of scholars continuing Longmore's project while also integrating early feminist film critique. Feminist cinema scholars relied on Adorno's and Althusser's critical theories of ideology and work on the passive spectator. In addition, this corpus of scholarship expanded from engaging with contemporary Hollywood cinema to also including early silent and sound films.[66]

Animated Film and Disability is situated within the third and current phase, which began in the early 2000s. This phase focuses on the formulation of aesthetic methodologies that interpret film as a form of audiovisual art while integrating concepts from critical disability studies and crip theory.

Longmore's theory about film representations of disability relies on a critique of the classical Hollywood narrative, which constructs disabled antagonists through its melodramatic means of expression. This type of film links disfigurement of the body and disfigurement of the soul.[67] The disabled "villain" is represented in film as resenting their own impairment and therefore hating the "normal" or "healthy" and wishing to exact revenge upon it. In addition to such representations, portrayals of disabled people as inspirational, emotionally stunted, hypersexual, or asexual can also be found in abundance. Through such imagery, the audience receives justification for the exclusion and annihilation of disabled people from society, since they are seen as responsible for their own predicament. Longmore reaches these conclusions following an analysis of films such as *Whose Life Is It Anyway?* (John Badham, 1981) and *The Other Side of the Mountain, Parts 1 and 2* (Larry Peerce, 1975, 1978).[68]

Communication scholar Martin F. Norden's historical research includes Hollywood films with stereotypical depictions of people with disabilities. Norden examines these stereotypes starting with the silent film era—for example, *The Near-Sighted Cyclist* (1907) and *Invalid's Adventures* (1907)—and ending with films from the 1990s—for example, *The Waterdance* (Neal Jimenez and Michael Steinberg, 1992) and *Passion Fish* (John Sayles, 1992). In this way, he outlines the development of social perceptions about disability.

Longmore's and Norden's groundbreaking insights on film representations of disability continue to serve as the basis for any analysis of disability in film. However, *Animated Film and Disability* takes the approach of third-phase scholars, located at the intersection of cinema, television, and media studies and disability studies. The third phase is based in cinema and television studies and greatly focuses on the cinematic medium, its unique expression and apparatus, and the discourses around it.

One of the main components in third-phase scholarship is engagement with the means of expression, rather than just the films' narrative. Thus, for example, a reading of the films *The Elephant Man* (David Lynch, 1980) and *My Left Foot* (Jim Sheridan, 1989) might combine reference to the film's artistic uniqueness with disability studies critique. Such a reading suggests that cinematography functions as a crucial component in the spectators' experience of disability. For example, *The Elephant Man* is filmed in black and white using a static camera and features many close-up shots. This type of cinematography positions the cinematic spectator as the audience of a "freak show." In contrast, *My Left Foot* utilizes camera movements (mainly pan shots) that position the spectator as a family member of the protagonist, thus offering his subjective point of view.[69] Examining films about disability from this point of view allows us to expose the sensory-physical components of the relationship between the spectator-listener and the disabled bodymind represented.

In their chapter about body genres in disability-focused cinema, Sharon L. Snyder and David T. Mitchell criticize the way mainstream cinema has used the bodies of people with disabilities. Such bodies, they suggest, were used as spectacles for the gaze of audiences aspiring to behold what is hidden. Snyder and Mitchell endeavor to add the phenomenological interaction of the cinematic viewing experience to critical disability studies.[70] They argue that, within mainstream cinema, disability serves two seemingly opposed patterns of image consumption: on the one hand, the desire to behold physical spectacles, mostly provided through mainstream narrative cinema, and on the other hand, the desire to know an object empirically as a result of gazing at it, as offered through documentary film using the scientific gaze. Disability plays a central role in most Hollywood productions, since it allows the viewers to witness performances of physical difference, without the fear of having the objects return their gaze. In addition, social conventions of normalcy, as a historical product of gazing practices, are emphasized in mainstream cinema through the representation of people with disabilities. These representations reaffirm the belief that disabled bodies uncover a hidden or secret phenomenon.[71] This phenomenological state of spectatorship constructed for able-bodied/minded viewers resembles the disclosure trope trans characters are deemed to fulfill in those same mainstream films aimed at the curious gaze of cis viewers.

Located at the intersection of disability studies and film studies, third-phase scholarship has exposed films that represent disability "positively," as well as films that allow the spectators to experience various levels of identification. Over the past decade, this type of writing has expanded thanks to disability studies scholars writing about aesthetics, performance, and film—for example, David T. Mitchell and Sharon L. Snyder, Tobin Siebers, Carrie Sandahl, Eliza Chandler, Eunjung Kim, Petra Kuppers, Jay Dolmage, Sally Chivers, Nicole Markotić, Catalin Brylla, Raphael Raphael, and more. In addition, anthologies studying the connections between narrative and documentary cinema have also been published, as well as articles in film studies and disability studies journals.

For the first time, in 2019 the *Journal for Cinema and Media Studies* published an "In Focus" section dedicated to cripping cinema and media studies, edited by Robert McRuer.[72] In their "Studying Disability for a Better Cinema and Media Studies," Elizabeth Ellcessor and Bill Kirkpatrick, editors of *Disability Media Studies* (2017), note that the incorporation of feminist theory, critical race studies, queer theory, and postcolonial and global perspectives radically expanded our understanding of media and society, improved our ability to identify and critique the workings of power, and broadened our appreciation of how people with a diverse range of embodiments, identities, and subject positions engage with media technologies, industries, and texts.[73] The only animation discussed in the section is the children's film *Inside Out* (Pete Docter, 2015), analyzed by Nicole Markotić in regard to depression. In "The Many in the One: Depression and Multiple Subjectivities in Inside Out," Markotić argues that the animated film concludes that sadness is a way to navigate and live through and beyond depression.[74]

Most scholarship crossing between film studies and disability studies so far has focused on live-action film. The few studies that have been dedicated to animation have continued to focus on questions of representation related to the bodies on-screen rather than the spectators' bodies[75] Some of these excluded questions will be raised throughout the book and include what do lived experiences of disability look like when told in first person? How does the film mediate these experiences to the spectators? What may these mediations evoke in spectators' bodyminds? What are the sensory and ideological meanings of reliance on a "true" story? These questions allow an examination of the possible effects that crip animation may produce in looking at the history of traditional cinematic spectatorship by creating a bodily spectatorship experience that evokes other senses.

EMBODYING SPECTATORSHIP

Phenomenologist Maurice Merleau-Ponty (1908–1961) placed perception, which is necessarily physical, at the center of his philosophical inquiry. In his work *Phenomenology of Perception* (1945), Merleau-Ponty relies on the philosophical methodology of Edmund Husserl, who is considered the "parent" of phenomenology. According to Merleau-Ponty, the world is not composed of our consciousness of it, as suggested by Kant (1781), but is instead made up of everything that might be perceived by our bodily senses, rather than just thought, as suggested by Descartes (1641). In this way, phenomenology subverts the body/soul and object/subject binaries. Merleau-Ponty argues that our physical intentionality allows us to give meaning to our experiences through the promise of possibilities of other places, times, and human situations. Our bodily senses are central to this concept, since they organize our experiences and construct the physical world and our experiences within it.[76]

In order to focus on spectatorship, I apply Merleau-Ponty's phenomenological theory of the "sensible body" to the spectator because, like any social interaction, viewing is intercorporeal. Furthermore, a phenomenological approach to disability studies emphasizes bodily experience as inseparable from the everyday experiences of disabled people. In my analysis of spectatorship in crip animation and its use of corporeal metaphors, I follow Merleau-Ponty's concept of the sensible body—a body in carnal interaction with the world. In his book chapter "The Intertwining—The Chiasm" (1968), Merleau-Ponty focuses on the reversibility and interconnections between bodily senses and our perception of the world. The body is "flesh in the flesh of the world."[77] As flesh, the body is simultaneously sensible ("objective") and sentient ("phenomenal"). The chiasm of senses binds our bodies with other objects/subjects in the world: "If it touches them and sees them, this is only because, being of their family, itself visible and tangible ... because each of the two beings is an archetype for the other, because the body belongs to the order of the things as the world is universal flesh."[78] Theoretical-phenomenological writing about film was developed by scholars such as Linda Williams, Vivian Sobchack, Laura U. Marks, and Jennifer Barker.[79]

In her now-canonic article in film theory based on psychoanalytical and phenomenological tools, Linda Williams examined three (bodily) genres: horror, pornography, and melodrama.[80] Williams argued that these genres have a low cultural status because of their sensational representation of bodies and their effect on the bodies watching them. What gives them this low status is their perception as genres that entrap the spectator in an almost-involuntary mimicry of the bodily sentiment or sensation presented on-screen. The success of these genres is measured by the correlation between the audience's sentiments and what is shown on-screen. The most significant characteristic of these genres is bodily excess. Therefore, their examination bears great ideological importance, since culture uses the term *gross* to mark this excess and exclude it. This physical excess is conveyed through both bodily ecstasy (shouts of fear or woeful sobbing) and bodily spectacle (orgasm, violence, sobbing).[81]

Bodily excess is present in crip animation, both through direct engagement with sensory overload (for example, in autism) and by criticizing the concept of sensory "compensation" (for example, blind people's sense of hearing). However, this book seeks to demonstrate that crip animation evokes bodily responses that do not mimic the bodies represented on-screen but rather evoke sensory incoherence, disorientation, and reflexivity.

Vivian Sobchack's scholarship, influenced by Merleau-Ponty, examines the cinematic body and the sensory experiences it evokes for the spectators. Sobchack argues that cinema's technological mechanism is analogous to the cinematic body; cinema is made possible thanks to its apparatus in the same way that the human body is made possible thanks to its senses. The cinematic body is made up of human organs such as the eyes, ears, and mouth. The camera is analogous to the cinematic eyes and ears while the projector is analogous to the mouth. The projected image is like a cinematic skin, both because it defines the "fleshy" boundaries of the cinematic body and because it is analogous to the way our "flesh" enables our bodily movements.[82] In this way, the introspective relations between the spectator and the film also include the cinematic apparatus.

Furthermore, applying Merleau-Ponty's sensible/sentient body to spectatorship, Sobchack argues that we "know" what we are seeing on-screen not merely through our eyes but also our entire bodies. As viewers, "we possess an embodied intelligence that both opens our eyes far beyond their discrete capacity for vision, opens the film far beyond its visible containment by the screen, and opens language to a reflective knowledge of its specific carnal origins and limits."[83]

Vivian Sobchack's writing may also be read within the framework of the embodiment model of disability studies. She examines her body's intentionality toward the world in various situations: sitting through epic historic films in "Surge and Splendor"; her fingers, skin, nose, lips, tongue, and stomach in "What My Fingers Knew"; and all other parts of her body in *The Address of the Eye* and "Surge and Splendor."[84] In her book *Carnal Thoughts*, Sobchack thoroughly explores the phenomenology of living with a prosthetic leg.[85] She articulates her own concepts, methodology, and style, which derive from her embodied phenomenology. In addition to her film analysis, in these three essays, Sobchack directly addresses the phenomenology of living with a disability.

Laura U. Marks broadens the traditions of Williams and Sobchack and uses phenomenological theory to analyze experimental diasporic intercultural cinema. Marks notes that films created by immigrants and exiles, who live in between cultures, are intensely engaged with sensory memory. Such people inhabit two sensoriums—that of their culture of origin and the one in which they live.[86] Therefore, their works are ambivalent about their ability to represent the traditional sensory experience. This distinguishes them from films that exoticize the senses of the "other" culture. Marks argues that the hierarchical organization of senses is as cultural as it is personal and therefore changes from one culture to another as it changes from one person to another. Thus, the intercultural filmmakers included in Marks's study stretch the boundaries of the cinematic apparatus in order to fit their sensory relationships with the world. These experimental filmmakers explore the relationships between physicality and perception and offer an alternative to mainstream sensory experiences.[87]

Animated Film and Disability demonstrates how crip animation filmmakers act similarly to intercultural filmmakers. In these films, senses are organized in ways that force spectators to "see" with their ears and "understand" through all their body's senses. In addition, such animated films offer a spectatorship experience in which the hierarchies of mainstream cinema, particularly in regards to the visual and the auditory, collapse one after the other, moving the spectator to a level in which imaginative rules prevail over reality's anchors. According to Walter Benjamin, this experience is shared by wandering around the city (flâneur), dreaming, viewing surreal art, and experimenting with drugs.[88] Based on the insights of phenomenological film scholars, *Animated Film and Disability* argues that experimental animated films about disability subvert the conventional sensory hierarchy, as well as the primacy of sight, in film spectatorship experiences and theory.

The first chapter, "Resisting the Ableist Gaze: Between Mainstream and Experimental Forms," discusses the construction of the ableist gaze in mainstream live-action film genres and various attempts to subvert it. This chapter offers a historical and thematic analysis of the construction of the ableist gaze in horror and melodrama films and demonstrates how this type of gaze was embedded within cinematic conventions. After laying the groundwork linking the conventional gaze and the construction of the ableist gaze, the chapter goes on to discuss films located at the heart of the mainstream, which simultaneously use avant-garde expression to represent subjective experiences of disability. These films depict the inner world of characters with disabilities, as well as their perceptions of the external world, by using a subjective camera. However, this diversity is left on the technical level only, while their contents and ideologies still conclude by annihilating or denying disability. The chapter concludes with a discussion of the possible alternatives animation offers for exploring disability. This chapter suggests that live action's move away from the conventions of narrative cinema and toward animation-like points of view targets cinephiles and allows for a critical examination of being-in-the-world in a sensual body and of the privileges or the lack thereof that attach to our bodies.

The second chapter, "Embodying Spectatorship: Intersubjective Ways of Being-in-the-World," looks into animated films produced through various levels of collaboration between filmmakers with and without disabilities. This discussion focuses on the aesthetic and political meanings arising from the introspective relationships created among these filmmakers, making a distinction between films produced by people with disabilities, and those produced through collaborations between disabled and nondisabled filmmakers. First, I introduce the first-person crip category through an analysis of animated films created exclusively by people with disabilities. These are autobiographical, and autoethnographic animated films, produced by people (mostly women) with disabilities, center first-person self-exploration and exercise the demand for self-representation. Following this, I discuss intersubjective encounters in animated films that, at first glance, may seem to be first-person crip films because the intersubjective process is concealed. The concluding section focuses on reflexive collaborative projects and addresses animation as a result of cooperative intersubjectivity between disabled and temporarily able-bodied filmmakers, who expose spectators to the power relations between these bodyminds. The analysis of these collaborations produces another distinction: that between intersubjective encounters of abled and disabled filmmakers. The animation's production process requires physical closeness and obfuscates the differences between projects of collaboration that expose social power relations between disabled and nondisabled people. Analyzing such films allows for insights with regard to creative collaborations and the ways they evoke diverse bodily spectatorship experiences among viewers.

The third chapter, "Blinding the Spectator: Non-Vision-Centric Pleasures," offers haptic spectatorship as an alternative to the primacy of vision in film theory. This chapter analyzes animated films about sight disabilities, blindness, color blindness, and strabismus. These films subvert spectators' presumptions by suggesting that conventional perception/sight is constructed by ableist models. Some animated films offer disorientation and reflexivity with regard to the way they direct themselves at objects in the world. On the other hand, other animated films offer their spectators a shift in perception by evoking their sense of touch.

The fourth chapter, "Deafening the Spectator: Rethinking Sonic Pleasures and Audism," discusses the centrality of the soundtrack in crip animation. Following the previous chapter, this chapter examines the function of indexical voice-overs in animated documentary and the ways they construct crip authorities. Simultaneously, these animated films also make heightened use of music as an empathetic tool for increasing the spectator's emotional identification. In addition, this chapter looks into the "sound movement" that characterizes crip animated documentaries. Finally, the chapter suggests that crip animated documentaries emphasize the sonic aspects of the cinematic spectatorship-listenership experience. This emphasis is made by relying on the sense of hearing, which evokes other senses. The soundtracks of such animated films address the spectator's body in a synesthetic manner. This is done by using voices indicating the existence of a sensual body outside the cinematic frame, in addition to empathetic music and sounds that offer movement beyond the limitations of the "flesh." The combination of these techniques creates a process that "deafens" the spectator by evoking a synesthetic spectatorship experience that mixes among the senses, offering a reading of images as an extension of sign language.

The fifth chapter, "Toward Accessible Spectatorships," concludes the theoretical approach that combines disability studies and phenomenology in analyzing the spectatorship experience offered by animated films about disability. While most popular films and television shows continue to depict disability as a spectacle, a field of crip animation is growing that engages with disability through various genres and techniques. *Animated Film and Disability: Cripping Spectatorship* uses animation—a popular and accessible cinematic format—to explore alternative bodily spectatorship experiences. This book focuses on representations of internal psychological worlds and conditions, as well as the subjective viewpoints of people with disabilities. It suggests that these experimental or independent animated films advance the development of artistic styles that subvert traditional forms of the medium and breach the spectator's comfort. The book studies the possibilities that arise from experiences in which spectators are forced into a lack of sensory orientation, which, in turn, evokes awareness of their own bodies and, in certain cases, also their social privileges.

NOTES

1. His second film, *Le Labyrinthe* (2013), also emphasizes the phenomenological experience of time as experienced by a prisoner.

2. *Live action* is a term describing the normal production process of film imagery. This term is mainly popular in the context of animation since it allows a theoretical and practical distinction between the traditional image-production process and that of animated images. In animation studies, the use of *live action* can be seen in writings about its integration with animated texts. For more about the various uses of *live action* in animation, please see: Alison McMahan, *The Films of Tim Burton: Animating Live-Action in Contemporary Hollywood* (New York: Continuum, 2006).

3. Annabelle Honess Roe, *Animated Documentary* (New York: Palgrave Macmillan, 2013).

4. Margaret Price, *Mad at School: Rhetorics of Mental Disability and Academic Life* (Ann Arbor: University of Michigan Press, 2011), 9.

5. The official website of ReelAbilities: http://reelabilities.org.

6. Starting with the formulation of the Americans with Disabilities Act in the United States in 1990. Please see: http://adata.org.

7. Please see Giannalberto Bendazzi's three comprehensive books about the history of world animation—especially the third volume, dedicated to

contemporary animation (1990–2015): *Animation: A World History*, vol. 3, *Contemporary Times* (New York: Routledge, 2017).

8. A search for the words *autism* and *sensory overload* produces thousands of results, including animated films created by people on the autistic spectrum. For example: "Sensory Overload," by Alkurhah, uploaded January 16, 2015, www.youtube.com/watch?v=K2P4Ed6G3gw.

9. Vivian Sobchack, "Animation and Automation, or, the Incredible Effortfulness of Being," *Screen* 50, no. 4 (2009): 375–391.

10. For example: Martin F. Norden, *The Cinema of Isolation: A History of Physical Disability in the Movies* (New Brunswick: Rutgers University Press, 1994), and Paul K. Longmore, "Screening Stereotypes: Images of Disabled People in Television and Motion Pictures," in *Images of the Disabled, Disabling Images*, ed. Alan Gartner and Tom Joe (New York: Praeger, 1987), 65–78.

11. Tobin Siebers, "Disability in Theory: From Social Constructionism to the New Realism of the Body," *American Literary History* 13, no. 4 (2001): 737–754, and Tom Shakespeare and Nicholas Watson, "The Social Model of Disability: An Outdated Ideology?" *Research in Social Science and Disability* 2 (2002): 9–28.

12. Carrie Sandahl, "It's All the Same Movie: Making Code of the Freaks," in "In Focus: Cripping Cinema and Media Studies," special issue, *JCMS: Journal of Cinema and Media Studies* 58, no. 4 (2019): 148.

13. Thomas Baldwin, introduction to *Maurice Merleau-Ponty: The World of Perception*, trans. Oliver Davis (New York: Routledge Classics, 2009), 1–11.

14. Alison Kafer, *Feminist, Queer, Crip* (Indianapolis: Indiana University Press, 2013), 15.

15. Please see: Maurice Merleau-Ponty, "The Intertwining—The Chiasm," in *The Visible and the Invisible*, ed. Claude Lefort, trans. Alphonso Lingis (Evanston, IL: Northwestern University Press, 1968), 130–155.

16. A term coined by Martin Heidegger in *Being and Time*, trans. John Macquarrie and Edward Robinson (New York: Harper & Row, 2008), 78–90, as well as Hubert Dreyfus, *Being-in-the-World: A Commentary on Heidegger's Being and Time* (Cambridge, MA: MIT Press, 1991), 40–59.

17. For more about bodily genres, please see: Linda Williams, "Film Bodies: Gender, Genre and Excess," *Film Quarterly* 44, no. 4 (1991): 2–13.

18. For more about this term, please see Judy Rohrer, "Toward a Full-Inclusion Feminism: A Feminist Deployment of Dis-ability Analysis," *Feminist Studies* 31 (2005): 34–63.

19. Michael O'Prey argues that animated film achieves omnipotence by combining music with movement that allows the spectator to experience pleasure because they desire this movement for themselves. Moreover, Eisenstein described animation as having independent life and the artwork as having influence and control over the spectator by the creator-magician.

"Eisenstein and Stokes on Disney: Film Animation and Omnipotence," in *A Reader in Animation Studies*, ed. Jane Pilling (London: John Libbey, 1997), 197–199.

20. Referring here to Donna Haraway's vision as conveyed through "A Cyborg Manifesto: Science, Technology and Socialist-Feminism in the Late Twentieth Century," in *Simians, Cyborgs and Women: The Reinvention of Nature* (New York: Routledge, 1991), 149–181.

21. A type of gaze that assumes the supremacy of abled bodies, mental states, and cognition over that of disability. Please see: Sherene H. Razack, "From Pity to Respect: The Ableist Gaze and the Politics of Rescue," in *Looking White People in the Eye: Gender, Race, and Culture in Courtrooms and Classrooms* (Toronto: University of Toronto Press, 1998), 130–156, concerning the legal system's "ableist gaze," as well as Fiona Kumari Campbell's article "Refusing Able(ness): A Preliminary Conversation about Ableism," *M/C Journal* 11, no. 3 (2008): 46–55, concerning the "ableist gaze" in academic scholarship in general and cultural studies in particular. This is discussed in detail in chapter 1.

22. For more about the sensory hierarchy in experimental culture and film, please see chapters 3 and 4, as well as Laura U. Marks, *The Skin of the Film: Intercultural Cinema, Embodiment, and the Senses* (Durham, NC: Duke University Press, 2000), 194–242.

23. Jean-Louis Baudry and Alan Williams, "Ideological Effects of the Basic Cinematographic Apparatus," *Film Quarterly* 28, no. 2 (1974): 39–47.

24. Nichola Dobson, Annabelle Honess Roe, Amy Ratelle, and Caroline Ruddell, introduction to *The Animation Studies Reader* (New York: Bloomsbury Academic, 2018), 1.

25. Alan Cholodenko, "The Animation of Cinema," *Semiotic Review of Books* 18, no. 2 (2008): 1–10, and Lev Manovich, *The Language of New Media* (Cambridge, MA: MIT Press, 2001). See Koch in note 27 below.

26. Paul Wells, *Animation: Genre and Authorship* (London: Wallflower, 2002), 29.

27. Gertrud Koch, "Film as Experiment in Animation: Are Films Experiments on Human Beings?" trans. Daniel Hendrickson, in *Animating Film Theory*, ed. Karen Beckman (Durham, NC: Duke University Press, 2014), 135.

28. Susan Buchan, "The Animated Spectator: Watching Quay Brothers' Worlds," in *Animated Worlds*, ed. Suzanne Buchan (London: John Libbey, 2006), 27.

29. Sobchack, "Animation and Automation," 378.

30 Walter Benjamin, "The Work of Art in the Age of Mechanical Reproduction," trans. Harry Zohn, in *Illuminations*, ed. Hannah Arendt (New York: Schocken Books, 1968), 217–251. Also, please see: Stéphane Symons, "'The Creature That Can Still Survive': Walter Benjamin on Mickey Mouse and Rhythmic Movement," *Telos*, no. 176 (2016): 165–186, and Miriam Bratu Hansen,

"Micky-Maus," in *Cinema and Experience: Siegfried Kracauer, Walter Benjamin, and Theodor W. Adorno* (Berkeley: University of California Press, 2012), 163–182.

31. Halberstam, *The Queer Art of Failure*, 22–23.

32. Halberstam, 174–175.

33. Halberstam.

34. For example, *Zootopia* (Bryon Howard, Rich Moore, and Jared Bush, 2016), an animation that uses the physical differences of animals in exploring different types of urban accessibility. In one remarkable scene, differently shaped and sized animals ride on a train that is able to accommodate all of them.

35. J. Jack Halberstam, "Finding Nemo and Transgender Creatures," in *21st Century Sexualities: Contemporary Issues in Health, Education, and Rights*, ed. Gilbert Herdt and Cymene Howe (London: Routledge, 2007), 63–66.

36. Producer Michael Warch said about the film that "working on a short is a special experience, it's a little bit off the radar and you get a lot more freedom to explore different techniques and subject matter." See: "Pixar's 'Loop' Gives an Autistic Lead Character a Powerful Voice," ABC7, January 10, 2020, https://abc7.com/5837089/.

37. Fox, Comedy Central, HBO, and CBS.

38. Featured on the Adult Swim programming on Cartoon Network.

39. Season 4, episode 11.

40. Season 2, episode 5.

41. John Reid-Hresko, "Deconstructing Disability: Three Episodes of South Park," *Disability Studies Quarterly* 25, no. 4 (2005): np.

42. Moritz Fink, "People Who Look Like Things: Representations of Disability in The Simpsons," *Journal of Literary & Cultural Disability Studies* 7, no. 3 (2013): 255–270.

43. In "Downer Ending," season 1, episode 11, Bojack gets high and his animated character loses its outlines. After he reflects on this by saying, "There's no boundary between me and outer space," his colors fade away.

44. This is further discussed in the other chapters.

45. Sami Schalk, "Disability: Keywords for Gender and Sexuality Studies," New York University Press, accessed October 22, 2021, https://keywords.nyupress.org/gender-and-sexuality-studies/essay/disability/.

46. Janet Price and Margrit Shildrick, "Bodies Together: Touch, Ethics and Disability Theory," *Disability/Postmodernity: Embodying Disability Theory*, ed. Marian Corker and Tom Shakespeare (London: Continuum, 2002), 62–75.

47. Michael Oliver, *Understanding Disability: From Theory to Practice* (New York: St. Martin's, 1996), 32–33.

48. Shakespeare and Watson, "The Social Model of Disability," 22–28.

49. Nick Watson and Simo Vehmas, "Disability Studies: Into the Multidisciplinary Future," in *Routledge Handbook of Disability Studies*, 2nd ed. (London: Routledge, 2020), 5.

50. Anne Waldschmidt, "Disability Goes Cultural: The Cultural Model of Disability as an Analytical Tool," in *Culture—Theory—Disability: Encounters between Disability Studies and Cultural Studies*, ed. Anne Waldschmidt, Hanjo Berressem, and Moritz Ingwersen (Bielefeld, Germany: Transcript Verlag, 2017), 24.

51. Waldschmidt, "Disability Goes Cultural," 26.

52. Waldschmidt, 26.

53. Alexandre Baril, "Transness as Debility: Rethinking Intersections between Trans and Disabled Embodiments," *Feminist Review* 111 (2015): 62.

54. Jasbir K. Puar, "Disability," *Transgender Studies Quarterly* 1, no. 1–2 (2014): 78.

55. Puar, "Disability," 79.

56. Puar, 79.

57. Madeline Stump, "The Rambling of a Chronically Ill Mad Trans Femme," *Queer Disability Studies Network* (blog), November 3, 2021, https://queerdisabilitystudies.wordpress.com/the-ramblings-of-a-chronically-ill-mad-trans-femme/?fbclid=IwAR2MLgjSMWStAe7nshChhbowLDaMrouFolrtYhkt-1qkcm_w3NfifhoTAfw.

58. Niamh Timmons, "Towards a Trans Feminist Disability Studies," *Journal of Feminist Scholarship* 17, no. 17 (2020): 47. Also see: Niamh Timmons, "My Gender Is Crip: Engaging the Experience of Being Trans and Disabled," in *TransNarratives: Scholarly and Creative Works on Transgender Experience*, ed. Kristi Carter and James Brunton (Toronto: Women's Press, an imprint of CSP Books, 2021), 249–261.

59. Faye Ginsburg, "Foreword to the *Routledge Companion to Disability and Media* (Or: A Companion on the Ramp Less Traveled)," in *Routledge Companion to Disability and Media*, ed. Katie Ellis, Gerard Goggin, Beth Haller, and Rosemary Curtis (London: Routledge, 2020), xxii–xxvi.

60. Elizabeth Ellcessor and Bill Kirkpatrick, *Disability Media Studies* (New York: New York University Press, 2017).

61. Ginsburg, xxiii.

62. Mara Mills and Jonathan Stern, "After Word II: Dismediation—Three Proposals, Six Tactics," in *Disability Media Studies*, ed. Elizabeth Ellcessor and Bill Kirkpatrick (New York: New York University Press, 2017), 366.

63. Ginsburg, "Foreword," xxiv.

64. Christopher Smit and Anthony Enns, *Screening Disability: Essays on Cinema and Disability* (Lanham, MD: University Press of America, 2001).

65. Longmore, "Screening Stereotypes."

66. For example, Norden, *The Cinema of Isolation*.

67. One salient example for this is the character of Dr. Strangelove, the ultimate antagonist who causes the world's destruction in Stanley Kubrick's critical and anti-war film, *Dr. Strangelove* (1964). Not only is Dr. Strangelove a

wheelchair user, but he also suffers from inexplicable spasms, causing him to strangle himself.

68. Longmore, "Screening Stereotypes."

69. Thomas B. Hoeksema and Christopher R. Smit, "The Fusion of Film Studies and Disability Studies," in *Screening Disability: Essays on Cinema and Disability*, ed. Christopher R. Smit and Anthony Enns (Lanham, MD: University Press of America, 2001), 33–43.

70. As formed by scholars such as Teresa De Lauretis, Linda Williams, and Vivian Sobchack.

71. Sharon L. Snyder and David T. Mitchell, "Body Genres: An Anatomy of Disability in Film," in *The Problem Body: Projecting Disability on Film*, ed. Sally Chivers and Nicole Markotić (Columbus: Ohio State University Press, 2010), 180–181.

72. Robert McRuer, introduction to "In Focus: Cripping Cinema and Media Studies," special issue, *JCMS: Journal of Cinema and Media Studies* 58, no. 4 (2019): 134–139.

73. Elizabeth Ellcessor and Bill Kirkpatrick, "Studying Disability for a Better Cinema and Media Studies," in "In Focus: Cripping Cinema and Media Studies," special issue, *JCMS: Journal of Cinema and Media Studies* 58, no. 4 (2019): 139–144, and *Disability Media Studies* (New York: New York University Press, 2017).

74. Nicole Markotić, "The Many in the One: Depression and Multiple Subjectivities in Inside Out," in "In Focus: Cripping Cinema and Media Studies," special issue, *JCMS: Journal of Cinema and Media Studies* 58, no. 4 (2019): 162–168.

75. For example, Moritz Fink's "People Who Look Like Things" and John Reid-Hresko's "Deconstructing Disability."

76. Baldwin, introduction to *Maurice Merleau-Ponty*.

77. Merleau-Ponty, "The Intertwining—The Chiasm," 136.

78. Merleau-Ponty, 137.

79. Williams, "Film Bodies"; Vivian Sobchack, "Film's Body," in *The Address of the Eye: A Phenomenology of Film Experience* (Princeton, NJ: Princeton University Press, 1992), 203–248, and "What My Fingers Knew: The Cinesthetic Subject, or Vision in the Flesh," *Senses of Cinema*, 2000; and Marks, *The Skin of the Film*.

80. Williams, "Film Bodies."

81. Williams, 2–13.

82. Sobchack, "Film's Body," 203–248.

83. Sobchack, "What My Fingers Knew."

84. Vivian Sobchack, "'Surge and Splendor': A Phenomenology of the Hollywood Historical Epic," *Representation* 1, no. 29 (1990): 24–49, and "Film's Body."

85. Vivian Sobchack, *Carnal Thoughts: Embodiment and Moving Image Culture* (Berkeley: University of California Press, 2004).

86. A relevant example of inhabiting two sensoriums is the series *Sense8* (J. Michael Straczynski, Lana Wachowski, and Lilly Wachowski, 2015–2018), which alludes to both trans and crip experiences. Over the span of the first two seasons, eight characters learn that they are not human but *homo sensorium*, i.e., species secretly living among humans able to sense the members of their cluster. For an extensive phenomenological and trans studies analysis of the series, see: Cáel M Keegan, "Epilogue—Event Horizon: Sense8," in *Lana and Lilly Wachowski* (Urbana: University of Illinois Press, 2018), 106–129.

87. Marks, *The Skin of the Film*, 194–242.

88. Miriam Hansen, "Benjamin, Cinema and Experience: 'The Blue Flower in the Land of Technology,'" *New German Critique*, no. 40 (Winter 1987): 211, and Walter Benjamin, *On Hashish* (Cambridge, MA: Harvard University Press, 2006). For more about this issue, please see chapter 3.

ONE

RESISTING THE ABLEIST GAZE
Between Mainstream and Experimental Forms

HAVE WE "PROGRESSED" TO A new post-ableist, antineoliberal-PC, "woke" era in the representation of people with disabilities in film and television? And, in retrospect, have all previous representations of disability been derogatory? This binary opposition between an ableist past and an evolved present is negated with yet another dichotomy: those separating mainstream and experimental forms by crowning the latter as radical and dismissing the first due to its conservatism. Instead, this chapter proposes a discussion about the construction of the ableist gaze through time and across genres, from mainstream to the experimental and back again. My aim is to lay the ground to explore the possibilities that lie beyond live action and questions of representation and divert the focus to the alternatives that dwell in a different way of communicating with audiences. I turn to animation—not only because it is not bound by any physical laws or representational conventions but rather because it evokes spectators' bodies in ways that may open up a space to discuss the experience of crip embodiments and states of mind.

Although the construction of the ableist gaze took place simultaneously with the formulization of cinematic conventions, it is important to note that the subversion of this gaze is neither a new nor a current phase but rather can be identified throughout film history. The tension between mainstream cinema and avant-garde, independent, experimental, or animated films has existed from the beginning of cinematic production and continues to this day.

Films such as *Freaks* (Tod Browning, 1932), *Mask* (Peter Bogdanovich, 1985), *The Elephant Man* (David Lynch, 1980), and *Million Dollar Baby* (Clint Eastwood, 2004) construct the able-bodied spectator's point of view over the bodily difference of people with physical disabilities as a spectacle. Furthermore, the narratives of these films suggest that contemporary medicine is unable to assist such people and therefore there is not much point in sustaining their lives. These films provide spectators with a guilt-free glance into what is outside the ordinary field of visuals. According to Sharon L. Snyder and David T. Mitchell, the spectators in such films gaze at the abnormal body, which is presented as visually excessive. This presentation reiterates the practice of clinical diagnosis from a medical point of view.[1] In this way, the disabled body is used as a spectacle in mainstream cinema for the gaze of the temporarily able-bodied viewer.

Over the past decade, it has become more difficult to distinguish between mainstream and marginal cinematic aesthetics as many films are now combining classical Hollywood expression and experimental scenes. These avant-garde scenes rely on the alternative point of view of a disabled character. Films such as *Thumbsucker* (Mike Mills, 2005), *Cake* (Daniel Barnz, 2014), and *The Diving Bell and the Butterfly* (Julian Schnabel, 2004) are shown from the characters' points of view (point-of-view shots and subjective camera), thus potentially replacing the medical/ableist gaze with disabled subjectivity. These films offer momentary deviations from the Hollywood gaze through scenes emphasizing the subjective physical or emotional experience. Such scenes are unique in that they emphasize the body and its senses, allowing space for a political-ethical point of view.

As this chapter shows, short avant-garde animation concerning the lived experiences of people with disabilities subverts the ableist gaze and offers an alternative to previous cinematic representations of disability. Avant-garde film is defined by cinema scholars and historians as a counterreaction to mainstream cinema[2]—and therefore marginalized compared with commercial cinema.[3] As opposed to mainstream filmmakers, avant-garde filmmakers tend to have lower budgets, work independently, and use unconventional distribution methods. Avant-garde cinema is arguably celebrated thanks to its artistic value but also for its opposition to kitsch, sentimentality, melodrama, and banality. In addition, it frequently has been argued that avant-garde cinema is freer compared to mainstream cinema, which limits directors' artistic creativity in accordance with public demand.[4]

However, the distinction between avant-garde and mainstream cinema is not so clear cut historically. Many avant-garde filmmakers have never categorically avoided the commercial field. Indeed, they often have relied on it for financial reasons or even for the creative opportunities its resources allowed.[5] The clay animation company Aardman Animations rests within this tension, especially in the context of a series such as *Creature Discomfort*, which consists of collaboration between the company and a charity serving people with disabilities.

The spectatorship experience in alternative films and animation strives to invoke all the spectators' senses. According to Merleau-Pontian phenomenology, each single-sensory experience arouses another sense due to the overlap between them. This means that viewing any mainstream or avant-garde film affords the experience of hearing through sight and, similarly, of touch through hearing as well. Any film may arouse our bodily senses, even if it mostly relies on traditional cinematic conventions; however, animation celebrates the possibility of disconnecting from the conventions that structure cinematic spectatorship and listenership in particular and our sensory perceptions in general. Although mainstream live-action cinema contains individual scenes that challenge traditional conventions by using a subjective camera (as I discuss later in this chapter), animation allows for reflection about the way we view cinema and perceive the world.

The first part of this chapter analyzes the construction of the ableist gaze in the well-known horror films *Freaks* and *The Elephant Man*, as well as the popular melodrama films *Mask* and *Million Dollar Baby*. I explore the way these films are in negotiation with both the ableist gaze and avant-garde film. The second part of this chapter examines films that are located at the heart of the mainstream but simultaneously occasionally use avant-garde expression. The films *Thumbsucker, Cake,* and *The Diving Bell and the Butterfly* rely on the subjective points of view of people with disabilities and use experimental methods like the subjective camera for representing their inner world. The third part of this chapter focuses on some of the alternatives offered by animated film that relies almost completely on the subjective points of view of people with disabilities. I highlight the animated series *Creature Discomforts*, produced by Aardman Animations, and discuss the potential of this type of animated film to create a spectatorship experience that forces audiences to abandon some of their traditional conventions.

THE CONSTRUCTION OF THE ABLEIST GAZE IN MAINSTREAM GENRES

Before focusing on the ableist gaze as constructed by cinema, I need to first differentiate it from the off-screen and out-of-theater type of looking, defined by Rosemarie Garland-Thomson as the stare. Her *Extraordinary Bodies: Figuring Physical Disability in American Culture and Literature* positions a distinction between the erotic gaze and the stare that is directed at disabled bodies.[6] In *Staring: How We Look*, Garland-Thomson articulates looks exchanged in the world, in particular between able-bodied starers and visibly disabled "starees."

She suggests that "once triggered, a stare can yield its bearer myriad responses, from curiosity to confusion, attraction, discomfort, even repulsion. Starees, of course, are sometimes reluctant participants in their starers' visual search for something new; they have their own lives to live."[7] However, Garland-Thomson distinguishes the stare from the gaze. While the gaze "has been extensively defined as an oppressive act of disciplinary looking that subordinated its victim," the stare engages in many variations of intensive looking: for example, "blank stare, baroque stare, gold-driven stare, and the dominating stare."[8] Garland-Thomson unsettles the common understanding that staring is rudeness, voyeurism, or surveillance and that starers are perpetrators and starees victims. In cinematic spectatorship the gazer is secured by the darkness of the theater, social conventions, the distance from the subject of the image, and the fact that the image cannot gaze back.

Laura Mulvey's well-known argument—that mainstream Hollywood cinema constructs the male gaze on women's bodies as visual objects for satisfying its scopophilia and to ease its anxieties—is fundamental to tracing the ableist gaze. Building on her study, I show that the ableist gaze provides satisfaction for the abled viewer's desires through the disabled body/mind. According to Mulvey, mainstream cinema reflects social psychological obsessions—those being patriarchal in the case of the male gaze and ableist in the case of the able-bodied/minded gaze. Mulvey suggests that Hollywood cinema is distinct from alternative cinema by serving the dominant ideology: "However self-conscious and ironic Hollywood managed to be, it always restricted itself to a formal mise-en-scène reflecting the dominant ideological concept of the cinema. The alternative cinema provides a space for a cinema to be born which is radical in both a political and an aesthetic sense and challenges the basic assumptions of the mainstream film."[9]

The male-gaze theory as well as its critique have inspired the articulation of the cissexist gaze, defined by film and trans studies scholar Cáel M. Keegan as "the investment in the realness, perceptibility, and meaningfulness of assigned sex"[10] and by media scholar McKenzie Wark as "a looking that harbors anxiety about the slippages and transformations between genders, but which also harbors desires for those transitions as well."[11]

Similar to patriarchy, which is entangled in misogynist ideology, and cissexism, which is entangled with transphobia, ableism is entangled with eugenicist ideology. This paradigm makes it necessary to separate "healthy" from "sick" while providing justifications and explanations for doing so. Therefore, exposing the ableist gaze in cinema might subvert visual pleasure in similar ways to those suggested by Mulvey. The ableist gaze in mainstream cinema is constructed by satisfying the scopophilic desire to know the "other" body. I focus on the traditional gaze as constructed within the horror and melodrama genres and explore its dual function—as a physical spectacle that eases the fear of disability and as the suggestion of death or exclusion as a way of eradicating radical physical difference.

Applying Linda Williams's examination of the fantasies that body genres allow their spectators to experience, within horror, the fantasy is that of sadomasochism, while in melodrama, it is masochism.[12] Snyder and Mitchell examine the presentation of the excessiveness of the disabled body in mainstream cinema and analyze the cinematic genres of comedy, horror, and melodrama using nine main categories for the representation of disability.[13] Thus, for example, they argue that the source of the disability of characters in horror films is inborn monstrosity while melodrama films show maimed capacity. On the narrative level, the motivation of disabled characters in horror is revenge while in melodrama it is restoration.[14] Snyder and Mitchell offer the narratives of documentary film as an alternative to representations in mainstream cinema.[15] Their arguments concur with previous studies of the history of documentary film and its reproduction of the ableist and medical gaze.[16]

Continuing their work, I focus on two main genres, horror and melodrama, due to their great popularity in Hollywood. These genres serve as representative examples of mainstream cinema. By examining the horror films *Freaks* and *The Elephant Man*, I discuss the spectacle of physical difference meant to ease the anxiety of becoming a person with a disability. In analyzing the melodrama films *Mask* and *Million Dollar Baby*, I examine the use of physical difference for reinforcing eugenicist perceptions of death as both a narrative and an ethical solution.[17]

These four films were selected due to the broad recognition they received among audiences and film scholars over time and the critiques they have drawn from disability scholars. Most critiques focused on the presentation of disability based on the medical/individual model, which views disability as a tragedy requiring medical repair. Such films suggest that in the lack of a medical solution, the lives of people with disabilities are rendered unworthy. This reading is offered to exemplify the third phase of the theoretical intersection between film and disability studies, characterized by a combination of aesthetic methods with the critical viewpoint of disability studies.[18] Such readings allow an examination of the ways cinematic expression works—sometimes as a reinforcement of the ableist narrative and sometimes as a subversion of it.

This discussion focused on mainstream live-action cinema and discussed the ways it constructs an ableist gaze on people with disabilities. This type of gaze visually enhances the physical difference and dependency of people with disabilities and provides narrative relief for the spectators by killing off the disabled character. In fact, the ableist point of view in cinema perpetuates the tradition of the medical point of view, with aesthetic and narrative additions.

THE HORROR OF BECOMING DISABLED

Although *Freaks* is categorized as a horror film on the Internet Movie Database (IMDb) website while *The Elephant Man* is categorized as a biographical drama, they both correspond with the horror genre's horizon of expectations.[19] Both films make use of the physical difference of people with disabilities to construct an ableist gaze over them. Nevertheless, I also wish to discuss the ways these films can be read as subverting this gaze. The depiction of the physical difference of people with disabilities can be interpreted as a reinforcement of mainstream cinema's dominant ideology. However, at the same time, the use of spectacle can also be read as a critical stance with regards to ableist social perceptions through an analysis of the expressionist cinematic style, the use of contrast lighting, and the horror genre's conventions. *Freaks* uses horror's conventions to critique Hollywood's idealized body and offers inner-community solidarity as an alternative to an ableist world. Similarly, *The Elephant Man* uses an expressionist cinematic style to create critical parallels between the gaze of the masses watching a "freak show" and the medical gaze. Both these gazes are perceived as gaining pleasure from the spectacular body's performance and are driven by similar motives.

The cult status of *Freaks* may be read through its description by the American Cinematheque in Los Angeles for a screening on 35mm:

> "Gooble gobble, gooble gobble, we accept her, we accept her, one of us, one of us!" Based on the simple moral that beauty is on the inside comes this inspired, documentary-like tale of circus life. Trapeze artist Cleopatra and strongman Hercules plot to kill the sideshow midget and gain his inheritance. Drawing from past experience working for the circus, DRACULA director Tod Browning cast [sic] people with disabilities instead of using special effects and makeup, something unthinkable for the time. Although banned in the U.K. for 30 years, FREAKS was selected for preservation in 1994 by the United States National Film Registry as one of the greatest films of all time.[20]

The narrative of the film *Freaks* follows Hans, a little person working as a circus performer, who falls in love with a woman with an ideal classical body for the films of 1930s Hollywood. The woman, named Cleopatra, together with her partner, Hercules, plots to kill Hans after their wedding and win his inherited fortune. In what was defined by Sally Chivers as the only classical horror scene in the film, the community of people with disabilities stalks Cleopatra, traps her, and turns her into a "human chicken."[21] It is interesting to note that in contrast with most films about disability, in which temporarily able-bodied actors are cast as people with disabilities, most of the participants of the film *Freaks* were, in fact, people with disabilities. In addition, the film includes a variety of disabilities—little people, conjoined twins, intersex people, and people with missing limbs.[22]

Years after the film's production, many artists and culture scholars cite it as having greatly influenced their affection for the horror film genre.[23] About one-third of the first anthology on film and disability was dedicated to Tod Browning's films—especially *Freaks*, as his most controversial work.[24] The film was banned in the Unites States and the United Kingdom shortly after being released and was the target of strong criticism on the part of both film critics and the general public.[25] In addition, some of its participants have stated that they regretted their involvement.[26] As mentioned in the introduction, *Freaks* is also the main point of reference in the recently released documentary *Code of the Freaks* (2020), which was made by disability studies scholars and activists, on the topic of disability representation in Hollywood.

This film is a classic example of Paul Longmore's argument about people with disabilities being constructed as antagonistic in horror films. Horror is invoked when disability functions as a melodramatic tool for representing the antagonist and is emphasized when villains are represented through physical deformity. As Longmore suggests, the disabled body symbolizes the disfigurement of the soul, and therefore such characters represent evil incarnate. The cross between the antagonist and disability radically reflects and reinforces three types of prejudice. The first is that disability is a punishment for evil, a notion that is easily observed in horror films. In *Freaks*, Cleopatra's transformation into a human chicken without the ability for speech or movement is her "punishment" for being an evildoer.[27] The second is that people with disabilities are bitter on account of their tragic "fate." The film suggests that this bitterness causes Hans's friends to enact the code of the freaks ("Offend one, and you offend them all") on Cleopatra. The third is that people with disabilities hold a grudge against nondisabled people and would annihilate them if they could. In *Freaks*, the group of people with disabilities exacts revenge on the desirable able-bodied Cleopatra, disfiguring her body. According to Longmore, people with disabilities receive this vilifying representation on film and television because of the social anxiety from encountering disability either personally or through loved ones. This anxiety manufactures images that concur with it, hence producing negative images of disability as a source of horror.[28]

Simultaneously with readings relying on the use of negative images in this film, Sally Chivers also suggests that *Freaks* lacks typical elements of the horror film genre and that its inclusion is related to its exceptional spectatorship position, which offers identification with people with disabilities. According to her, and in contrast with the typical narrative structure of horror films, the film consists of a rather coherent love story. The only aspect related to the characteristics of horror is that the spectator is forced into an unusual position of identification. Chivers argues that the film's opening sequence is reminiscent of melodrama or romance, and therefore, the only horror present in the film is the challenge presented to the ableist gaze. The film presents Cleopatra's body as inconceivable and impossible, thus forcing the viewers to realign their gaze on the ideal body as a deviation from the norm. The transformation of Cleopatra's body into a human chicken realizes the anxiety of bodily disfigurement, related to the spectators' horizon of expectations from the horror genre. Her body's transformation is the exact opposite of the way she perceived the "freaks." Hence, Cleopatra herself becomes the thing she feared most. Although the film does not show explicit violence, the spectator is terrified at the demonization of the body that the audience has become accustomed to perceive as the "protagonist." Positioning the disabled bodies, which operate morally, against the excessively able bodied, which operate immorally, encourages the spectators to come closer and join the disability community.

The discomfort offered by this film is caused by identification with a person deviating from the norms of the ideal Hollywood body of the time. The film's horror relies on this discomfort, which comes into play by changing the spectator's gaze from the abled body to that of a person with a disability as the subject of interest. Thus, Chivers's inevitable conclusion is that the only horror is identification with a body that is different from Hollywood norms of a health-ideal body.[29]

Similar to *Freaks*, *The Elephant Man* also tells the story of a person with physical difference who makes a living as a circus performer.[30] This is yet another film situated comfortably within the cinematic canon that was rarely read through a disability lens despite its centrality to the plot as well as the cinematography. After the protagonist, John Merrick, is discovered by Dr. Frederick Treves, he is transferred to a hospital, where he stays under medical supervision (not treatment). Merrick becomes a celebrity in the aristocratic Victorian society for writing prose, poetry, and an autobiography. At the end of the film, it is unclear whether Merrick passes away as the result of suicide or as an attempt to mimic the sleep position of "normal" people. Lynch wished to direct a black-and-white homage to both classical horror films and *Freaks*' aesthetics of German expressionism. The film's unique style, among other things, is expressed through the fact that the film's protagonist is first seen on-screen half an hour into the film's run time, and his voice is first heard after forty minutes.[31]

Film critics have raised similar questions with regards to both films: what makes the film into a horror? Noël Carroll argues that horror films consist of a paradox based on the question: how can audiences be attracted to that which repulses them? Carroll explains that the monsters typical of the genre are the subject of interest, curiosity, and inquisitiveness because they are anomalous. Their anomaly challenges familiar categories, and therefore they are simultaneously attractive and repulsive.[32] Following these questions, scholars have examined the source of the horror and the identity of the monster in horror films.[33] Shai Biderman and Assaf Tabeka mainly rely on the theory of alienation while examining the question of whether Merrick is doomed to be an outcast from society.[34] They argue that the film presents Merrick as an animal-like monster: he does not speak or walk properly, is first shown as lacking any cognitive capabilities, is disfigured, and is locked in a cage. This treatment changes after the doctor decides there's a gentle soul behind the monster. However, making him into a celebrity preserves him as a subject of the curious gaze.

The first scene that transforms the viewpoint of Merrick as a monster is the kidnapping scene, in which a violent crowd bursts into Merrick's room and forcefully returns him to the circus. Within this scene, Biderman and Tabeka argue, the presentation of the crowd's evil suggests that the real monstrosity lies with every person in society—and, indeed, the heart of the social order. Not recognizing their nature, humans victimize those they perceive as weak and different because of the monstrosity within them. Merrick is thus perceived as an object by both Mr. Bytes, the sideshow manager at the carnival, and Dr. Treves, as well as the medical team and society in general. Similar to the relationship among the community members in *Freaks*, inner-community friendship in *The Elephant Man* is presented as solidarity between people with disabilities, who selflessly save Merrick. However, the film's conclusion with Merrick's death, caused as a result of his wish to be "like everyone," suggests that only through death can Merrick join the social sphere. In addition, the viewpoint on Merrick is transformed by the treatment he receives after being discovered as a "gentle soul." However, if he had any cognitive or linguistic disabilities, he might have suffered social treatment similar to the one he had initially experienced while caged in the carnival by Bytes.

The stylistic choice of horror and expressionism, alongside surrealist scenes, draws a critical view of society, in particular in reference to medical institutions and the institutionalization of people with disabilities, physically alienating and segregating them. Through its cinematic expression, the film criticizes the clinical gaze over Merrick's body. This critique focuses on his transfer to the hospital for no apparent medical reason. The black-and-white cinematography of the film, with a static camera and close-up shots, positions the spectators as the audience of a freak show. Cinematically and politically equating three gazes—the mob, the doctors, and the intellectual elite—Lynch confronts the gaze of the spectators, deeming them as accomplices.

Both films, *Freaks* and *The Elephant Man*, make use of horror cinematic expression to reinforce the spectator's gaze on the physical difference of people with disabilities. Although both offer a critique of the ableist gaze, these films rely on the physical spectacle of people with disabilities. They do so by presenting physical excess as unable to exist within an ableist world. The conclusion of *The Elephant Man* marks the period in which it was produced; during this time, the liberal representation of disability was conveyed by relieving the spectators from the need to engage with social oppression—conveyed through the protagonist's death. This aspect of the film is related to its melodramatic components, as discussed in the context of the films *Mask* and *Million Dollar Baby* in the following section.

DEATH AS REDEMPTION FROM DISABILITY (MELO)DRAMA

The film *Mask* was produced after the formation of the disability rights movement in the 1980s in the United States yet before the Capitol Crawl (March 12, 1990) and the ADA, and it too seeks to satisfy the desire to stare at the physical differences of people with disabilities through offering spectators the scopophilic gaze. *Mask* is based on the story of Roy L. "Rocky" Dennis (1961–1978), an American boy with a syndrome that causes a deformation of the skull and face.[35] This film has garnered praise and positive reviews, both for Cher's remarkable performance as Rusty Dennis, which won her a Cannes award, and for what critics referred to as the choice to include positive elements, such as social integration, within its narrative.[36]

Mask relies on classical Hollywood conventions, narrating Rocky's coming-of-age alongside his mother, who is a member of a biker community. Similar to many coming-of-age films, *Mask* engages with issues of relationships and sexuality.[37] The love story between Rocky and Diana (a beautiful blind girl, played by Laura Dern, he meets at the Hollywood version of Camp Jened featured in *Crip Camp*) survives despite obstacles caused by the ableist attitudes of her parents.[38] The film not only addresses sexuality but also targets inequity, exclusion, and discrimination faced within the school by students with disabilities.[39] The plot focuses on the struggle of Rocky's mother against the school's discrimination and her success in attaining her son's right to education. Both the romantic and the political spheres remain undeveloped, since the film concludes with Rocky's death.

Despite the praise garnered by this film in the press, disability scholars—and Longmore, in particular—have criticized the choice to display Rocky's story in excess, as well as the film's particular choice to conclude the narrative with his death.[40] An analysis of this film according to the first and second phases of the conjunction between film theory and disability studies, which focus on exposing negative representations, gives way to a critique of the film's sentimental and melodramatic representation of disability. The main argument in this context is that melodrama constructs a paternalistic attitude toward characters with disabilities, evoking pity and thus a moral superiority in able-bodied spectators.[41] This approach maintains that the directors of the genre manipulate the spectators' response by exacerbating the physical aspects of the protagonist's condition and specifically do so in parts where the narrative requires extra drama.[42] Similar to *The Elephant Man*, in this case, too, *Mask* relieves the spectators from having to deal with questions of social justice and oppression by concluding with the protagonist's death. Moreover, such narratives reinforce the notion that the more apparent the disability, the more likely the person with said disability will be portrayed as not being able to integrate.[43]

Similarly, *Million Dollar Baby* also offers death as an appropriate solution for disability. This ableist portrayal was met with vibrant disability protests on one hand and box office success on the other. The "gap between the almost-universal adoration of the film, emanating from the moviegoing public at large, and the almost-universal condemnation of it, emanating from disability activist communities," is explained by Robert McRuer as part of neoliberal risk, and he finds the protests against the film to be most productively read "through the wide-spread, increasingly global generation of alternative disabled values and futures."[44] The neoliberal lessons of the film are that the market is everything and deregulation is best, privatization is an unequivocal good, social services are insufficient and corrupt, and personal "responsibility" should be valued. McRuer concludes with anti-ableist activism through the slogan at the heart of the next chapter—"Nothing about us without us" (or "Nothing Without Us," as Lawrence Carter-Long has rephrased it)[45]—as "always echoing in the background, however (and I imagine we always have yet to recognize just how radical that watch phrase is), we can continue to insist that integration into that order, or any order, is unacceptable if it leaves so many of 'us' behind."[46]

This film tells the story of Maggie, a thirty-one-year-old woman aspiring to become a professional boxer. As part of her training process, she seeks the help of Frankie, the owner of a boxing club who has refused to train women for years prior to her request. Frankie relents after she proves her skills and determination to him, and the two form a very close, almost father-daughter relationship. However, Maggie's dream is cut short when she is injured in a crucial fight and becomes paralyzed and bedridden at a hospital. The last part of the film focuses on the relationship between Maggie and Frankie, which is presented as the only source of hope in her life, since her family is exploiting her and the hospital is neglecting her. The film concludes as traumatized, depressed, and isolated Maggie asks for help to kill herself through euthanasia, which Frankie accepts.

Before going into any specific issues within the film, this abstract alone touches on many of the ableist tropes covered by *Code of the Freaks*. In fact, it even surpasses what Carrie Sandahl termed as "all the same movie" in combining so many of them in a single film: for example, a life not worth living, disabled women as asexual, films that end with euthanasia and a person with a disability advocating for his or her own worthlessness (see *Whose Life Is It Anyway*), films about paralysis that begin with an overly physically active character and center on his or her body's motion, a focus on the period immediately after a person first learns about his or her disability after a traumatic or sudden event, and representations of hospitals that should provide basic care but are unable to.[47]

In addition to the extremely ableist narrative, *Million Dollar Baby* also failed on issues of gender and race. Doris Zames Fleischer and Frieda Zames argue that superficially, this film may have seemed as supporting marginalized social groups—whether they be a blind Black boxer or a thirty-one-year-old poor woman aspiring to become a professional boxer. However, in actuality, the film's ableist narrative contributes to their depiction as inferior or unworthy. The film's narrative relies on the distorted assumption that euthanasia is an act of kindness toward people with disabilities. Maggie, the film's protagonist, has many reasons to be depressed—the loss of her dream to win the championship, neglect at the rehabilitation center, the preventable amputation of her leg as a result, family alienation, and more. The main problem with the film's conclusion lies with the fact that in the absence of a disability, she would likely not have been encouraged to die by suicide but would have been offered mental support.[48]

Similar to the hospitalization of *The Elephant Man*'s protagonist, the conclusion of *Million Dollar Baby* positions the film's protagonist in a hospital and constructs her as not merely invaluable but also, as per neoliberal values, too costly. Although the institution is called a "rehabilitation center," Karen Schwartz, Zana Mary Lutfiyya, and Nancy Hansen argue that the film lacks representation of any rehabilitative/medical processes; on the contrary, what we see is negligence. In addition, this part of the film focuses on Maggie's confinement to a hospital bed and enhances her physical immobility with a sense of mental stagnation, which is portrayed as the new permeant reality rather than possibly linked to said trauma, oppression, and depression. One example is a scene exacerbating the effort involved in her treatment and her life, emphasizing the slowness of the three hours it takes to help her sit in a wheelchair and deeming it a waste of time. Maggie herself does nothing in her free time; her depression is linked with her physical disability, and she is represented as awaiting her death. Even when Frankie speaks of getting her an electrical wheelchair and college classes, she seems to not be listening. The film concludes with the notion that her life is not worth living. Because she is doomed to suffering and self-hate, it seems that her only logical choice is to end her life.[49] *Million Dollar Baby* is an extreme case of the ableist gaze and is almost the architype that combines many tropes that further inscribe what Paul Darke articulated as using illnesses, impairment, and disability, as part of a process of invalidating disabled characters.[50]

As dramas, the films *Mask* and *Million Dollar Baby* use the physical difference of people with disabilities in order to arouse the spectators' sentimental emotions. The films' narratives expose various aspects of injustice, exclusion, and discrimination on several social levels yet end with the protagonists' deaths. In the lack of narrative continuity or indications of any social change, the audience is left with a paternalistic sense of pity toward people with disabilities. Therefore, while the ableist gaze in horror films exacerbates the anxiety of becoming disabled, the ableist gaze in melodrama films coincides with the medical one and relieves the viewers from any possible imagination of (social) change.

The ableist gaze over physical difference is established in these four films, and their representations of disability very much concur with the anatomy of bodily genres articulated by Snyder and Mitchell.[51] *Freaks* and *The Elephant Man* use horror to represent the characters' innate monstrosity, thus realizing the spectators' sadomasochistic expectations. *Mask* and *Million Dollar Baby* use melodrama to represent the disabled body as pathetic and in need of rehabilitation, thus realizing the spectators' masochistic expectations.

Despite this critique, starting from 2009, the third phase of the scholarship on disability and film has focused on cinema's desire to move spectators and manipulate their emotions, most forcefully by the scholarship's focus on embodied human experiences. Some scholars have argued for the melodramatic use of disability, suggesting that to deny the emotional reactions invoked by depicting disability means denying the power of film and misinterpreting the medium in question. Thus, an integrative analysis within the framework of the third phase would suggest that sentimentality is a basic element of any melodrama, and a comprehensive analysis of such melodramas and how sentimentality functions within them should also consider that sentimentality produces real feelings of loss for the spectators. A reading grounded in the context of melodrama locates sentimentality as related to these expectations.[52]

Nevertheless, the main issue with mainstream cinema in regards to disability, which this part of the chapter seeks to expose, is not its inability to move the spectators but the eventual preference of the ableist gaze, which often derives from the medical gaze, over other points of view in the films. Despite inclusion of scenes expressing criticism in even the most ableist of films, mainstream Hollywood live-action cinema has been merging the spectator with the ableist gaze since the beginning of cinematic history as means of luring able-bodied and able-minded audiences to the cinematic attraction of the disabled body to further reinforce Hollywood's norms for desirable bodies and minds that continue to rely on the medical gaze. Simultaneously, during the past decade, filmmakers have been experimenting with alternatives to this type of gaze by combining avant-garde cinematic expressions, made possible by less common cinematographic styles and editing technologies. Such filmmakers, discussed in the next part, do not abandon mainstream techniques and ideologies but, at the same time, insert alternatives into mainstream expression. Through analysis of *My Left Foot* (Jim Sheridan, 1989), Hoeksema and Smit suggest the alternative presented with the film's point-of-view scenes and subjective camera angles. The film, they suggest, uses the protagonist's point of view as well as camera movements to transform the spectator into a family member of a person with a disability.[53]

An alternative spectatorship experience, offering a cinematic expression that subverts conventions, would endeavor to detach the spectator's point of view from his or her hegemonic social position and allow the viewer to experience a reflexive spectatorship, which invokes sensory aspects and raises awareness of perception. Such possibilities are enabled through the subjective camera, which allows a merging of the spectator's point of view with the point of view of a person with a specific experience of a disability—including his or her inner and external world.

SUBJECTIVE POINTS OF VIEW AND EXPERIMENTAL CINEMATOGRAPHY IN MAINSTREAM CINEMA

Three films offer the subjective point of view of people with disabilities while also subverting classical continuity through avant-garde expression: *Thumbsucker*, *Cake*, and *The Diving Bell and the Butterfly*. The three films can be located between the mainstream and the margins, as they offer deviations from the traditional cinematic gaze that enhance the subjective sensory experiences. *Thumbsucker*, the most mainstream in its expression, is an independent film telling the coming-of-age story of an adolescent named Justin, who is coping with attention deficit disorder or something else, of which sucking a thumb is a symptom. Another explanation to the thumb sucking is given in the conclusion of the film. It does not mean anything; it is not indicative of neither a pathology not identity. *Cake* tells the story of a woman coping with chronic pain and suicidal thoughts after surviving a car accident that left her injured and killed her son. This film mainly relies on mainstream cinematography and, except for subjective scenes interrupting its continuity, offers a narrative from the point of view of a woman with an intermittently apparent disability.[54] *The Diving Bell and the Butterfly*, the most avant-garde in its expression, tells the autobiographical story of Jean-Dominique Bauby, who became paralyzed after a stroke and is dictating his memoir using his left eye. About half the film is shown through a subjective camera, alongside abstract scenes representing his memories and imagination. Despite its avant-garde expression, it also concludes with the protagonist's death, similar to mainstream films about disability.

HAPPY ENDINGS FOR THE ABLE-BODIED SPECTATORS

The independent film's *Thumbsucker* cinematography is quite conventional, but some individual scenes, representing the protagonist's subjective experience, do offer a brief exception. The film's narrative is also dual and ranges between engagement with classical coming-of-age stories, ending with a move away from childhood toward adulthood, and a circular narrative revolving around thumb-sucking. The film's dual expression and narrative give way to various readings of the gaze constructed by the film over the disabled body. Although Justin's point of view, adopted by the film, rejects the medical gaze and chooses to maintain his difference, at the same time, it also eschews the identity category of disability. The film can be read through the social model as it concludes with Justin rejecting the impairment label and proudly sucking his thumb away from those who shamed him for it, yet this overall rejection of the disability category is rooted in the neoliberal embrace of difference that does not interfere with his bright financial future.

This film, based on a novel by Walter Kirn (who plays the debate judge), is a cisnormative story about a shy adolescent boy falling in love with a girl and discovering his sexuality.[55] Although he fails in maintaining his romantic relationship, he matures and "comes out into the world" as an adult and a self-accepting person, despite his compulsive thumb-sucking. In times of distress or anxiety, the teen is shown sitting alone is some small space and sucking his thumb.[56] In these moments, Justin is infantilized by his parents in the ways they respond to this practice while, at the same time, they require him to call them by their first names so they do not have to age (to their mind). In this coming-of-age story, the protagonist subverts the genre by pausing his transformation from childhood to adulthood, allowing himself the possibility of being both simultaneously. In addition to this narrative, there is a dialogue taking place within the film about various categories of disability—placing thumb-sucking at the center of the plot as a problem requiring a medical solution echoes the ways cinematic representations of people with disabilities tend to rely on the medical gaze. The protagonist's father perceives his behavior as abnormal and requiring behavioral change.

The traditional medical gaze is reinforced through the school counselor, who offers Justin pharmaceutical treatment. While significant portions of the film are dedicated to the orthodontist, representing a different perspective, the counselor only appears in one short scene where she diagnoses his attention and concentration difficulties. In the presence of his parents, the counselor asks Justin: "Have you ever suspected that you were different from other teenagers? Not as patient? Can't finish what you've started? Terrified of being left alone, but angry when you feel crowded?" As expected of teens his age, Justin responds: "A little." The counselor finds this response sufficient and immediately pronounces: "It's classic hyperactive teen. Attention deficit hyperactivity disorder. ADHD. We'd like you to think about a stimulant drug treatment." Justin's mother (Tilda Swinton), a professional nurse, reads from an information pamphlet about attention deficit disorders and notes that the symptoms described seem rather vague. Justin smiles and asks: "So my problems are just because I'm hyper?" When he and his parents leave the counselor's office, Justin reads the benefits of the pharmaceutical treatment aloud and notes that he could have more confidence and self-control, as well as better relationships. His father (Vincent D'Onofrio) expresses the notion that this solution seems too easy, while Justin is excited about just that.

An additional medical gaze in this film is represented by the orthodontist, Perry (Keanu Reeves), who holds an alternative approach that expands on his profession's boundaries. While his role is supposed to be limited to treating Justin's dental problems caused by his thumb-sucking, the doctor perceives him as a whole person—and, in particular, as an adolescent. Perry offers an observation of the teen's subconscious to resolve his behavioral thumb-sucking problem. The doctor offers the teen the chance to speak honestly about his anxieties and treat them with the help of hypnosis. This solution works partially, and Justin can no longer find comfort in sucking his thumb, since it now tastes like echinacea. When it becomes clear that Ritalin is not a sufficient solution for his coming-of-age transformations, Justin makes a special effort to seek out the orthodontist and ask for his help. Perry explains that he stopped trying to change and decided to accept himself the way he was, suggesting that Justin do the same. The doctor admits there is no medical or mental problem with his thumb-sucking, despite Justin's experience of it as a severe problem due to social misconceptions, as per the social model of disability.

Ritalin is represented in the film—through expression and narrative—as a euphoric drug that leads to momentary joy in dealing with coming-of-age processes. This comes in addition to explicit critiques made by his mother, the orthodontist, and a teacher, as well as a classmate who argues that only three molecules separate Ritalin and cocaine. In light of this, the most exceptional scene in the film, in terms of its cinematic expression, is dedicated to representing Justin's subjective experience under the influence of Ritalin. Colorful molecules float over a pink background. When they connect, the screen is lit up, while in the background we can hear a choir and echoing music. The scene changes with a shot of Justin opening a book. Following this, we see a sequence containing a number of scenes that share an identical structure—pages from the book are juxtaposed with short shots of Justin sifting through it. This scene utilizes common drug experimentation filming and editing techniques to critique Ritalin and the overall medicalization of what the film argues are natural adolescent processes. The positive change experienced by Justin is dismissed, and he is criticized for his overconfidence by friends and family, who state that it makes him arrogant and aggressive. Another scene that hones this argument shows the acceptance essay Justin writes to NYU under the influence of Ritalin. In this scene, in order to get accepted, the teen lies and writes that his parents are coping with a mental disability, thus tokenizing disability and disavowing it at the same time. Finally, Justin throws away all his Ritalin containers and quotes his opponent in the debate competition, who called him a "speed freak," thus rejecting the possibility of joining the disability community.

Thumbsucker uses Justin's anxiety as part of adolescence as a springboard or narrative protheses to argue against "drugging kids" and other oversimplified generalizations in pop culture—for example, *South Park*'s Timmy 2000—that expose the ableism at the root of their premises. This framing is coupled with the absence of discussion or recognition of ADHD as a valid condition, even if not experienced by Justin. Similar to *Million Dollar Baby*, which erases the various options for living with a disability, *Thumbsucker*, too, relieves itself from discussing mental disabilities and uses neurodiversity for the sake of arguing against medication for ADHD.

The film's final scene adopts the orthodontist's alternative approach. During Justin's flight to go to school in New York, he falls asleep and dreams about being a famous television anchor. He wakes up to find that while asleep, he has been sucking his thumb, and he sees a young woman in the next seat now smiling at him. He smiles and confidently introduces himself to her. From here the film skips to Justin's "happy" ending, as he is running through an avenue in Manhattan. This conclusion completes both narratives offered by the film about thumb-sucking—the coming-of-age narrative and the disability narrative. According to the first one, the teen sucks his thumb as an oral obsession that is merely a symptom of his adolescent anxiety. Justin's wish to come out into the world of adulthood, without giving up the comfort of thumb-sucking when he feels anxious, offers a critical point of view about the coming-of-age process in light of what the films argues to be overmedicalization. Within the second narrative, thumb-sucking, which serves as the grounds for discussing the disability categories of anxiety and attention deficit hyperactivity disorders and brushes on learning disabilities, is rendered as a sourceless symptom or quirky habit by the final scene.

This means that a reading of thumb-sucking as part of a successful coming-of-age story challenges the assumption of a dichotomous shift from childhood and adulthood. At the same time, thumb-sucking is described as a symptom of anxiety related to attention deficit disorders. As such, it requires at least two types of medical interventions—one neurological and one dental—while the first one is rejected within the film. From a disability studies perspective, Justin not only rejects the normalizing medical gaze represented by the school counselor but also disability's identity categories. The teen chooses individual acceptance of his "flaws" and refuses the medical diagnosis rendering the behavior classification as a disorder as well as the disability identity it offers, but most of all, he refuses to join the disability community. The coming-of-age narrative makes use of thumb-sucking to suggest visible difference but disregards the meaning of identification with the group of people with disabilities. Thus, despite some individual scenes, *Thumbsucker* does not challenge traditional ableist spectatorship.

The film *Cake* depicts the subjective experience of a woman coping with chronic pain.[57] The film consists of traditional cinematography and editing, combined with scenes offering the protagonist's point of view over her inner and external world. Claire's (Jennifer Aniston) point of view—from a lowered car seat angle—as a woman coping with chronic pain, who is unable to sit up straight on account of that pain, is presented many times throughout the film. In addition, several scenes that represent Claire's dreams and hallucinations include Nina, a fellow participant of her chronic pain support group, prior to her death by suicide. Similar to *Thumbsucker*, *Cake* also raises repeated criticism against the fast use of psychiatric drugs and overmedicalization. The film's writer based this story on a murder in his family that happened as a result of antidepressant drugs.[58] Both films use mental disability as narrative prosthesis for their critique of the medical and psychiatric institutions.

As in *Thumbsucker*, disability in *Cake* is nonapparent and therefore seems to be implicit. Despite the protagonist's participation in a chronic pain support group for women, the film ranges between representing Claire's physical pain and representing her emotional pain since the accident that killed her son. The film exceptionalizes Claire from the other women in the group by hinting at a temporality that corresponds with chronic disability and yet differs from it by being temporary. Discussing crip time from the point of view of chronic pain, Ellen Samuels writes, "The medical language of illness tries to reimpose the linear, speaking in terms of the chronic, the progressive, and the terminal, of relapses and stages. But we who occupy the bodies of crip time know that we are never linear, and we rage silently—or not so silently—at the calm straightforwardness of those who live in the sheltered space of normative time."[59] However, *Cake* does not offer the simultaneity Samuels describes; instead, it relies on a progression narrative of emotional recovery that, in turn, further discredits women's experiences with nonapparent physical pain. Therefore, the film's narrative, as well as its expression, offers the subjective experience of disability but at the same time negates the possibility of joining a community of people with disabilities. On the one hand, the film represents life with nonapparent or intermittently apparent and physical pain, while, on the other hand, it suggests that physical pain is the expression of emotional pain and therefore can be overcome. It is also worth mentioning that the film's approach toward Claire's bodymind's pain is that she confuses her emotional pain with the physical rather than that they are inseparable.

In contrast with the montage scene in *Thumbsucker*, which was intended to criticize the use of Ritalin, the montage scene in *Cake* is used to create a link between Claire's physical and emotional pain. The unspoken reason for Claire's pain and suffering is only revealed to the spectator toward the film's end. Claire takes a step toward choosing life, as she invites Nina's partner and son to her house. This meeting also motivates her to enter her son's room, which she had not done in a long time. Her euphoria from the possibility of having a new family dissolves as the driver who caused her son's death unexpectedly arrives at her house. This meeting reveals the source of Claire's pain to the spectators and is concluded with her emotional and physical reactions, including dissociated staring, vomiting, and losing consciousness. The montage showing the protagonist's experience while unconscious consists of shots of her son at different ages, juxtaposed with shots and sounds from Nina's accident and death by suicide. The montage is concluded with an image out of Claire's dream in which she is strangled by Nina. When Claire regains consciousness, a blurry point of view shows Silvana (Adriana Barraza), her official housekeeper and unofficial caregiver, sitting next to her in the hospital and praying for her health. Additional shots show Claire tossing and turning in her bed, restless on account of her pain.

The film is concluded as Claire visits her son's grave together with Silvana, who provides her with emotional and physical support. The film's conclusion hinting at an emotional solution for her physical pain is problematic as the assumption that chronic pain is solely psychological is one of the main barriers to receiving proper care. Adi Finkelstein studied the experience of women living with chronic fatigue and fibromyalgia in Israel and discovered that they negotiate the very recognition of their condition, both against institutions and against the people close to them, due to the vague nature of this medical diagnosis. Finkelstein offers the point of view of women who state that they know their bodies better than any other person, thus subverting the order controlled by external "experts." Her study also indicates that social alienation and exclusion may exacerbate the physical suffering of people living with chronic illnesses.[60] Similar to the women interviewed by Finkelstein, offering Claire's subjective point of view could have contributed to the political appearance of nonapparent or intermediately apparent disabilities; however, the conclusion of the film may, in fact, achieve the opposite.[61]

In addition to representing Claire's experience alongside other women participating in the group, and her relationship with Nina's haunting image, the film presents Claire's closest relationship as with Silvana. This is so despite their obvious socioeconomic, racial, and class gaps, in addition to the employer-versus-employee hierarchic structure. Silvana's housekeeping job is constantly expanding to include physical and emotional care for Claire. The differences between relationships with friends and relationships with caregiver have been explored by Janet Price and Margrit Shildrick through their conceptualization of the ethical experience of "being-in-the-world with others." The type of closeness built up through the shared history between Price and her friends is also apparent in Claire and Silvana's relationship. The process of becoming closer peaks in the scene where they sleep together in a highway motel after their car was stolen. Price states that during her most difficult period, there were actions she was unwilling to let friends do for her; she preferred them to be performed by a partner or caregiver due to the differences in mutuality, sacrifice, and separation in such relationships. However, according to Price, such actions can also be performed by close friends and thus establish a new type of relations: "It is clear that any alternative ethic of relationality, of mutuality, that did not rely on strictly autonomous agency of the singular, detached self would go at least some way toward forestalling the anxiety, and even hostility, evoked by proximity. It means taking seriously the notion of becoming-in-the-world-with-others."[62] Claire and Silvana's caregiver-housekeeper-friend relationship is represented as an opposition to the support group, where the facilitator proudly asserts the group to be a "super supportive" female environment while simultaneously removing Claire from the group. Nevertheless, crossing the boundaries between housekeeper and caregiver is a highly gendered and racialized phenomenon, and the film only alludes to the exploitation of her labor in a brief scene where her daughter confronts her about it.

Claire's second most important relationship is with the phantasmatic Nina, the woman who participated in her support group and died by suicide and now appears in her dreams and hallucinations. Claire uses this imaginary relationship to constantly question her choice to keep living with her pain. When Claire is hospitalized, she hallucinates Nina coming to visit her with a cake. They remember that when the facilitator of their support group asked about their wish for a life without chronic pain, Claire replied that she wanted to have sex with the entire Madrid soccer team. Nina's dream was to bake a cake for her son. This hallucination motivates Claire to realize that she is, in fact, addicted to painkillers, and she addresses the "real" source of her grief. The last scene in which Nina appears is when Claire lies down over train tracks and Nina validates her coping without medication. Suddenly, Nina's ghostly appearances become tangible to the spectators when Claire says, "I was a good mother" and rises up from the train tracks. This moment of reckoning allows Claire and the spectators to identify, if not diagnose, her condition as yet another (as with

Thumbsucker) case of a transient process of mourning thus erasing an already less apparent disability. The film builds on Freud's depathologization of mourning as transient and temporary (like adolescence), in contrast with the disabling mental disorder—melancholia—that requires medical intervention. Interestingly, in "Mourning and Melancholia," Freud also discusses the physical pain accompanying emotional pain in the process of mourning and argues that in contrast with melancholia, mourning is a natural and temporary process. In addition, it is easier for society to accept a person in mourning since unusual behavior is perceived as an understandable reaction to loss.[63] Although the film concludes with a dismissal of the disability category, through some subjective point-of-view scenes, it offers the sense of a moment from a lived experience of a person with chronic pain.

Cake contains some scenes that subvert the conventional gaze through the subjective point of view where the camera adopts the protagonist's perspective. These scenes are filmed from unusual angles from a lying-down position, forcing the spectator to look at the world from Claire's point of view. The inclusion of such scenes in a film that mostly consists of conventional cinematography and editing styles emphasizes the gap between these two points of view. In *Thumbsucker*, moments like this take place in scenes representing the influence of Ritalin, but *Cake* offers realistic subjective scenes, which reflexively contrast with the film's "normal" point of view. The spectator is required to rethink traditional camera angles aimed at the sitting position of the audience at the theater and the meanings arising from this seating architecture.

ADOPTING DISABLED SUBJECTIVITIES

The Diving Bell and the Butterfly is based on Jean-Dominique Bauby's autobiography, which he wrote using his eye following a stroke that resulted in a condition called "locked-in syndrome,"[64] in which the person maintains full mental, emotional, and sensual functions but most of their body parts are paralyzed. Out of the three films discussed in this part, *The Diving Bell and the Butterfly* is the most avant-garde in expression and narrative. Although Schnabel took a risk in using unusual camera angles, the film gained even greater commercial success than both *Thumbsucker* and *Cake* combined.[65] The film avoids satisfying the spectator's ableist desires by using a subjective camera in representing external space, as well as through editing that emphasizes internal space. Only after seventeen minutes do we first see the film's protagonist, revealed to the spectators through a mirror reflection. The subjective camera forces the spectator to adopt Bauby's point of view. Simultaneously, the film also represents

Bauby's experience by depicting his inner world, including his imagination and memories, as well as the repeated image of the diving bell in the depths of the sea, which serves as a metaphor to his condition.

The subjective camera not only depicts the point of view of the character, Bruce Kawin suggests, but is assimilating the spectator into the character's experience.[66] The camera is an active presence that usually is not constrained to any particular character's point of view. In the late works of Rene and Buñuel, the subjectivity of the camera and voice-over merge with those of the film characters. This subjectivity is vital for a first-person narrative structure. The subjective camera can be used in two ways: depicting what the character sees or thinks. The first is related to the physical eye, the second to the mental eye, but both are related to each other.[67] The films *Cake* and *The Diving Bell and the Butterfly* contain subjective camera scenes depicting both what the characters see and what they think—that is, using both physical and mental points of view.

The Diving Bell and the Butterfly does not prepare the spectators to the subjective camera, Christian Quendler argues.[68] The change in form created by switching to the subjective camera references various cinematic styles ranging from avant-garde to mainstream. In addition, the film explores new sensory and symbolic patterns, thus offering an unfamiliar mental and physical condition.[69] The first time Jean-Dominique's eyes are opened, we see a blurry image of the medical team and can hear dim speaking voices alongside the sound of breathing. The camera goes in and out of focus, and members of the medical team speak to the protagonist, asking him questions. His responses cannot be heard by the doctor and are only audible to the hearing spectators. The sequence depicts the protagonist's point of view through a blurry depiction of everything in his field of vision, combined with his voice-over narration. Therefore, the doctors approaching to talk to him become the object of the gaze rather than its subject, simultaneously reversing both the medical and the ableist cinematic gazes. The first scene in which a doctor approaches him to break the news of his diagnosis—"In the past, we would have said you'd had a massive stroke. You would very probably have died. But now . . . we're able to prolong life."—maintains the protagonist's point of view. Unlike the doctor, the spectators can hear the protagonist's response: "Is this life?" In addition to emphasizing Bauby's point of view through the camera, the scene is concluded with images that seek to animate his subjective feeling. A person screaming in a diving suit, in the depths of the sea, appears for a few seconds and then disappears. This image of the diving bell is repeated throughout the film to represent Bauby's inner world.

The subjective camera allows a phenomenological spectatorship experience, since it connects the protagonist's body to that of the spectator. An important scene in the film, which especially enhances this experience, is the one in which Bauby's eyelid is stitched due to an inflammation in his eye. In this scene, shown from the protagonist's point of view, a doctor comes in to stitch Bauby's right eye while he is fully conscious. The protagonist begs the doctor not to do it, but his voice remains unheard by the doctors. The spectators see his field of vision as it closes up, and a similar emotional and sensory effect is created as the screen is filled with water, representing Bauby's tears. These embodied experiences allow the spectators to experience subjective perception as well as bodily identification. In this way, the spectator's physical sensory experience is enhanced. Nevertheless, the film focuses on Bauby's joy at the sight of the vitality of his children's bodies, alleviating his inability to touch them. In another scene, Bauby imagines himself as nondisabled, sitting at a luxury restaurant with the woman who types his book, while the camera emphasizes the erotic pleasure of eating.

Through editing, in addition to the subjective camera, the film includes scenes that present Bauby's subjectivity. These subjective scenes increase in number starting from the point in the narrative when Bauby declares that he will stop feeling sorry for himself, since his imagination and memory are still active, in addition to his sense of sight. This scene consists of a montage composed of superimpositions of nature films, home movies images of him and his family, sexuality, surfing, and matadors. While Bauby's physical space is narrowed into his hospital room, his mental space is boundless, Açalya Allmer argues.[70] The scenes showing the material space, as seen through the protagonist's eyes, are presented alongside poetic depictions of his broad imagination.

And so, what answer does this film provide to the question asked by Bauby in the beginning? Is his life worth living? The film offers a number of possible answers, as well as two possible endings. Despite concluding the film with a text slide about his death, Bauby himself is conflicted about the ending he would give himself in his book and play. Quendler argues that this film has two endings. One is conveyed through the last shot of the film, showing a collapse of snowy mountains from end to start in slow motion, thus, in fact, presenting their reconstruction. This enigmatic image can be read as symbolizing Bauby's desire to escape death by literally turning back time. A different ending, which continues this shot, shows Selene, Bauby's speech therapist, sitting near him and reading his book. This offers his autobiography as evidence of the protagonist's success at staying alive.[71]

Primarily, the conclusion of *The Diving Bell and the Butterfly* appears to also reflect an ableist view of life with a disability. Similar to *The Elephant Man*, *Mask*, and *Million Dollar Baby*, *The Diving Bell and the Butterfly* also concludes with a repudiation of the possibility to continue living with apparent disability. The film presents a similar narrative to *Million Dollar Baby* and *Whose Life Is It Anyway?* in depicting an active person whose life was destroyed after becoming disabled. Letting people with physical disabilities live is presented as requiring many resources, and medicine is shown as not providing any good rehabilitative solutions, and therefore the films conclude with their deaths. Moreover, and similarly to *Whose Life Is It Anyway?*, the protagonist forms an indictment against himself. The first time Bauby assembles a sentence using his eye, he expresses his wish to die. However, and in contrast with Maggie (*Million Dollar Baby*) and Merrick (*The Elephant Man*), Bauby is visited by his supportive family members and friends and receives proper medical and rehabilitative treatments. In contrast with the films discussed previously, considerable parts of *The Butterfly and the Diving Bell* allow the spectator to see the value of this person, alongside his dependency on relationships with other people, even if those include the performance of daily activities.

Though the classical ableist gaze, which relies on the physical difference of people with disabilities as a spectacle, is not present in the three films discussed in this section, their narratives do include ableist views about devaluation of people with disabilities. Such views are conveyed through their answers to the question of what life is worth living and are most apparent within the films' conclusions. *Thumbsucker* ends with a "happy ending" of running through the streets of New York City. This happens after the protagonist realizes that the disability category is unable to provide him with good solutions to his experience. In this way, the happy ending relies on the repudiation of the disability category, suggesting that life can only be lived fully without it. *Cake* ends with a similar "positive message": Claire's physical disability is a natural emotional reaction to the loss of her son, and upon her completion of the mourning and healing process, her body will be healed as well. Here, too, the disability category is repudiated against a suggestion of the "temporariness" of her disability.[72] In contrast, however, *The Diving Bell and the Butterfly* offers a loving and appreciative gaze of a man with physical paralysis.

Although films such as *Thumbsucker* and *Cake* offer the subjectivity of being with a disability while relying on avant-garde expression, they both repudiate identification with the group of people with disabilities. Instead, they offer a "positive" life philosophy of self-acceptance by overcoming disabilities. In contrast with these films, *The Diving Bell and the Butterfly* offers the subjective camera, as well as scenes relying on the memory and imagination of a person with a disability, as an alternative to the medical or ableist gaze. These examples hint at the transformation undergone by the ableist gaze, from a complete repudiation of difference to a certain neoliberal inclusion of it. Therefore, the next part discusses animated films that reject live action along with traditional cinematic expression and directly addresses the ableist gaze embedded into live-action cinematic conventions.

TOWARD CRIP ANIMATION AND CINEPHILIA

The avant-garde scenes within the live-action mainstream films discussed rely on subjective camera angles, extensive editing techniques, flashbacks, and flash-forwards. They all seek to represent disability through unconventional aesthetics and to provide an experience that is closer to disabled subjectivities. Yet even the most obscure attempts of live action to detach itself from the normative conventions of cinema are limited by the indexical nature of film. Regardless of how realistic it may strive to be, animation lies further away from the physical laws of reality. Thus, when depicting disability, animation is not only forced to recreate the body but also its disabling environments.

Avant-garde and experimental animated films have relatively small audiences, consisting of cinephiles, film buffs, art house enthusiasts, and film festival attendees. These films are usually created by independent filmmakers or film students funded by national funds (e.g., NFB, BFI). Only rarely do studios, like Aardman Animations, also experiment with animation for adults. Similar to more mainstream animation, these films vary both in length and technique. However, animators tend to mix up these elements, thereby creating hybrid styles: for example, clay animation and film noir, musical and animated documentary, or animation and life action. By analyzing Aardman's *Creature Comforts* (1989) and *Creature Discomforts* (2007–2008), I suggest that animated experimentations challenge not only overall ableist perceptions and the medical gaze in live action but also the logic of conventional spectatorship hierarchies, possibly evoking viewers' bodily reflexivity.

Cinematic spectatorship, and especially the love that people bear for it, has received considerable attention within film studies. However, animaphilia, the love of animation, has received much less. That notwithstanding, recent interest in new forms of spectatorship has been increasingly available for potential inquiry. The classic cinephile was defined in the 1960s as based on the love of the actual medium and the moviegoing experience. However, according to Melis Behlil, the new cinephile "is closely related to technology, in the way that it relies on the gadgets that make home theatres possible: first the VCR, then the hi-fi surround sound systems, and lastly the DVD. The new cinephiles may be called videophiles instead, but it is the same love for an art form." Currently, the cinephile can watch any film at home, including free, repeated, rewound, and rewatched viewing available legally or illegally online.[73] Thus, the distribution, curation, and spectatorship of short animated films are heavily based on digital platforms and contemporary archives.[74] All these invite intertextual play that indulges cinephilia.

Aardman Studios, founded by Peter Lord and David Sproxton in 1972, is a prominent example of an animaphile haven within the field of animation. Their clay animations are used in short experimental films, television shorts and series, and commercial feature animation for children and adults, as well as public service announcement for nonprofit organizations. Aardman's most well-known animated films include *Wallace and Gromit* (1989, 1995, 2005, and 2008), *Chicken Run* (2000), and *Shaun the Sheep Movie* (2015). In 1989, Nick Park joined Aardman, where he animated and directed his first short animation for the company, a clay animation titled *Creature Comforts* (35mm, color, 5 min.) and described on IMDB as "a humorous and thought-provoking view of what animals in zoos might be thinking about their captivity and surroundings."

The film was very well received because of its integration of documentary and animation. Michael Brooke explains: "What really caught the public imagination was the inspired conceit of interviewing zoo animals about their living conditions. The voices were actually drawn from the inhabitants of a housing estate, an old people's home and assorted others."[75] The film received the Academy Award for best short animated film in 1990. Following this, the clay animation was adapted into a television series, which aired on ITV (UK) between 2003 and 2006 (two seasons, twenty-six episodes), and then readapted by CBS in 2007 under the title *Creature Comforts America*. In 2007–2008, Aardman produced the *Creature Discomforts* sequel, focusing on people with disabilities through the same concept of entrapped animals accompanied by a documentary voice-over.

The short animation *Creature Comforts* presents clay animals being interviewed about captivity in zoos: a family of polar bears, a couple of armadillos, a Brazilian puma, two baby hippos (with a fragment of the mother's body as the background), five terrapins, a large family of rodents, a gorilla, a blind galago (bush baby), and a couple of roosters (in order of appearance). The animals speak about captivity in enclosed zoo spaces, confined both by prison-like cells and the visual frame closing in on them. Not only are these clay animals uprooted from their natural habitats, but they are also placed in a humanized prison. For example, throughout the interview with the Brazilian puma, he complains about the weather and food in the UK. Similarly, during the interview with a gorilla, we can see her markings for imprisonment days drawn on the wall. The interviews are shown using full shots. They focus on the bodies of the speaking animals, confined within closed frames that reveal small fragments of their new surroundings. Alongside its comparison between zoos and prisons, the animated experiences in *Creature Discomforts* also draw attention to other heterotopic spaces—in particular, residential institutions for people with disabilities.

One central technique in the original *Creature Comforts* short, which also carries through to the sequels, is animal entrapment in a zoo as seen through a human gaze. In his book *Animals in Film*, Jonathan Burt begins his inquiry of the visibility (and disappearance) of animals in cinema with the zoo: "Indeed, film's emphasis on action and event was from a spectator's point of view much closer to the ideal zoo exhibit and provided a contrast to those many hours when actual zoo animals do very little and zoo exhibits are minimally eventful. Thus in film the already edited life of the captive animal was edited even further."[76] Burt suggests that the zoo gaze can be positioned between the pornographic and the ethnographic gazes, in a triangular relation with them. Furthermore, "this version of the zoo gaze does not have any qualities specific to looking at animals but is derived from those gazes that most emphasize the elements of desire, voyeurism and power over other human beings."[77]

However, the gaze in *Creature Comforts* is not on live-action animals but rather clay representations of human perspectives on entrapment. The short begins by equating animal captivity with nursing homes and other residential institutions. The baby polar bear says: "Emh, well, the zoo is very important to animals, they're a bit like homes, like nursing camps, and for poor animals and . . . emh . . . people like old people. And there is old people which are . . . dead, and people in the wild have . . . don't have much to eat so they have to kill their own people, to have something to eat." This opening scene sets the ground for the film's critical intervention in institutions that segregate others purportedly "for their own protection"—for example, conservation facilities for animals, shelters for women survivors of intimate partner violence (IPV), or residential institutions for people with disabilities.[78]

In their overview of *Disability Incarcerated*, Liat Ben-Moshe, Chris Chapman, and Allison C. Carey set out four primary goals for the anthology: (1) situating disability within current scholarship about prisons, criminal justice, and incarceration—that is, utilizing disability in understanding the rationales, practices, and consequences of incarceration; (2) expanding notions of "incarceration" to encompass a wider variety of social settings and practices; (3) theorizing interlockings of incarceration and disability—that is, similarities and differences across constructed categories of identity (gender, race), sites of incarceration, and geographical boundaries; and (4) encouraging further dialogue among unconnected scholars and activists to promote social change.[79]

Though it utilizes animals as a metaphor for human social conditions, *Creature Comforts* confronts the segregation, confinement, and captivity that affect both animals and people with disabilities to different extents. By placing clay animals in a zoo and integrating the voyeuristic gaze on animals with the ableist gaze on people with disabilities, animal confinement is animated as a metaphor for human ableism.

This approach echoes ecofeminist philosophy, particularly Edna Gorney's suggested intersections among restrictive social spaces, nature reservations, and shelters for women IPV survivors.[80] Following the persuasive arguments of ecofeminist philosophy, Gorney suggests that, through the subjugation of woman and nature,[81] "these constructed 'Others,' parallel to postcolonial study of Native and Nature as 'Others,' have been represented by Western patriarchy as being wild and powerful, and yet, also weak and helpless, and therefore in need of taming and protecting, respectively." By this logic, securing women IPV survivors in shelters and exploiting nature in reservations are touted as symbols of progress and modernism. Similar to zoos, residential institutions, nature reservations, and shelters for women IPV survivors are all part of the problem rather than the solution. Gorney discusses four ways these reinforce the dominant ideology: the victims of violence are the ones being incarcerated; a temporary solution becomes permanent; social power relations are recreated inside the shelters; and patriarchal power constructs the problem and the solution.[82]

The "creatureness" that captive animals and institutionalized people share with disability is reflected in the short's title, *Creature Comforts*. This title reflexively comments on what was meant to provide bodily comfort and accommodation but is, in fact, part of the problem. Concurrently, the title of the series *Creature Discomforts* holds a promise for addressing the lack of suitable solutions.

Aardman Studios commented more directly on disability in *New Mindset* (Danny Capozzi, 2018) and in their interactive website for the award-winning CBeebies show *Something Special*. The website is accessible to children with a broad range of interests and needs. However, the most prominent example of their commitment to disability rights was in collaborating with the UK charity organization Leonard Cheshire Disability on the production of *Creature Discomforts*.

All eight shorts in this series are clay animations narrated by people with physical disabilities who came to the project through the organization's services. The first four episodes were produced in 2007 and screened on ITV on Christmas night. Four additional episodes were produced during the summer of 2008. The eight episodes present different clay animals with physical and apparent disabilities, which resemble the characters in the *Creature Comforts* short and series. The most prominent formal characteristic of the series is its "talking heads" documentary style. Different animals look straight into the camera and speak about their experiences with disability using a microphone that occasionally pops into the frame. The use of clay animal figures discussing human disability experiences positions what is seen in conflict with what is heard. Such comic effects can be seen throughout the series: for example, a stick insect using a walking stick or a blind chameleon.

Both *Creature Comforts* and *Creature Discomforts* show different animals looking at the camera and speaking to a microphone about their experiences with disability. In this way, the films arouse discomfort through three conflicts: First, a conflict between image and sound, which refuses the automatic attribution of the narration to a single particular body.[83] Second, discomfort caused by the realization that what we hear is a testimony and that the actual voice belongs to people who have experienced the oppression of ableism. Moreover, the testimonies are presented by animals looking into the camera and addressing spectators directly. Third, at the same time, the incoherence between what is seen (humorous and comic clay animals) and what is heard (testimonies about ableist oppression) creates an ironic effect that flips the viewer's expectations of a purely tragic-emotional portrayal of disability.[84] Here, the incommensurability of animal characteristics with human disabilities serves to subvert these traditional conventions.[85]

Despite its creative response to ableism through animals, *Creature Discomforts* does not go as far as its prequel, *Creature Comforts*, when it comes to aligning animal and human struggles against captivity and segregation. *Creature Comforts* uses the kinship between what Mel Y. Chen refers to as nonhuman and human animals in its exploration of animacy by merging queer of color scholarship with critical animal studies and disability theory.[86]

While *Creature Comforts* contests captivity and confinement, *Creature Discomforts* remains on relatively safer grounds of advocating for public accessibility. Liat Ben-Moshe proposes thinking of disability and incarceration from an intersectional perspective. This perspective might encompass "a variety of locales that disabled and/or nonnormative bodies and minds are being swept into, such as psychiatric hospitals, residential institutions for those with intellectual and developmental disabilities, and prisons."[87] Ben-Moshe focuses on alternatives to incarceration (broadly defined) across three movements with an abolitionary framework: antipsychiatry, prison or penal abolition, and the movement to close down institutions for those labeled intellectually and developmentally disabled. She writes: "These movements seek not to reform prisons, psychiatric hospitals, and residential institutions for those labeled as developmentally disabled, but to do away with them altogether." Building on the work of activists and scholars within these movements, Ben-Moshe discusses incarceration from a critical and abolitionary framework. She provides a thorough outline of some alternatives: alternatives to imprisonment, alternatives to psychiatry and hospitalization, and community living as an alternative to institutionalization.[88]

Creature Comforts, the prequel to *Creature Discomforts*, explicitly compared zoos, prisons, and residential institutions and hinted that they were all part of a problem rather than its solution. In this light, knowing the premises of its prequel, *Creature Discomforts'* disregard for the confinement of people with disabilities is even more disconcerting. The series seems reluctant to critique the ableist segregation—or, in Ben-Moshe's term, "decarcerating disability"—of people with disabilities through restrictive institutions.[89] This reluctance may be understood through Aardman's collaboration with the Leonard Cheshire Disability charity, an organization criticized by the UK disability rights movement and especially by disability scholar, filmmaker, and activist Paul Darke.[90]

That notwithstanding, both *Creature Comforts* and *Creature Discomforts* illuminate the mechanisms of othering, particularly those rendering animals, women, people of color, and people with disabilities as being in need of protection. Concurrently with these mechanisms, the solution proposed to this supposed problem is captivity. While zoos and nature and native reservations play a dual role of simultaneously creating distance and exhibiting, prisons and residential institutions for people with disabilities reinforce alienation and segregation and keep them out of the public eye. Thus, what *Creature Comforts* suggests, more so than *Creature Discomforts*, is a cine-zoo animaphilia, the love of watching animation transforming living beings into creatures, allowing for a reflection on the shared experiences of incarceration, reservation, and confinement.[91] *Creature Comforts* thus utilizes avant-garde clay animation in a mainstream narrative about disability and its place. Much like the ableist gaze, the human gaze frames and entraps the subject rather than allowing for a fresh look from a disabled point of view.

The uniqueness of experimental animation about disability, as I show in the following chapters, is not only derived from the fact that it is produced independently, with a low budget, targeting cinephiles, and that it deviates from cinematic conventions. Rather, it mainly derives from the level of involvement of people with disabilities and their intimate relations in the production process. Despite the animated films' formal, technical, genre, and thematic differences, grouping them together allows us to read aesthetic and political alternatives endeavoring to create a shift in perception—that is, their cripping spectatorship.[92] The following chapter examines animated projects according to the involvement level of filmmakers with disabilities in the production process and the animation of their subjective point of view in arousing the spectators' bodies. The two following chapters each, in turn, discuss the arousal of the spectators' sense of sight and sense of hearing, consequently subverting traditional viewing hierarchies.

NOTES

1. Snyder and Mitchell, "Body Genres," 180–181.
2. See Peter Wollen's comments concerning the two types of avant-garde. "The Two Avant-Gardes," *Studio International* 190, no. 978 (November/December 1975): 171–175.
3. Michael O'Pray, *Avant-Garde Film: Forms, Themes and Passions* (London: Wallflower, 2003).
4. O'Pray, *Avant-Garde Film*, 1–2.
5. O'Pray, 3. One example for this is the abstract animator Oskar Fischinger, who created advertisement films in the 1920s and was involved with the production of Disney's masterpiece *Fantasia* (1941).
6. Rosemarie Garland-Thomson, *Extraordinary Bodies: Figuring Physical Disability in American Culture and Literature* (New York: Columbia University Press, 1997).
7. Rosemarie Garland-Thomson, *Staring: How We Look* (Oxford: Oxford University Press, 2009), 7.
8. Garland-Thomson, *Staring*, 9.
9. Laura Mulvey, "Visual Pleasure and Narrative Cinema," *Screen* 16, no. 3 (1975): 7–8.
10. Cáel M. Keegan, *Lana and Lilly Wachowski* (Urbana: University of Illinois Press, 2018), 24.
11. McKenzie Wark, "The Cis Gaze and Its Others (for Shola)," *E-Flux Journal* 117 (2021): 1–12, https://www.e-flux.com/journal/117/387134/the-cis-gaze-and-its-others-for-shola/.
12. Williams, "Film Bodies," 2–13.
13. Bodily display, emotional appeal, presumed audience, disability source, originary fantasy, resolution, motivation, body distortion, and genre cycles "classic." Snyder and Mitchell, "Body Genres," 188.

14. Snyder and Mitchell, 186–193.
15. Snyder and Mitchell, 193–203.
16. Ann Pointon, "Disability and Documentary," in *Framed: Interrogating Disability in the Media*, ed. Ann Pointon and Chris Davies (London: British Film Institute/The Arts Council of England, 1997), 84–92.
17. *Eugenics* is a term describing scientific viewpoints that encourage the genetic improvement of the human race by controlling breeding. This view was widespread in the United States from 1880 until World War II. For detailed information about the expressions of eugenics in US medicine and film, please see Martine E. Pernick, "The Black Stork," in *The Black Stork: Eugenics and the Death of 'Defective' Babies in American Medicine and Motion Pictures since 1915* (New York: Oxford University Press, 1996), 143–158.
18. Smit and Enns, *Screening Disability*.
19 The "horizon of expectations" is a phrase coined by Hans Robert Jauss in his book about the aesthetic of reception. Robert Hans Jauss, *Toward an Aesthetic of Reception* (Minneapolis: University of Minnesota Press, 1982), 79. It refers to the reader's general approach, including the knowledge and experience accumulated by them in encountering previous texts. See Steve Neale, "Questions of Genre," in *Film and Theory: An Anthology*, ed. Robert Stam and Toby Miller (New York: New York University Press and Blackwell, 1991), 166.
20. "Julie Delpy Presents Freaks," American Cinematheque, October 24, 2021, https://www.americancinematheque.com/now-showing/julie-delpy-presents-freaks/.
21. Sally Chivers, "The Horror of Becoming 'One of Us': Tod Browning's Freaks and Disability," in *Screening Disability: Essays on Cinema and Disability*, ed. Christopher R. Smit and Anthony Enns (Lanham, MA: University Press of America, 2001), 58.
22. Only Werner Herzog's film *Even Dwarfs Started Small* (1970) comes close to this, being made up of a cast of little people.
23. Chivers, "The Horror of Becoming 'One of Us,'" 57.
24. Smit and Enns, *Screening Disability*.
25. Distributed by MGM in 1932.
26. Chivers, "The Horror of Becoming 'One of Us.'"
27. The most extreme physicality compared with all circus performers.
28. Longmore, "Screening Stereotypes," 65–78.
29. Chivers, "The Horror of Becoming 'One of Us.'"
30. The film and play are based on the story of the Englishman Joseph Carey Merrick (1862–1890). In 1979, Lynch directed a play about Merrick written by Bernard Pomerance and shown on Broadway. One year later, the play was adapted to film.

31. This technique of delaying the vocal representation of the protagonist is similarly used by *Third Body* (Zohar Melinek-Ezra and Roey Victoria Heifetz, 2020) to explore transfeminine experiences.

32. Noël Carroll, "Why Horror? The Paradox of Horror," in *The Philosophy of Horror: Or, Paradoxes of the Heart* (London: Routledge, 1990), 159–195.

33. Cleopatra and Hercules, the people with disabilities, Merrick, the crowd, the doctors.

34. Shai Biderman and Assaf Tabeka, "The Monster Within: Alienation and Social Conformity in The Elephant Man," in *The Philosophy of David Lynch*, ed. William J. Devlin and Shai Biderman (Lexington: University Press of Kentucky, 2011), 207–223.

35. Craniodiaphyseal dysplasia, also called lionitis or CDD, is a rare autosomal recessive disorder that causes calcium to build up in the skull, disfiguring the facial features and reducing life expectancy. Please see Alan C. Richards, Caroline Brain, and Christian Martin Bailey, "Craniometaphyseal and Craniodiaphyseal Dysplasia, Head and Neck Manifestations and Management," *Journal of Laryngology and Otology* 110, no. 4 (1996): 328–338.

36. Please see the reviews on the major film websites IMDb and Rotten Tomatoes, as well as the review by Vincent Canby published by the *New York Times* on March 8, 1985, following the film's release: "Film: Mask, Bogdanovich Tale of a Rare Disease," *New York Times*, March 1985, accessed September 2018, https://www.nytimes.com/1985/03/08/movies/film-mask-bogdanovich-tale-of-a-rare-disease.html.

37. Similar to *Thumbsucker*, which is discussed in the following part.

38. The use of blind women in films to engage with men's physical disabilities reinforces views about the both the women's and the men's lack of desirability and is widespread in many films, as I discuss in chapter 3.

39. Similar to Forrest's school principal in *Forrest Gump* (Robert Zemeckis, 1994), Rocky's school principal also prefers that he study at a "special" school.

40. See, for example, Paul Darke, "No Life Anyway: Pathologizing Disability on Film," in *The Problem Body: Projecting Disability on Film*, ed. Sally Chivers and Nicole Markotić (Columbus: Ohio State University Press, 2010), 97–108.

41. For an extensive account of the pity discourse, see Lois Keith's "Punishment and Pity: Images and Representations of Disability, Illness and Cure," in *Take Up Thy Bed and Walk: Death, Disability and Cure in Classic Fiction for Girls* (New York: Routledge, 2001), 15–32.

42. Hoeksema and Smit, "The Fusion of Film Studies."

43. Longmore, "Screening Stereotypes."

44. Robert McRuer, "Neoliberal Risks: Million Dollar Baby, Murderball, and Anti-National Sexual Positions," in *The Problem Body: Projecting Disability on*

Film, ed. Sally Chivers and Nicole Markotic (Columbus: Ohio State University Press, 2010), 160.

45. Lawrence Carter-Long, "A Manifesto: Where Have You Gone, Stephen Dworkin? On Disability Film," *Film Quarterly* 72, no. 3 (2019): 26–29, quoted in Ginsburg, "Foreword," xxiv.

46. McRuer, "Neoliberal Risks," 175.

47. This trope is so popular that it even appears in a contemporary series about superheros. In season three of *The Boys*, Stormfront, the Nazi superhero, kills herself after a period of hospitalization due to a disabling injury. Similarly to Maggie, she is never treated nor offered rehabilitation on screen.

48. Doris Zames Fleischer and Frieda Zames, "Compassionate Killings," *Disability Studies Quarterly* 25, no. 3 (2005): np.

49. Karen Schwartz, Zana Mary Lutfiyya, and Nancy Hansen, "Social Imagery in the Film Million Dollar Baby: An Analysis Based on Wolf Wolfensberger's Social Role Valorization," *Disability Studies Quarterly* 25, no. 3 (2005): np.

50. Darke, "No Life Anyway."

51. Snyder and Mitchell, "Body Genres."

52. Hoeksema and Smit, "The Fusion of Film Studies."

53. Hoeksema and Smit, 33–43.

54. I follow Margaret Price's (*Mad at School*, 2011) term *intermittently apparent* and Sami Schalk's (*Bodymind Reimagined*) use of *nonapparent, intermittently apparent*, and *apparent* rather than *visible* and *invisible* to distance myself "from the ocular-centric nature of visibility and shift the onus for noticing or not noticing disability onto the perceiving person rather than onto the visibility via a person's bodymind, accoutrements, or behaviors" (Schalk, 124). I prefer *apparent* over *visible* because of its sematic proximity to *passing*, thus allowing me to further align disability studies with trans studies.

55. Walter Kirn, *Thumbsucker: A Novel* (New York: Anchor Books, 1999).

56. For example, after the debate teacher exposes Justin's admiration of his classmate, Rebecca, or after his mother suggests that he apply to a local college.

57. Chronic pain and fibromyalgia are discussed later on. Please see: Adi Finkelstein, "Estrangement and Alienation in Chronic Illness Experience: Narratives of Women Suffering from Chronic Fatigue Syndrome and Fibromyalgia Syndrome" (PhD diss., The Hebrew University, 2008) [Hebrew].

58. Ryan Parry, "The True Story behind Jennifer Aniston's Cake—How Movie's Scriptwriter Was Inspired by the Brutal Murder of His Brother's Wife, Baby Daughter and Mother-in-Law," *DailyMail*, February 24, 2015, https://www.dailymail.co.uk/news/article-2962358/The-true-story-Jennifer-Aniston-s-Cake-movie-s-scriptwriter-inspired-brutal-murder-brother-s-wife-baby-daughter-mother-law.html.

59. Ellen Samuels, "Six Ways of Looking at Crip Time," *Disability Studies Quarterly* 37, no. 3 (2017): np.

60. Finkelstein, "Estrangement and Alienation."

61. Slava Greenberg, "(Dis)abling the Spectator: Embodying Disability in Animated Documentary," in *Documentary and Disability*, ed. Catalin Brylla and Helen Hughes (London: Palgrave Macmillan, 2017), 129–143.

62. Price in Price and Shildrick, "Bodies Together," 72.

63. Sigmund Freud, "Mourning and Melancholia," in *The Standard Edition of the Complete Psychological Works of Sigmund Freud Volume XIV (1914-1916): On the History of the Psycho-Analytic Movement, Papers on Metapsychology and Other Works*, trans. James Strachey, ed. Anna Freud, Alix Strachey, and Alan Tyson, (London: Hogarth Press and the Institute of Psycho-Analysis, 1964), 237–258.

64. Please see: Thomas Mallon, "In the Blink of an Eye," *New York Times*, June 15, 1997, https://www.nytimes.com/1997/06/15/books/in-the-blink-of-an-eye.html.

65. Based on box office data as published on IMDB, according to which *Thumbsucker* made $1,325,073 and *Cake* made $1,873,547, whereas *The Diving Bell and the Butterfly* made $5,990,075.

66. Bruce F. Kawin, *Mindscreen: Bergman, Godard, and First-Person Film* (Rochester, NY: Dalkey Archive Press, 2006). Originally published 1978.

67. Kawin, *Mindscreen*, 5–7.

68. Christian Quendler, "Subjective Cameras Locked-In and Out-of-Body," *Image and Narrative* 15, no. 1 (2014): 79. In contrast with *Lady in the Lake* (Robert Montgomery, 1947).

69. Quendler, "Subjective Cameras Locked-In and Out-of-Body," 81.

70. Açalya Allmer, "The Poetics of the Real in Julian Schnabel's The Diving-Bell and the Butterfly," paper presented at Design Cinema: International Design and Cinema Conference, Istanbul, Turkey, 2008. Another good example for the use of mental space in representing people with disabilities is *Orgesticulanismus* (Mathieu Labaye, 2008), which is discussed in the next part of this chapter, as well as in chapter 4, about the use of sound in documentary disability animation.

71. Quendler, "Subjective Cameras Locked-In and Out-of-Body," 81.

72. For a fascinating exploration of crip time, see Kafer, *Feminist, Queer, Crip*, particularly "Time for Disability Studies and Future for Crips," 25–46.

73. Melis Behlil, "Ravenous Cinephiles: Cinephilia, Internet, and Online Film Communities," in *Cinephilia: Movies, Love and Memory*, ed. Marijke de Valck and Malte Hagener (Amsterdam: Amsterdam University Press, 2005), 111–123.

74. For example, YouTube, Vimeo, Hulu, Amazon, Netflix, and Ubu, as well as searchable databases such as IMDB, Latern, Internet Archive, Scholarly Literature on Film, Museum of the Moving Image Research Guide, film blogs and websites, newspaper reviews, and Twitter.

75. Michael Brooke, "Creature Comforts (1989)," BFI ScreenOnline, accessed December 28, 2018, http://www.screenonline.org.uk/film/id/588459/index.html.

76. Jonathan Burt, *Animals in Film* (London: Reaktion Books, 2002), 19–20.
77. Burt, *Animals in Film*, 41–42.
78. Inspired by the short animated documentary *Some Protection* (Marjut Rimminen, 1987), based on the story of Josie O'Dwyer, who was incarcerated to protect her from sexual abuse.
79. Liat Ben-Moshe, Chris Chapman, and Allison C. Carey, *Disability Incarcerated: Imprisonment and Disability in the United States and Canada* (New York: Palgrave MacMillan, 2014), x–xi.
80. Edna Gorney, "'If Only I Had Petals, My Situation Would Be Different': The Curious Case of Nature Reserves and Shelters for Battered Women," in *Ecofeminism in Dialogue*, ed. Douglas A. Vakoch and Sam Mickey (New York: Lexington Books, 2018), 77–92.
81. Val Plumwood, *Feminism and the Mastery of Nature* (New York: Routledge, 1993), and Karen Warren, *Ecofeminist Philosophy: A Western Perspective on What It Is and Why It Matters* (Lanham, MD: Rowman and Littlefield, 2000).
82. Gorney, "'If Only I Had Petals,'" 77.
83. The same voice may have come from other humans and been portrayed through different animals.
84. Van Norris, "Taking an Appropriate Line: Exploring Representation of Disability within British Mainstream Animation," *Animation Studies* 3 (2008): 67–76. The comic tone of the series also comes from its references to *Creature Comforts*.
85. Michael Hayes and Rhonda Black, "Troubling Signs: Disability, Hollywood Movies and the Construction of a Discourse of Pity," *Disability Studies Quarterly* 23, no. 2 (2003): np.
86. Mel Y. Chen, *Animacies: Biopolitics, Racial Mattering, and Queer Affect* (Durham, NC: Duke University Press, 2012).
87. Ben-Moshe, *Disability Incarcerated*, 255.
88. Ben-Moshe, 255–272.
89. Ben-Moshe, *Decarcerating Disability*.
90. See Paul Darke's short *Say No to Leonard Cheshire* (2001). Also see: Helen Hague, "Wiped Out: Activist's Anti-Charity Website Blocked," *Guardian*, May 2, 2001, https://www.theguardian.com/society/2001/may/02/guardiansocietysupplement2.
91. Anat Pick coined the term *cine-zoos* in her *Creaturly Poetics: Animality and Vulnerability in Literature and Film* (New York: Columbia University Press, 2011), 103–130.
92. I use Sandahl's active use of the words *queer* and *crip* as analytical tools: *queering* and *cripping*. *Queering* describes the practices of exposing the queer subtext of mainstream representations, imposing a new meaning on the image, or deconstructing its heterosexism of representation. Similarly,

cripping entails the practices of revealing the assumptions of the ableist body and its exclusionary effects. Significantly, "both queering and cripping expose the arbitrary delineation between normal and defective and the negative social ramifications of attempts to homogenize humanity." Carrie Sandahl, "Queering the Crip or Cripping the Queer: Intersections of Queer and Crip Identities in Solo Autobiographical Performance," *GLQ* 9, no. 1–2 (2003): 25–56.

TWO

EMBODYING SPECTATORSHIP
Intersubjective Ways of Being-in-the-World

ANIMATED FILMS ABOUT DISABILITIES, ALONG with the plethora of subgenres on which they rely, emphasize crip subjectivity at every level of production. Thus, they attempt to depart from the ableist/medical/universalist point of view presented in the previous chapter. Discussing contemporary documentary cinema's integration of the avant-garde in its depiction of disability, Snyder and Mitchell argue that "phenomenology means not only the capture of disability perspectives on film but also the meaningful influence that disability has upon one's subjectivity and even cinematic technique itself."[1] Although all the films examined in this book foreground crip subjectivities by utilizing animated expressions that challenge previous typical representations of people with disabilities, both in content and form, only a small portion of them were produced by people with disabilities.

Despite the political commitment of able-bodied filmmakers and allies to portray crip subjectivity while resisting cinematic techniques used to load it with derogatory meaning, their products are the result of experiences presented after extensive mediation. Mediation is, of course, inherent to all cinematic processes; however, when addressing power relations, self-identification and the publicly stated motivation of the creators may play an important role both in the analysis of the works and in their production and reception.

This chapter proposes that the phenomenology-inspired approach of disability studies scholars regarding the relationships inherent in the intersubjective process of encounters between disabled and nondisabled people offers a renewed examination of socially constructed power relations. The process of animation production, which requires touch among people and between people and materials, emphasizes intersubjectivity and its reversibility. The physical touch in animation production evokes intersubjective interactions that embrace, if only to a certain extent, the disparities and discontinuities in all corporeal encounters. David Sarlin dates the fear of touch as a means of sustaining the boundary "of sexual danger or inappropriate conduct or as an epidemiological vector of cognition" to the early twenty-first century.[2] Furthermore, Sarlin suggests that for certain members of the population—"those on the autism spectrum, for example, or the chronically ill, the elderly, or people with mobility or other physical impairments"—touch "might sometimes carry a different set of meanings."[3]

Utilizing Merleau-Ponty's approach to intersubjectivity to emphasize the reversibility of touch, Janet Price and Margrit Shildrick place the disabled body at the center of inquiry of embodiment while considering its coming into contact with the masculine, white, able, "universal" body. By depicting the disabled body as an object of phenomenological research, they maintain that the reversible nature of touch, which characterizes intersubjective relationships, challenges the binary feasibility of slave/master, object/subject, and disabled/nondisabled interactions. Merleau-Ponty's famous example of the chiasm of senses through touch, whereby a hand that touches another blurs the line between the person touching and the one being touched, takes on additional significance concerning people with disabilities. The dichotomy of power relations can be challenged by examining them in situations in which a stranger touches the body of a person with a motor disability against the latter's will, in contrast to situations in which a deaf or blind person touches a stranger for the purpose of communication or direction. This phenomenological approach maintains that complete mastery of able-bodied people over people with disabilities is impossible. Despite the fact that power relations are involved in every touch between bodies, the mutuality and reversibility of touch emphasizes the fact that "we are in a continual process of mutual reconstruction of our embodied selves."[4] So, for example, when a hand that has lost feeling is grasped by someone else, the hand becomes clumsy. That is, the instability of the disabled body is an extreme case of the instability of all bodies. Thus, "it is not just that anybody can 'break down' in illness or as a result of accident, but that, for all, the 'bits and pieces' are held together in contingent ways. Final integration is never achieved."[5] The challenge in distinguishing between the disabled and the nondisabled in the relationships inherent in touch is that the distinction is not at all obvious because of less apparent disabilities, late-diagnosed or undiagnosed people, those who do not self-identify, and so on, as well as their power dynamics reshuffles through touch. These intersubjective relations are further intensified in crip animation, as in other cinematic texts that extensively rely on touch in the production process.

This chapter presents the ways crip subjectivity is expressed in animation. Each of the three sections refers to the different levels of involvement by people with disabilities in the production process. The discussion begins with autobiographies in animation about disabilities, which express the subjectivity by means that convey the disabled "I"—that is, first-person crip—through an analysis of the films *Rocks in My Pockets* (Signe Baumane, 2014) and *My Depression: The Up and Down and Up of It* (Elizabeth Swados, 2014). Such films fulfill the disability rights movement's demand for "nothing about us without us," (or, "nothing without us") as well as the feminist critique opposing the universalist approach of philosophy. The second section, "Intersubjective Encounters and Touch Ethics," analyzes films that, at first glance, may seem to be first-person crip films because the intersubjective process is not revealed to the spectators. The chapter focuses on films produced in collaboration between artists with and without disabilities, particularly *John and Michael* (Shira Avni, 2005) and *Petra's Poem* (Shira Avni, 2012). Nonetheless, even when produced by other members of the disability community, their focus is on people with a disability they do not share; despite their solidarity practices, such animation projects are still the result of work *about* people with disabilities. Studying these processes through disability studies' reading of Merleau-Ponty's phenomenology enables the analysis of the relationships between producers and their objects/subjects and the touch involved in the production process that undermines the boundaries between object and subject. The third section, "Reflexive Collaborative Projects," addresses animation as a result of cooperative intersubjectivity between disabled and temporarily able-bodied filmmakers, who expose spectators to the power relations between these bodyminds particularly in *A Is for Autism* (Tim Webb, 1992) and *Tying Your Own Shoes* (Shira Avni, 2009). The three sections constitute a proposal for possible categories of crip subjectivity that characterizes animated films involving people with disabilities.

FIRST-PERSON CRIP

In reaction to the ableist gaze—medical/psychiatric and cultural—which devalues those unfit of the unmarked norm, social movements of people with disabilities throughout the world demand to be their own speakers in matters pertaining to them. Alongside political involvement, more and more people with disabilities express themselves in autobiographies focusing on crip experiences and rewriting narratives previously written about them without them. This has become even more apparent after the film that highlighted the activists who participated in the establishment of the movement, *Crip Camp*

(James LeBrecht and Nicole Newnham, 2020), won best feature (the top prize) at International Documentary Association Documentary Awards 2021.[6] A historic opportunity for Hollywood to do justice with the disability community was missed when the film lost the documentary Academy Award to *My Octopus Teacher*.

The two animated autobiographies examined in this section may also be classified under definitions of autoethnography, which integrates autobiography and ethnography, proposing a self-narrative. These narratives locate the self in a social context and seek to expand viewers' horizons by thinking critically about the experiences of people they see.[7] Both *Rocks in My Pockets* and *My Depression* explore the subjectivity of women coping with mental disability, like schizophrenia, manic depression, and depression, in the first person. The two animated autoethnographies constitute an exploration of one's self, combined with an examination of society.

Both autoethnographic animated films echo the literary subgenre of auto-antipathology. In their book about autobiographies, *Reading Autobiography: A Guide for Interpreting Life Narratives*, Sidonie Smith and Julia Watson propose six subgenres of autobiographies, among them autosomatography/autopathology, which they apply to personal narratives that challenge stereotypes that people with disabilities are abnormal. G. Thomas Couser suggests that these narratives can be called antipathological and that the motivation to write such a narrative in the first person stems from the desire to depathologize one's experience. Courser therefore proposes using the term *autosomatography* to distinguish such a first-person narrative from narratives written about a person with disabilities in the third person by a nondisabled person. Such first-person narratives "critique social constructions of the disabled body and incorporate a counter-narrative of survival and empowerment that reclaims the individual's ... body from the social stigmatization and the impersonalization of medical discourse." Courser observes that "a few ... diseases or disabilities have generated ... more autobiographical writings than have others. Foremost among them are ... breast cancer, HIV/AIDS, Deafness and paralysis." More recently, narratives about blindness, depression, and autism have been added to this list.[8]

The genre of animated autobiographical documentary developed simultaneously with people with disabilities writing autobiographies. Annabelle Honess Roe posits that "animated documentaries show us how animation can function as an alternative way to recall the past. In fact, I think that animation is a representational strategy that is particularly suited to documentaries that explore fragmented pasts of forgotten, perplexing, yet often formative memories."[9] Moreover, animated documentaries about personal memories and histories can be read as a reaction to hegemonic power relations. "By the 1990s, autobiographical, personal and subjective filmmaking had become a means to protest political and social injustice and inequality."[10] Similar to the motivations of people with disabilities to write their autobiographies, filmmakers with disabilities want to depathologize themselves and redefine the narratives of their lives. Despite the fact that animated autobiographical films are cheaper to produce, very few such films have been animated and directed by people with disabilities. Two of the most outstanding animated documentaries in this genre, *Rocks in My Pockets* and *My Depression*, were almost single-handedly made—that is, produced, written, directed, filmed, animated, edited, and distributed—by their authors, women with disability. In both films, use of the first person is not only a narrative tool; it also appears in many of the creative and technical methods used.[11]

Despite the similarities between the two films, they reflect subjective and particular experiences, which are animated by means of various visual metaphors. The films emphasize the subjective experience by relying on humor and the hereditary aspects of mental illness in general and depression in particular. Both directors explore their personal mental disabilities through their family heritage and fragmented memories of the past. Swados (*My Depression*) reveals her mother's death by suicide after coping with depression, as well as her brother's schizophrenia. Baumane (*Rocks in My Pockets*) describes the deaths by suicide of her grandmother and her cousin, coping with her own mental illness, and other cousins who deal with various mental disabilities. All of these are framed in a way meant to make the viewing experience easier on the audience. Baumane does this primarily by means of the voice-over; Swados uses upbeat music to the same end. At the beginning of the film, Swados states that depression can manifest in different ways in different people but, at the same time, wants to present her own subjective depression. At first, the depression Swados deals with is portrayed as a black cloud in her film, *My Depression*; later, it turns into a hole leading to spiraling suicidal thoughts. In *Rocks in My Pocket*, Baumane represents her depression first as a physical pain, animated by blowing up a balloon made up of pointy blades (see figure 2.1), with the accompanying negative feelings presented as rocks in her pockets.

The characters in *Rocks in My Pockets* are two-dimensional pencil-on-paper drawings placed on top of three-dimensional photographs of different materials, lit and shot with a digital camera and then scanned and edited on computer. The project is an outstanding example of an extremely high level of involvement by a filmmaker, disabled or nondisabled, throughout every level of the production process. As noted, Signe Baumane wrote the script; produced,

Fig. 2.1. Depression wheel: images of pain © Signe Baumane, *Rocks in My Pockets*, 2014

animated, and directed the film; and participated in editing, distributing, and raising the funds for it. In light of all that, the film's impressive achievement is worth noting. Despite the film's tiny budget ($100,000), Baumane won the award for best film at the Latvian National Film Festival and was Latvia's entry for an Oscar as best foreign film.[12] *Rocks in My Pockets* is Baumane's first feature film, although she had previously made thirteen short animated films on various subjects.

In *Rocks in My Pockets*, Baumane describes a process of self-discovery started in response to a psychiatric diagnosis. Baumane's sister reveals Baumane's diagnosis, which was changed from schizophrenia to bipolar disorder by a psychiatrist, at their parents' request, becomes the object of an investigation and is used to challenge psychiatric categorization. In the film, Baumane seeks to reconstruct the circumstances of her grandmother's death and learn more about her life in Latvia during the 1920s in an effort to understand what she and her cousins have in common. In parallel to the narrative of her familial investigation, Baumane deepens the phenomenological descriptions that present her physical pains, accompanied by a sense of the emptiness of depression. Baumane describes them in subjective terms and figures: pain that begins like a needle puncture, which spreads throughout one's body like a big, empty balloon, the ends of which are like hundreds of razors cutting her soul (see figure 2.2). These feelings are accompanied by physical pain and high fever. Socially,

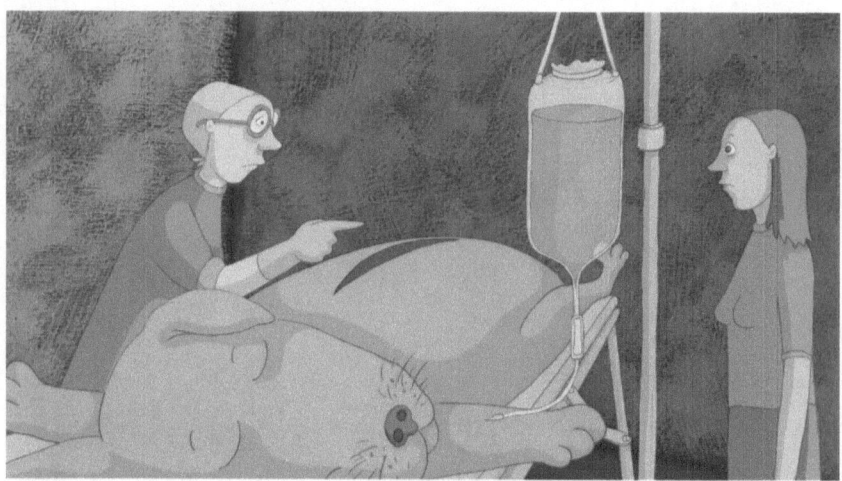

Fig. 2.2. Diagnosis reveal © Signe Baumane, *Rocks in My Pockets*, 2014

Baumane describes the pain as a source of shame and embarrassment, so she tries to hide it from people.

Bauman's visual description of her experience with depression relies on various visual metaphors, the most prominent one being rocks. The animation opens with a scene in which a woman pushes a large rock uphill, even before the film's opening credits are shown. When the woman reaches the top of the hill, a monster bursts from the rock and threatens her. She tries to flee downhill, but her way is blocked by a huge boulder. While she is still trying to escape from the monster, the boulder begins to roll down, accelerating toward her. The screen darkens until only her screams are audible. The following scene describes how a poacher found Baumane's grandmother in the river. Baumane interprets it as an unsuccessful suicide attempt—her grandmother did not succeed because she forgot to put rocks in her pockets. The actual rocks, which her grandmother apparently "forgot," become a visual metaphor throughout the film and are used by Baumane as a metaphor to describe her own depression. The metaphorical function of the rocks is revealed in a scene in which Baumane begins to feel "a sort of needle stabbing deeply into her chest, under the heart," while she is packing up her purchases at the supermarket. The negative thoughts that accompany her daily routine are expressed by the things she places on the checkout counter of the supermarket and by her lit figure, trying to make her way opposite that of the moving conveyor belt. At the end of the animated film, Baumane gets to the six rocks that comprise her condition: Dread, Pain,

Obsessive Thoughts, Confusion, Guilt, and Self-Destructive Behavior. In describing her feelings about not taking psychiatric medications, Baumane takes the rocks and puts them in her pockets, completing the process of coming to terms with her mental disability.

Baumane's autoethnography about coping with mental illness enables the revelatory process of renewed self-discovery. In the first autobiographies written about lived experiences of disability, the authors tended to present themselves as victims of impairment rather than of ableism. They portrayed their disabilities as personal tragedies that had to be overcome through extraordinary means. More recently, changes have occurred in the way life with disabilities is presented; written autobiographies that project a binary view of conquering or winning versus victimhood are rejected.[13] Contemporary autobiographies utilize alternative genres that incorporate classical social structuring. Smith and Watson define such works as "writing back"—that is, a reaction to earlier autobiographies, which relied on narratives of victimization. Writers located on the margins of the discussions at various points in time, like women, slaves, and people with disabilities, offer narratives of physical experiences as a means to intervene in the existing social order. Accordingly, an expanding and strengthening trend of people writing about living with disabilities has been identified.[14]

The ambiguity of the psychiatric diagnoses of Baumane and her family members reinforces the antipathologization aspects she presents in the animation. After a detailed description of the lives of her grandmother and cousins, Baumane returns to addressing her own experiences. In the last part of the film, Baumane portrays her own antipathologization, which began with a chance meeting with an old woman who hears the "the sweetest, most glorious music in the world" in her head. Baumane asks herself how the woman was entitled to hear that fantastic music while her own cousin heard destructive voices that led to her death by suicide. That question leads Baumane to investigate her own psychiatric diagnosis, which she had previously not known, because the psychiatrist who treated her had claimed that her case was so difficult she would never be able to teach or undertake any other position of responsibility. The psychiatrist had determined that she was a "mental cripple" who would be unable to function without taking pills all her life. Later, Baumane finds out that her parents had bribed the psychiatrist to give her a "less serious" diagnosis to enable her to complete her studies in Latvia. At that time, people who were diagnosed as schizophrenic were not permitted to study or work, and so her parents paid off the doctor to change the diagnosis to bipolar disorder. Many years later, as a result of her cousins' deaths by suicide, Baumane's sister tells her about the original diagnosis and describes her as "a certified nutcase," which the family had to keep secret to avoid her (and them?) being ostracized. Baumane utilizes the film to verbalize her criticism of such problematic psychiatric diagnoses: "As if anyone even today knows what schizophrenia is. Anybody and anything could be schizophrenic." At the end of the film, Baumane further reinforces her criticism of her diagnosis, as she had achieved a successful career and creative life without taking pills.

Like Baumane, scholars aligned with the social model of disability studies and members of the Mad Pride movement maintain that psychiatry has not yet found a clear, consistent source or explanation for mental illness. People who identify as coping with, users of, or survivors of the psychiatric system organized into a separate movement (from the broader disability rights movement) called Mad Pride, which criticizes the oppressive way the psychiatric establishment relates to them, depriving them of their autonomy while simultaneously stigmatizing them. Specifically, they argue that psychiatrists rely on diagnostic tools that have not been scientifically proven, primarily related to the prognosis of "schizophrenics." Evidence of this is that psychiatrists themselves disagree whether this or that individual "suffers from" a "mental disturbance or a mental illness" and, if so, which one. In other words, one psychiatrist may diagnose someone as mentally ill while another psychiatrist will diagnose the same person completely differently. Herb Kutchins and Stuart Kirk argue that the *DSM* is a defective illusion.[15] The illusion is inherent in the process of drawing it up: new "disorders" included in the *DSM* are voted on because the psychiatrists who make up the committee often do not agree on them. Another example substantiating their claims is that pharmaceutical companies that make and sell psychiatric medications have succeeded in their lobbying efforts to set the definitions and categories of mental disorders and illness. Despite the ambiguity in many psychiatric diagnoses, a disorder or mental illness remains in a person's medical records forever from the moment they are diagnosed because it is characterized as chronic.[16]

Baumane's antipathologization is carried out through her opposition to the psychiatric diagnosis she was given by refusing to take the pills prescribed for her. In Baumane's lived experience, the drugs dull her senses. Thus, paradoxically, they reinforce the negative symptoms of her illness: "The soft pillow of pills would enwrap my existence and distort the perspective. My perspective, which is that I have to walk the thin line between sanity and insanity, keeping a fragile balance. If my pain is dulled, I might forget that I am prone to insanity and might make a decision that only normal people are allowed to make." The film's critical process, challenging the psychiatric diagnosis and its ramifications and concomitant stigma, ends with the undermining of the efficacy of psychiatric medication.

Social aspects of living with mental disability are presented as they are experienced through Baumane's, point of view. These experience rely on the intersubjectivity of other people—a legacy that her mother bequeathed to her, requiring that she leave her room and meet with family members. The first-person crip—that is, autoethnography or autobiography—presented in *Rocks in My Pockets* describes Baumane's voyage of self-discovery, of breaking her relatives' silence about mental illness in the family; at the same time, her film relies on the social aspects of autoethnography. Alongside Baumane's particular expressions of crip subjectivity in the figure of the rocks, she also deals with the social aspects of disability, expressed in the encounter with her psychiatric diagnosis and the accompanying social stigma.

Similar to *Rocks in My Pockets*, the film *My Depression* is autobiographical, told in the first person, about crip subjectivity. This film, too, derives from the desire for self-discovery and to depathologize the creator's experience. This short animated documentary is an adaptation of Elizabeth Swados's graphic novel, which was published in 2014 under the same title. Swados was the composer, painter, stage manager, and cowriter and codirector; she died two years after producing the film. In both the graphic novel and the animation, Swados describes how she coped with depression, as well as relates the deaths by suicide of her mother and brother—the latter coped with schizophrenia. Swados cowrote and codirected the film with Robert Marianetti and David Wachtenheim. In adapting the novel for film, the three turned it into an animated documentary musical.[17] In this way, Swados was able to communicate her experiences through her passion for writing, painting, and music.

On one level, Swados's animated documentary, which was nominated for best documentary at the Tribeca Film Festival, continues the tradition of documentary films of the 1970s, reflecting the influence of the civil rights, student, and antiwar movements. According to Michael Renov, the prevailing approach before the 1970s—that documentary films were supposed to be objective—was replaced by the subjective point of view, emphasizing the filmmakers' perspectives. The women's movement "helped to usher in an era in which a range of 'personal' issues—namely, race, sexuality, and ethnicity—became consciously politicized..."[18] In all cases, subjectivity, grounding in the personal and the experimental, fueled the engine of political action."[19] The preoccupation of these films with the "personal" constituted a political reaction to the silencing of certain voices in the new documentary cinema. In the current generation of documentarists' "explorations of the (social) self, they are speaking the lives and desires of the many who have lived outside 'the boundaries of cultural knowledge.'"[20]

In the spirit of these live-action documentaries, yet using cel animation, *My Depression* begins with Liz, a sketched character, talking directly into the "camera" and announcing the importance of telling her personal story. Liz begins from the social aspect: that depression is nonapparent or intermittently apparent ("Many people don't really know about it"). She continues by presenting her motivation to describe her subjective experiences in animation. The film's opening sequence is a self-declared musical. Using a lighthearted, happy song and colorful figures arranged rhythmically, the sequence describes various positive aspects of her life, her talents and abilities, her passions, the public acclamation she had received, her relationships with her partners and lovers, and other unique achievements, such as her meeting the Dalai Lama. Without interfering with the uplifting spirit of the song and the colorful figures, interwoven into the song is the "disorder": a dark cloud that accompanies Liz throughout her life. The cloud, which in the beginning appears only as a sense of sadness that disrupts all the good, gradually expands and takes a larger share of the song's words and the figures. In the end, the cloud completely envelops the protagonist and fills the entire frame. Through a simple, easily understood, and relatable use of the dark cloud, Swados visualizes (her) depression.

In addition to the cloud, Swados's crip subjectivity is described by means of various visual metaphors. This state is emphasized by means of another visual metaphor: small holes that appear in her body, with the word *self-confident* spilling out through the widening holes. At the same time, similar to Baumane's description of the shame she felt, Swados elaborates on her fear of sharing her feeling of depression. She lies to her friends and tells them she is feeling great, thereby enhancing her negative feelings. These emotions are animated by a dark hole from which emanates the possibility of suicide. These intensified emotions are represented by a less common visual metaphor and introduce the humorous perspective that Swados and Baumane share: the suicide mobile. Through visual metaphors, *My Depression* connects subjective descriptions to the political aim of increasing the visibility of nonapparent disabilities.

Similar to Baumane, Swados examines the social restrictions on people with disabilities, particularly those labeled mad, by means of the clinical encounter portrayed in the film. In an effort to find a solution for her situation, Swados searches the Internet, but the clinical terms discourage her, and she focuses on alternative solutions like yoga, healthy foods, books, music, and so on. After some time, she decides to go to a psychologist, a step she defines as encountered by most people who cope with depression. The psychologist explains that her depression is caused by hereditary and chemical factors and so offers a pharmacological solution. Unlike the ableist gaze of mainstream cinema, the discussion with the psychologist is animated from Liz's point of view. Her eyes close when hearing the neurological explanations, and the scene changes to describe them in song and animation from the mouths of the antidepressant pills. Despite her decision to take antidepressants, she notes that it took three years of trial and error before she found the right dosage that finally helped her. Later, she emphasizes that pharmacological treatment is not effective for everybody and that antidepressants have a lot of side effects. Nevertheless, the film primarily deals with the ways Swados copes with depression and the mental and emotional work she does to "survive a little at a time." The film concludes by addressing spectators with chronic depression: "So if that little cloud shows up again, hopefully next time you'll be stronger. Remember, you got through it once and you can do it again."

Although Swados is critical of the psychiatric establishment, and the antipathology motif of crip autobiographies is obvious in the film, her criticism is much more restrained than Baumane's. Despite the similarities of depression portrayed in both films, in *Rocks in My Pockets*, Baumane undermines the psychiatric diagnosis with which she was labeled and completely rejects the efficiency of psychiatric medication. The difference in the depth of critique leveled at the medical establishment can be explained by the different psychiatric diagnoses and their stigmatization at the heart of each film. Baumane's diagnosis is perceived as more serious because she is diagnosed as schizophrenic, which is labeled under psychosis. By contrast, Swados is diagnosed with a less severe clinical depression, which is labeled under neurosis. These diagnoses are socially and politically loaded; they determine the binary division in assumptions between those considered dangerously insane and those thought sane and not dangerous. The distinction between psychosis and neurosis structures the "otherness" of psychosis, which is perceived to be more severe. The danger associated with psychosis is the reason for forced hospitalization and additional constraints on the freedom of people so diagnosed.[21] Because depression is much less stigmatized than schizophrenia or manic depression, *My Depression* does not negate the possibility of proper care from psychiatrists.

As noted, despite the differences in the two films, both animated autobiographies utilize visual metaphors to describe the first-person crip subjectivities. The films rely on the antipathologization that characterizes autobiographies of women with disabilities: "In positioning themselves as disabled subjects who address the history of their own marginalization, disabled writers reframe their impairment by refusing the diagnosis of disability or stigmatized abnormality."²² In the case of mental illness, the principal social constraints are social stigma and shame. Both these animated works are characterized by the creators' processes of self-revelation and desire to share their experiences with other people with mental disabilities as well as educate able-minded/sanist spectators regarding possible aspects of nonapparent disabilities in general and mental illness in particular.

Both animated films constitute rare examples of a high level of involvement by people with disabilities in the cinematic process about their own lived experience; in fact, they manifest crip and mad self-representation. The next two sections of this chapter focus on films in which the level of involvement by people with disabilities was much lower; however, they provide insight into the intersubjective relations within animation production.

INTERSUBJECTIVE ENCOUNTERS AND TOUCH ETHICS

As shown in the previous chapter, there are mainstream films disguised as first-person crip by using avant-garde forms and expressions. As with live action, many experimental animators have a desire to expose spectators to ableism, are aware of the problematics of their ally position, and thus rely on the point of view of a person with a disability to do so. These aspirations are reflected at every level: the narrative, soundtrack, image, and so on. In addition, the production techniques of short animated experimental films invite closeness and touch between the creators and their objects, thereby challenging the boundaries between object and subject. This section shows that the production process of animation requires work *with* and not only *about*, thus fundamentally undermining the feasibility of an I/them, object/subject relationship. This analysis relies on disability studies' phenomenology presented by Price and Shildrick's "touch ethics."

Two of Shira Avni's animated films devoted to the experiences of people with Down syndrome, *John and Michael* and *Petra's Poem*, allow for an examination of collaborative animation projects. While the first film is declaratively *about* crip-queer subjectivity, the second is produced in full collaboration *with* artists with Down syndrome. Both films were produced, written, and animated by Avni—a neurodivergent filmmaker—and her cinematic language as an animator using clay and painting on glass is clear as well as her sensibilities and affiliation to the disability community and her commitment to disability activism. In addition, all the participants that appear in the films had ongoing contact with Avni before, during, and after the films' productions. Avni began to work with people with Down syndrome at the end of 1980. That's when, she says, she fell in love with the community and began volunteering in schools and camps, working with young adults with Down syndrome. During the production of *John and Michael*, Avni became interested in working with people with Down syndrome as creators, artists, storytellers, teachers, and partners, not solely as subjects. Avni's animated films deal with diversity and social justice; they aim to break through the spectator's regular barriers regarding representations of disability. Avni argues that when her animated films are projected in a darkened movie theater, her work involves the spectator in a personal, emotional, and embodied experience.[23]

John and Michael is an animated film using clay on glass, backlit to create the effect of stained glass in motion. The film describes the intimate relationship between two gay men with Down syndrome, based on the story of a couple whom the director met at a summer camp for people with cognitive disabilities. The colors of the backlit clay on glass fuse with the nostalgic atmosphere of the film, blended with Michael's mourning, as he describes the close relationship he shared with John, which ended with John's death.[24] The narrator, Brian Davis, an actor with Down syndrome, was in fact responsible for part of the script. Brian described what he saw in the storyboard drawings so sensitively that Avni changed the script accordingly.[25] Davis's emotional reaction to the story and his own closeness to the subjects influenced the final version of the animated film.

Addressing love, intimacy, sexuality, gay and queer experiences, bereavement, and death among people with Down syndrome, and in the community of people with mental or developmental disabilities, is an innovative breakthrough. At the same time, presenting a love story between people with disability is also a novelty within queer cinema and television.[26] The intersecting of sexuality and disability is not only a philosophical or theoretical topic but an issue that has an impact on the everyday experiences of people with disability. The eugenic approaches to a "life worth living" discussed in the previous chapter are manifest in policies with tight control of the sexuality and reproduction of people with disabilities. According to Margrit Shildrick, who has meticulously studied sexuality in relation to disability: "The western discomfort with many manifestations of erotic desire ... is most clearly invoked by forms of differential embodiment that cannot be subsumed unproblematically under the rubric of the normative body."[27] According to this approach, the animating of John and Michael as sexual subjects of desire is in itself a unique political act in light of the absence of public discussion of the subject.

In mainstream cinema, the sexuality of people with disability often tends to align with perceptions of the sexual subject as related to the cis- and hetero-normative body. The anthropologist Robert F. Murphy posited that people with disabilities are perceived as hypersexual or asexual.[28] Anne Finger added the gender distinction, arguing that it is women with disabilities who are imagined to be asexual while men with disabilities are imagined to be hypersexual.[29] In turn, James L. Cherney concludes that "just as sexism employs a masculine perspective of sex to subordinate the feminine, ableism constructs an able-bodied perspective that positions people with disability as sexual others."[30] In *Crip Theory*, Robert McRuer constitutes a theory of "compulsory able-bodiedness" and argues that its system produces disability and is interwoven with the system of compulsory heterosexuality that produces queerness: "compulsory heterosexuality is contingent on compulsory able-bodiedness, and vice versa." McRuer also suggests that the "changing economic, political, and cultural conditions at the turn of the millennium, the relations of visibility have shifted significantly."[31]

Exposure of these tropes led to attempts by mainstream filmmakers to shift representation by humanizing disabled characters through presenting them as expressing sexual desire. However, Eunjung Kim shows that these films subordinated subjectivity to the heterosexual mechanisms of masculinity and femininity. According to Kim, "Cinematic representation of disabled men's sexuality often aims to externalize their humanity by presuming that heterosexual male desire is universal. The dichotomy between a sexually promiscuous, non-disabled woman and a chaste, disabled woman plays a pivotal role in establishing this desire."[32] The narrative and cinematic expressions of films like *Breaking the Waves* (Lars von Trier, 1996), *Born on the Fourth of July* (Oliver Stone, 1989), and *Oasis* (Lee Chang-dong, 2002) present fictional characters and developments that fit heterosexual expectations. With the exception of *Oasis*, all the films mentioned present the sex industry as enabling disabled men to integrate into heterosexual society. The cinema is rife with characters who go on journeys to fulfill gender expectations, and such a narrative, which reinforces heterosexuality, is what rehabilitates the protagonists from their disabilities. When the heterosexual mechanism is perceived as what "heals" the protagonists' disabilities, sexuality is diminished to its physical and psychological aspects. This perception erases the sexual range experienced by people with disabilities. The subjugation derives from the assumption that the disabled body is undesirable and therefore the person with a disability must be asexual. Following this, the assumption is that asexuality is an inferior way of life, rather than an identity.

By contrast to these mainstream live-action films, *John and Michael* does not revolve around the characters' rehabilitation through compulsory heterosexuality; rather, it focuses on the love and intimacy they feel for each other

Fig. 2.3. Kissing: images of intimacy © Shira Avni and NFB English Animation Studio, *John and Michael*, 2004

(see figures 2.3 and 2.4). In addition, unlike the compulsory able-bodied tendency of many live-action mainstream films to end with the death of a disabled character, Avni chooses to continue the film after John's death and focuses on his mourning partner and his memory. The animated film continues to describe Michael's longings and how he copes, and, after the narrator announces John's death, his heartbeats continue to accompany the soundtrack.[33] One scene stamps it as unique by emphasizing the possibilities of animation in sensual, emotional, experiential, and imaginative representation. While Michael is sleeping, John's spirit returns to give him a last hug; John looks at Michael through the window and his animated figure envelopes the small, sleeping Michael in his wings. Michael wakes up fueled with the spiritual embrace and is able to get out of bed and go outdoors to make snow angles. By means of this ending, the spectator is denied the ableist catharsis of John's death but remains with Michael's grief.

According to Avni, animation provides the spectators with a window into an alternative reality. This reality visually, poetically, and symbolically presents difficult or even socially taboo subjects, thereby evading common criticism and opposition.[34] Furthermore, Avni argues that experiences, memories, and feelings, which cannot be described by regular cinematic means except in the third person, can best be expressed through animation. Use of animation requires

Fig. 2.4. In bed: images of intimacy © Shira Avni and NFB English Animation Studio, *John and Michael*, 2004

that spectators watch and listen with greater focus precisely because their expectations formed by traditional cinema are unmet.

In contrast to the melancholic colors of *John and Michael*, the animated documentary *Petra's Poem* presents the soliloquy of Petra Tolley—an artist with Down syndrome—in a rainbow of colors. In its visual characteristics and first-person narrative, *Petra's Poem* resembles the autobiographical genre presented in the previous section of this chapter. The visual and auditory narrative of being-in-the-world with a disability presented in the first person is achieved by live action, animated images, and words accompanied by Petra Tolley's voice-over. Although the film relies almost entirely on Petra's point of view, subverting normative cinematic and linguistic grammar, the animation and direction are credited to the filmmaker, Avni. Avni was responsible for most of the film's creative and technical aspects. The complex dynamics between an animator, who is neurodivergent, and her subject with Down syndrome, who is an artist herself, the animated film presents Tolley's aesthetic language and narrative through image and sound. This may not completely restore the power balance, but recognition of the existence of an imbalance does allow them to address it.

Fig. 2.5. Petra explains the opposite of the middle © Shira Avni, NFB English Animation Studio, and Petra Tolley, *Petra's Poem*, 2012.

By using cel animation, live action, and their juxtaposition, Avni animates Tolley's feelings of "being in the middle." Even though no clear definition of "being in the middle" or "being on the side" is given in *Petra's Poem*, the terms may be interpreted via the animation and the words illustrated in the film. A line of animated characters is illustrated while, in the soundtrack, Petra invalidates them from the description of "being on the side." At the scene's end, colorful figures appear alongside Petra's shade (see figures 2.5 and 2.6). Moreover, the effect of the shaded figure separated from the collective is revealed when the shadow moves from its place and the words *lonely, shame, fear, anger, doubt, isolated*, and *sadness* appear and form Petra's animated figure. Similarly, the sense of "being in the middle," among others, is described by Petra as being like a tree or octopus with arms spread wide. Avni adds validating words of her own—*profound, sensitive, confident, inner strength, dignity, knowing, respect*, and *trust*—around Petra's live-action scene. Petra conveys the sense of "middle" as the experience of being in touch with others, which hones the Merleau-Ponty intersubjectivity and its intersection with disability studies. Tolley's intersubjective experience does not necessarily derive solely from Down syndrome, although that's an inseparable part of her. The narrative and expressions of Avni's films indicate the subjectivity of people with disabilities as part of interdependency, intersubjectivity, and being-in-the-world with others, which possibly grew out of Avni's physical and emotional closeness to the subjects in

Fig. 2.6. Petra explains being in the middle © Shira Avni, NFB English Animation Studio, and Petra Tolley, *Petra's Poem*, 2012

her films consequently establishing the intersubjective relationships creatively revealed.

Both animated films discussed here rely on intersubjective relationships among Shira, John, Michael, and Petra. The physical closeness required by the animation process, too, enabled an intersubjective collaboration, in which disabled subjectivity gets its proper place in the films, despite the power relations off-screen. Petra Tolley described Avni as an ally: "Shira's work comes from her caring heart, which cares for us. She's the one who did everything for us, is beside us."[35] The phenomenological aspects of the touch ethics of disability studies invite discussion of power relations via haptics. Avni's animated films enable examination of the possibilities inherent in the requirement for physical touch between various people conducting a dialogue about experiencing their different lives. Furthermore, alongside the animated films about crip subjectivity that were produced in collaboration with disabled artists, some of these films also make that collaboration apparent to the audience.

REFLEXIVE COLLABORATIVE PROJECTS

While, on some levels, *John and Michael* and *Petra's Poem* were produced through collaboration with people with disabilities, it was not their main focus or agenda. In what follows, I examine two animated documentaries that set out to be collaborative artistic projects between artists with different disabilities and nondisabled artists. The films, *A Is for Autism* (Tim Webb, 1992) and *Tying Your Own Shoes* (Shira Avni, 2009), emphasize crip subjectivity at the various levels of production and for the most part maintain self-representation of people with disabilities.[36] In addition, they play with the reflexive dimension of animation, which reveals the production process to the spectators. *AIFA* addresses being a cinematic product that is aimed toward both neurodivergent and neurotypical spectators.[37] *TYOS* adds the reflexivity of bodyminds' differences in intersubjective relationships to the director's exposure of the production process. This reflexivity also recognizes the possible power relations.

Art collectives use creative labor to change power structures, April Durham argues. She states, "Participants resist everything from the loss of individual status to the chaos of egalitarian governance, and thus collaboration sometimes appears to fail in its bid to provide an escape from alienation and oppression."[38] Proposing the term "trans-subjectivity" as a means of studying these practices, Durham focuses on the creation of space for the intersection of an array of types of subjectivity under "extreme conditions of exchange."[39] These efforts often involve "crossing boundaries through the cataclysmic rupture of coherent limits around the individual subject and offer, to use Donna Haraway's formulation, a 'troubling' of worlds."[40] Many collaborative animated documentaries rely on the subjectivity of a person with a disability, which is expressed in the narrative and soundtrack, although the animation remains in the hands of the "professionals," who do not identify as people with disabilities. So, for example, the filmmakers of animated series like *Animated Minds* and *Creature Discomforts* strived to present the lived experiences of people with disabilities by means of their indexical voices and animation of their subjective points of view. These collaborations leave their subjects solely with the tasks of speakers-narrators, but the fact that they are not first-person crip is never revealed to spectators.

By contrast, Tim Webb's pioneer animated documentary *AIFA* relies on crip intersubjectivity both in the soundtrack and in its aesthetic choices. The animation was commissioned by British Channel 4 and was widely acclaimed, nominated for and winning several awards; the short received a lot of academic interest as well. The film was produced in 1992, at the beginning of the wave of animated documentaries, and is considered to be one of the outstanding examples of the genre.[41] The uniqueness of the film is that it uses the drawings of its subjects. Honess Roe contends that "it is not only the contributors' drawings, but also the way these drawings are brought into motion and combined with live-action imagery that encourages an understanding of autism."[42] So, for example, the appreciation of the soothing effects of repetitive motions shared by some neurodivergent people is expressed in the animation by trains that pass like threads throughout every part of the film, both visually and aurally.[43] It is important to mention that the trope of autistic people being fascinated by trains has also been heavily gendered.[44]

"Auti-biography," a first-person narrative on autism, was defined by Thomas G. Couser to distinguish it from one written by family members or physicians—that is, separate from the domestic ethnographies and the medical gaze.[45] *AIFA* is not an animated auti-biography, however, as the stories were directed, animated, and edited by neurotypicals yet composed of first-person narratives about crip subjectivity. This ambiguity in *AIFA* is reinforced by the animated images of the subjects, which enable communicating in several languages simultaneously. Thus, the film speaks in the first person about autistic and neurodivergent people but is translated to a cinematic creation by a neurotypical filmmaker. By means of these relationships, the film's language makes it possible to reflexively reach both neurotypical and autistic spectators.[46]

Webb's animated documentary includes reflexive elements directed toward neurodivergent spectators, in addition to aspects that mediate crip subjectivity for neurotypical viewers. The experience of being-in-the-world with autism is presented to the neurotypical spectator via the animation and editing of the illustrations combined with live action and at the same time remains relevant to neurodivergent spectators. While the film is aimed at neurotypical spectators, a number of its characteristics make it not merely accessible but also pleasurable to the neurodivergent viewer. First, sequences of short shots show live-action images of opening and closing doors, faucets, turning lights on and off, monotonously tearing paper, and spinning coins, all of which are described by the participants as producing joy. Second, the animated images of trains continue visually throughout the film and potentially provide aesthetic enjoyment to some autistic spectators (as well as some neurotypical viewers). Third, the film opens and closes with statements from one of the participants: "The film begins and it is exactly eleven minutes long" and "The film is over." These statements are meant to reduce the anxiety shared by neurodivergent and neurotypical spectators by establishing a clear framework.

Moreover, the temporal reflexivity of *AIFA* may illuminate another form of autistic, autistic-trans, and crip "trap doors," as suggested by Jake Pyne in his "Autistic Disruptions, Trans Temporalities." Pyne uses Reina Gossett, Eric Stanley, and Joanna Burton's *Trap Door* anthology to marry concepts from trans studies with crip time, arguing that on trans people's list of costs for seeking belonging, "the demand for normativity could be reread as an incitement to able-mindedness."[47] Drawing on the trans studies concept of the trap door and using critical autism studies, Pyne shows how autistic-trans stories generate their own temporalities by claiming autism and gender nonconformity as mutually inclusive, foregrounding alternative sensory life, and "disrupting the mandate to get better."[48] The temporal laps of trains, time markers, and sensorial pleasures celebrated in *AIFA* may be best understood through Pyne's suggestion to read "autistic disruption—through the narratives of those who, by choice or by circumstance, defy the chrononormative mandate of the able-minded future."[49]

Films that openly declare that they are aimed at nondisabled people and those with (specific) disabilities are rare. An example of a recent film aimed at both deaf and hearing audience members is *The Sign for Love* (El-Ad Cohen and Iris Ben Moshe, 2017), which relies on the subjectivity of a deaf gay man and is directed by his and a hearing director. The film was originally produced with no sound, but during discussions between the directors, it was decided to add music to make it more accessible to a hearing audience.[50] The film *Black Sun* (Gary Tarn, 2005) can also be read as produced while mindful of blind spectators.[51]

The Sign for Love's direct address to the spectator-listener and reference to the process of spectatorship are reinforced by the animation's reflexive nature. Lev Manovich states that animation, in contrast to live-action cinema, never attempts to hide its representative nature: "Animation foregrounds its artificial character, openly admitting that its images are mere representations. It is discrete and self-consciously discontinuous—crudely rendered characters moving against a stationary and detailed background, sparsely and irregularly sampled motion . . . , and finally space constructed from separate image layers. . . . In contrast, cinema works hard to erase any traces of its own production process, including any indication that the images we see could have been constructed rather than simply recorded."[52] María Lorenzo Hernández adds, "From the earliest age of cartoons, their high degree of self-reflexivity has reinforced the status of animation as an invented environment, building what has been labelled as the language of animation. In addition, the evidence of these images as an optical illusion has accelerated a formalist search for narrative processes, questioning the conventions of filmmaking as can be noticed on a heterogeneous but characteristic corpus of works: the independent short animated films, which lines exceed the regular routines of screenwriting."[53] Like other short animated films, *AIFA* reflects on its own cinematic creation; its attraction lies in the fact that it exposes itself being produced by and for both neurodivergent and neurotypical people.

The cinematic reflexivity—or, in other words, the recognition that an animated film, by its nature, is an entity meant for audience members—is made manifest by revealing the imaginary spectator, or "general audience," biases. This reflexivity can be expressed in other ways that expose the cinematic apparatus, the involvement of its creators, or the spectators. So, for example, in two shots of Adam Eliot's first trilogy, the director's first name is shown on-screen.[54] In *AIFA*, Tim Webb participates actively in making the film, but he does not appear on-screen. Despite their careful consideration of the audience's potential mental diversity, the production process, and mention of the director's name, characteristic of avant-garde animated films centering disabilities, the uniqueness of Shira Avni's *TYOS* is in the blending of these various elements into one animated film. The animated documentary *TYOS* presents the collaborative process between Avni and artists with Down syndrome in producing the animated film and reveals her image alongside those of the participants. However, she is still not a subject of inquiry in the same way as the others.

TYOS is the result of a creative collaboration among the subject-creators—from writing the script through illustrating and animating the film, recording the sound, and editing it. The film is composed of four parts, each devoted to one of the participating artists, and a reflexive prologue and epilogue that expose the film's production process to spectators. The prologue shows the editing room, with the subject-creators of the film in live action. After showing Petra, Matthew, Daninah, and Katherine, the film shifts to show Avni working with them on the light board, part of the producing apparatus of the film we are viewing. The prologue ends with Avni's narration, asking how to begin the film; what could have been merely a performative gesture turns into an embodied practice. The film proceeds from there to its different parts, focusing on each of the four protagonists. This process, to a certain extent, enables the self-representation process. In an interview, Avni talked about the artists' role in the production: "Animation allowed the artists to truly be the driving creative forces behind the film—they not only provided the visual and audio material, but were involved and consulted in every part of the editing and production process. I was very moved by the disability-rights movement's rallying cry, 'Nothing about us without us,' and I wanted to integrate that motto into the very structure of the project."[55] The film's epilogue presents the four protagonists as Avni animated them, combined with illustrations and animations by the participant-creators. This process expresses the centrality of the haptic intersubjectivity discussed in this section.

Avni self-evidently inscribes herself into the film, making the intersubjective relations visible to spectators without concealing the physical differences.

Although, according to Merleau-Ponty, the reversibility of the senses symbolizes the reflexive nature of the body and therefore strives to address the connection to "the other," the formulation of the argument ignores the range of possibilities inherent in the human body.[56]

This reflexivity of the senses, and, more particularly, touching another person, according to feminist scholars like Sara Ahmed, Janet Price, and Margrit Shildrick, requires knowing that person. That is, the flesh is part and parcel of reflexivity precisely because it comes into physical contact with the flesh of other bodies.[57] Nevertheless, touching oneself is not like touching someone else, as Stawarska and other feminist philosophers propose. Stawarska offers the body as an interpretive tool, including addressing the differences of gender, race, and status, because the involvement of others takes place via physical gestures, facial expressions, eye contact, touch, and language, which are dictated by corporeal society.[58] These differences constitute life experiences that are affected by physical differences and the way society relates to them.

The intersubjective relationships reflexively presented in animated films are the result of close physical relationships, woven during and into the production process. This closeness, according to phenomenological approaches as formulated by disability studies scholars Price and Shildrick, exists in the social interaction with other bodies. Price and Shildrick posit that our interactions with other bodies are what constitute our bodies. These interactions build mutual effects that impact the social relationships between us. This point of view requires recognition of the fact that our sense of self is related to the bodies around us.[59] *TYOS* depicts the close interaction that results from the animation production process and reveals its role in the film. Similarly, *AIFA* enables some description of the experience of crip subjectivity in the first person.

Animation entails all levels of life: movement, feelings, cognition, friendship, intersubjectivity, communication, and language, as Maxine Sheets-Johnson maintains: "That key concept is *animation*: we are essentially and fundamentally animate beings. In more specifically dynamic terms, we are animate forms who are alive to and in the world, and who, in being alive to and in the world make sense of it. We do so most fundamentally through movement, unfolding a temporal-spatial-energic dynamic, a kinetic aliveness that is in play through the course of our everyday lives from the time we are born to the time we die."[60] The way we understand the world derives from our touch with parents, lovers, partners, friends, caregivers, neighbors, colleagues, and others, Sheets-Johnson suggests. Thus, intersubjective animated films enable a reflexive look at the way we are in the world and, at the same time, focus on being with others. In this way, the animated films discussed offer diverse types of being-in-the-world in a range of bodies that are in touch with each other.

In their attempts to challenge the compulsion of able-bodiedness/able-mindedness/neurotypicality, the animated documentaries discussed in this section may also be read as a subgenre of the new wave of documentary films about disabilities. In their analysis of the documentary *Forbidden Maternity* (Diane Maroger, 2002), Snyder and Mitchell discuss the film's struggle against the eugenic past by using various cinematic techniques, among them long shots, close-ups, and unconventional framing. The film refuses to allow the nondisabled spectators to distance themselves from the presence of the physical differences of people with disabilities.[61] In response, the new documentary film proffers a cinematic alternative to eugenics: "*Whereas the proselytizers of the eugenic period denoted the disabled body as the objectionable object within a sea of normalcy, new disability documentary cinema designates degrading social contexts as that which need to be rehabilitated.*"[62] Intersubjective crip animation adds a reflexive dimension, beyond the subjective presentation of people with disabilities.

In *AIFA*, Tim Webb centers on the subjectivity of neurodivergent people, who express their being-in-the-world by means of voice-over, animation, hand drawings, and live action. Webb's contribution to the narrative of the film's characters is in his editing, which is intended to make the film accessible to neurodivergent and neurotypical spectators at different levels of the film. Nonetheless, the film leaves the director concealed from the spectators; his role in the relationships is implied but not exposed. Similarly, Shira Avni's animated film *TYOS* presents the subjectivity of artists with Down syndrome in the first person, as well as emphasizes the intersubjective aspects of the creator-subjects. The intersubjectivity is explicitly manifest by exposing Avni's role in the production process and the apparatus she used. Both films utilize the reversibility of touch in the creative process in a way that reinforces the possibility of self-representation and highlights the recognition of social power relations off-screen. These collaborative projects shed light on the possibilities of intersubjective artistic work's reflexive potential. The film's exposing of the haptic relations in the production process may evoke similar sensation in spectators.

Although different in animation techniques, each one of the three categories evokes a different type of spectatorship and presumes the existence of a typical spectator. However, revealing the apparatus of animation provides the viewer with a look at the power relations "behind the scenes" and in the nondiegetic world. In addition, making the film accessible to an audience of both neurodivergent and neurotypical spectators proffers an experience that requires the viewer to be in the world next to other bodyminds in the movie theater. In this way, the films challenge the ableism at the core of the presumed able-bodied/able-minded/neurotypical spectator.

Animated films focusing on crip subjectivity challenge ableist, sanist, or neurotypical comfort by using visual metaphors, emphasizing intersubjective relationships, addressing diverse spectators simultaneously while reflecting on those differences, and revealing the production process that produce them. At the same time, experimental animated films that replace the corporeal body with illustrations and drawings, puppets and clay, and distorted and pixilated live action and stills may distance spectators from the lived experiences in the flesh. However, such animated projects, as shown in the following two chapters, directly address spectators' bodyminds through the senses—more specifically, the most dominant senses involved in the viewing process: spectatorship and listenership. Both processes of "blinding" and "deafening" spectators through experimental animation reflexively illuminate privileged embodied perceptions in the movie theater and outside of it, thus not only challenging the ableist gaze but also offering alternatives ways of experiencing cinema and being-in-the-world.

NOTES

1. Snyder and Mitchell, "Body Genres," 193–194.
2. David Sarlin, "Touching Histories: Personality, Disability, and Sex in the 1930s," in *Sex and Disability*, ed. Anna Mollow and Robert McRuer (Durham, NC: Duke University Press, 2012), 147.
3. Sarlin, "Touching Histories," 146.
4. Price and Shildrick, "Bodies Together," 70.
5. Price and Shildrick, 71–72.
6. Elizabeth Ellcessor and Catalin Brylla's discussion of the film in "Crip Camp," Docalogue, September 2020, https://docalogue.com/crip-camp.
7. Deborah Reed-Danahay, *Auto/Ethnography: Rewriting the Self and the Social* (New York: Berg, 1997) and Carolyn Ellis and Arthur P. Bochner, "Autoethnography, Personal Narrative, Reflexivity: Researcher as Subject," in *The Handbook of Qualitative Research*, 2nd ed., ed. Norman. K. Denzin and Yvonna S. Lincoln (Newbury Park, CA: Sage, 2000), 733–768 quoted in: Michael Jeremey Blair, "Animated Autoethnographies: Stop Motion Animation as a Tool for Self-Inquiry and Personal Evolution," *Art Education* 67, no. 2 (2014): 6–7.
8. The chapter "Sixty Genres of Life Narrative" in Sidonie Smith and Julia Watson, *Reading Autobiography: A Guide for Interpreting Life Narratives* (London: University of Minnesota Press, 2010), 261–262.

9. Honess Roe, *Animated Documentary*, 142.

10. Honess Roe, 144.

11. Another example of an animated film with autobiographical characteristics is the animated series *Laser Beak Man* (Igor Coric, 2011) by Tim Sharp, who has autism. However, the series is not included in this study because most of the productions were inspired by Sharp rather than done by him or with his extensive involvement.

12. Dan Sarto, "Signe Baumane, Mental Health and Her Brutally Frank 'Rocks in my Pockets,'" Animation World Network, March 26, 2015, http://awn.com/animationworld/signe-baumane-mental-health-and-her-brutally-frank-rocks-my-pockets.

13. Smith and Watson, *Reading Autobiography*, 142–143.

14. Smith and Watson, 141.

15. Herb Kutchins and Stuart A. Kirk, *Making Us Crazy: DSM—The Psychiatric Bible and the Creation of Mental Disorders* (London: Constable, 1999). Please see preface.

16. Anne Wilson and Peter Beresford, "Madness, Distress and Postmodernity: Putting the Record Straight," in *Disability/Postmodernity: Embodying Disability Theory*, ed. Miriam Corker and Tom Shakespeare (London: Continuum, 2002), 143–158.

17. The musical aspects of the film and the involvement of famous actors to voice it—for example, Sigourney Weaver and Steve Buscemi—are discussed in chapter 4.

18. Evidenced by the post-Stonewall gay rights movement as well as the intensification of racially or ethnically based political initiatives.

19. Michael Renov, "New Subjectivities: Documentary and Self-Representation in the Post-Vérité Age," in *Feminism and Documentary*, vol. 5, *Visible Evidence*, ed. Diane Waldman and Janet Walker (Minneapolis: University of Minnesota Press, 1999), 89.

20. Renov, "New Subjectivities," 94.

21. Wilson and Beresford, "Madness, Distress and Postmodernity." In the analysis of *Creature Comforts* in the previous chapter, I compared the captivity of zoo animals, nature, and native reservations with prisons and residential institutions for people with disabilities in addressing the dual role these institutions play in distancing and exhibiting simultaneously, reinforcing alienation and segregation. Also see Ben-Moshe, Chapman, and Carey, *Disability Incarcerated*, discussed in the previous chapter.

22. Smith and Watson, *Reading Autobiography*, 143.

23. Avni in Ann Fudge Schormans, "Media Review: Tying Your Own Shoes—One Film, Four Perspectives," *Journal on Developmental Disabilities* 17, no. 1 (2011): 84.

24. The music of the film's soundtrack is played by the band that was playing in the café Avni was sitting in when she received word of John's death; she created the film's storyboard there as well.

25. Schormans, "Media Review," 84–85.

26. It was not until 2019 that a series like *Special*, featuring a gay man with cerebral palsy, was released on Netflix.

27. Margrit Shildrick, "Sexuality, Subjectivity and Anxiety," in *Dangerous Discourses of Disability, Subjectivity and Sexuality* (London: Palgrave Macmillan, 2009), 81.

28. Robert F. Murphy, *The Different World of the Disabled: The Body Silent* (New York: W. W. Norton, 1990), 195–196. This distinction also relates to the sexuality of the aging.

29. Anne Finger, "Forbidden Fruit," *New Internationalist*, no. 233 (1992): 9.

30. James L. Cherney, "Sexy Cyborgs: Disability and Erotic Politics in Cronenberg's *Crash*," in *Screening Disability: Essays on Cinema and Disability*, ed. Christopher R. Smit and Anthony Enns (Lanham, MD: University Press of America, 2001), 166.

31. Robert McRuer, "Introduction: Compulsory Able-Bodiedness and Queer/Disabled Existence," in *Crip Theory: Cultural Signs of Queerness and Disability* (New York: New York University Press, 2006), 2.

32. Eunjung Kim, "'A Man, with Same Feelings': Disability, Humanity, and Heterosexual Apparatus in Breaking the Waves, Born of the Fourth of July, Breathing Lessons, and Oasis," in *The Problem Body: Projecting Disability on Film*, ed. Sally Chivers and Nicole Markotić (Columbus: Ohio State University Press, 2010), 133.

33. See Longmore, "Screening Stereotypes," discussed in the introduction and chapter 1. Also see my exploration of the death trope in films about disability in "Disorienting the Past, Cripping the Future in Adam Elliot's clay animation," *Animation: An Interdisciplinary Journal* 2, no. 12 (2017): 123–137.

34. Avni in Schormans, "Media Review," 86.

35. Tolley in Schormans, 88.

36. Hereafter, *A Is for Autism* will be referred to as *AIFA* and *Tying Your Own Shoes* will be referred to as *TYOS*.

37. The term *neurotypical* was coined by the community of people on the autistic spectrum and refers to a person who does not have autism or atypical neurological patterns of thought or behavior.

38. April Durham, "Slips, Breaks, and Tangles: Creative Collaboration and the Aesthetic Process of Trans-Subjectivity," *Camera Obscura: Feminism, Culture and Media Studies* 31, no. 3 (2016): 35.

39. Durham, "Slips, Breaks, and Tangles," 38.

40. See discussion about Donna Haraway in the introduction.

41. Honess Roe, *Animated Documentary*, 13.
42. Honess Roe, 125.
43. Honess Roe, 126.
44. The television series *Everything's Gonna Be Okay* (Josh Thomas) tackles this trope head on, as well as some others, with a premise of "if you've met one autistic person, you've met one autistic person."
45. Examples of auti-biography are the books written by Temple Grandin and Donna Williams and the YouTube film *In My Language* by the late artist, writer, and activist Mel Baggs, criticizing the language of the "normal." Also see: Smith and Watson, *Reading Autobiography*, 256.
46. I elaborate on the presumed able-bodied spectator and the ramifications of the situation in the conclusions of this book.
47. Jake Pyne, "Autistic Disruptions, Trans Temporalities: A Narrative 'Trap Door' in Time," *South Atlantic Quarterly* 120, no. 2 (2021): 344.
48. Pyne, "Autistic Disruptions, Trans Temporalities," 345.
49. Pyne, 356.
50. As stated by the directors during a discussion after its first screening, at the Docaviv film festival in 2017.
51. The film is discussed in chapters 3 and 4.
52. Manovich, *The Language of New Media*, 298.
53. María Lorenzo Hernández, "The Double Sense of Animated Images: A View on the Paradoxes of Animation as a Visual Language," *Animation Studies* 2 (2007): 36.
54. See Greenberg, "Disorienting the Past, Cripping the Future."
55. Avni in Schormans, "Media Review," 86.
56. Merleau-Ponty, "The Intertwining—The Chiasm," 130–155.
57. Beata Stawarska, "From the Body Proper to Flesh: Merleau-Ponty on Intersubjectivity," in *Feminist Interpretations of Maurice Merleau-Ponty*, ed. Dorothea Olkowski and Gail Weiss (University Park, PA: Penn State University Press, 2006), 97.
58. Stawarska, "From the Body Proper to Flesh," 105.
59. Price and Shildrick, "Bodies Together," 63.
60. Maxine Sheets-Johnstone, "Fundamental and Inherently Interrelated Aspects of Animation," in *Moving Ourselves, Moving Others: Motion and Emotion in Intersubjectivity, Consciousness and Language*, ed. Ad Foolen, Ulrike M. Ludtke, Timothy P. Racine, and Jordan Zlatev (Amsterdam: John Benjamins, 2012), 29–30.
61. Snyder and Mitchell, "Body Genres," 202.
62. Snyder and Mitchell, 196, italics in the original.

THREE

BLINDING THE SPECTATOR

Non-Vision-Centric Pleasures[1]

IN LATE FEBRUARY 2015, THE web was aflame with discussion about the colors in the photo of a dress.[2] The colors caused great controversy—many claimed seeing a dress in white and gold colors (71 percent) while others claimed the dress was blue and black (29 percent).[3] That is, objectively, as the dress was blue and black, most viewers failed to see "reality." In an interview with the *Guardian*, Ron Chrisley, Director of the Centre for Research in Cognitive Science at the University of Sussex, UK, explained that the problem lies with perception. According to him, "Which color we see isn't just a matter of the light coming into our eyes, it's the inferences that caused that input. . . . Some people see just what's in front of them and some people are affected much more by the context."[4] Science does not have the ability to determine whether this difference in perception is caused by genetic differences or by acquired abilities also affected by personality.[5] This approach, according to which "reality" is perceived in various manners depending on different perceptual filters, is shared by the four animated films discussed in this chapter. The four animated film add questions about the orientation of the ableist gaze to the discussion of perception—the way it is socially constructed and the possible implications of this.

From the beginning of the film era, narratives about people with vision disabilities and blindness have been an attraction for Hollywood. Silent films such as *The Near-Sighted Cyclist* (1907), *Near-Sighted Mary* (1909), and Charlie Chaplin's popular film *City Lights* (1931) relied on blindness to provide a slapstick effect.[6] Later on, in dramas, characters with vision disabilities were presented dichotomously—a criminal/evil man attempting to eradicate the nondisabled—for example, *The Blind Boy* (S. Lubin, 1908) and *A Patch of Blue*

(Guy Green, 1965)—or a female victim sharing the horror of "living in the dark"—for example, *Orphans of the Storm* (D.W. Griffith, 1921) and *Wait Until Dark* (Terence Young, 1967).[7] One common use of blind women characters in mainstream cinema is to emphasize the nondesirability of men with disabilities, with whom they have a relationship. One such example is Diana, a blind teen in a romantic relationship with Rocky, the protagonist of the film *Mask*, which is about a teen with an apparent physical disability.[8] In addition to the representation of women with vision disability and blindness as victims, many popular Hollywood films have also tended to depict them as lacking control over their lives, their destinies, and their bodies.[9]

One contemporary example of live-action narrative film's use of characters with blindness is Norwegian director Eskil Vogt's film *Blind* (2014).[10] This character serves as an intermediary between the spectators and the film's narrative through her voice and point of view. The protagonist, who is isolated and confined to her home, writes stories in which she imagines parts of the plot, thereby producing this film's visual and vocal layers. This near-complete reliance on the protagonist's point of view gives way to what one critic wrote about the film: "In some ways, as I watched, I also felt blind . . . figuratively speaking."[11] This film successfully arouses the spectators' senses, specifically through the blind protagonist's viewpoint, thus potentially providing a spectatorship experience based on crip subjectivity. This film may be read through the second category provided in the first chapter: mainstream films utilizing disability in presenting experimental cinematography.

In contrast with live-action narrative features, short animated films depicting vision disabilities and blindness rely on the voice and point of view of "real" subjects with vision disabilities in all levels of the text.[12] Moreover, the use of avant-garde animation techniques serves the purposes of "blinding the spectator"—that is, refusing to hierarchize the senses and offering a shift in the perception of vision and its role in "viewing." The film *Ishihara* (Yoav Brill, 2010) animates the point of view of a color-blind protagonist, thus forming a political and aesthetic critique of the ableist gaze responsible for designing the color vision test. Similarly, the animated documentary *An Eyeful of Sound* (Samantha Moore, 2010) makes use of subjects with synesthesia to bring forth a critique of the objective-coherent view-perception. The abstract animated film *Many Happy Returns* (Marjut Rimminen, 1996) and the animated documentary *A Shift in Perception* (Dan Monceaux, 2006) offer the point of view of blind women as an alternative to the dominant sensual hierarchy of film spectatorship. Through their use of varied animation techniques, enhanced by sound strategies, these films create the feeling of a dream or delirium, undermining the seeing spectators' reliance on their sense of sight.[13]

Disability studies scholar Georgina Kleege describes the portrayal of blind people in film in her *Sight Unseen*:

> The movie blind are a pretty sorry lot; they are timid, morose, cranky, resentful, socially awkward, and prone to despair. Actors represent blindness with the unblinking, zombie stare, directing their gazes upward to give the face a supplicating look of helplessness. Even characters that have been blind for a long time seldom seem to have mastered any of the skills that real blind people employ. They fumble with their canes and stumble over their guide dogs. The simplest daily task, such as dialing the phone, gives them no end of trouble. If they can read braille, they do so inexpertly. Their sighted companions marvel at the smallest show of skill. They say, "How did you know it was me?" or "How did you pour that without spilling?" And the blind reward them by announcing a pathetic longing for their lost sight, repeating their wish that they could catch one last glimpse of a lover's face, the old folks at home, a patch of blue.[14]

By "blinding the spectator," I draw from Kleege's politicizing not merely of the gaze of blind people (on- and off-screen) but also the cultural perspectives of sight and vision. Kleege writes that while she sees "less than 10 percent of what a normal person does," she describes herself as intensely visual. This is due to growing up surrounded by her parents' art and "an awareness that vision involves more than merely aiming the eyes at a particular object." For Kleege, viewing a movie requires the ability to decode a complex array of visual messages. She writes that "the pleasure I derive from visual media, and from the visible world in general, suggests that although my eyes are blind, my brain is still sighted. Through nature or nurture I know how to make the most of what I see."[15]

The four short avant-garde animated films examined here—*Ishihara, An Eyeful of Sound, Many Happy Returns*, and *A Shift in Perception*—go beyond merely challenging previous cinematic and cultural representations of people with vision disabilities and blindness but rather offer new insights into cinematic spectatorship and some of its naturalized sensual hierarchies. The films *Many Happy Returns* and *A Shift in Perception* criticize the construction of the cinematic spectatorship experience as vision-centric by providing a sensual-phenomenological alternative to social perceptions about vision in general and the primacy attributed to it within cinematic spectatorship in particular.

The primacy of vision in Western thought was analyzed in Martin Jay's book *Downcast Eyes: The Denigration of Vision in Twentieth-Century French Thought*.[16] In the chapter dedicated to the film camera, Jay criticizes the Cartesian construction of vision through its technological extensions, both literal and metaphorical, as establishing the dominance of the scopic regime.[17] Surrealist scholars and writers relied on photography and film while conceptualizing theories about the primacy of vision.[18] This trend was exacerbated during the merging of Marxist structuralists, psychoanalysts, and theoreticians at the end of the 1860s and 1870s. Utilizing Althusserian and Lacanian arguments against the humanist subject of the new novel of the previous decade, these scholars sought to locate ideology within the apparatus itself, rather than just "false consciousness." These theoreticians emphasized the problematic implications of new visual technologies.[19]

Following their analysis of the possible implications of the primacy of vision in cinematic spectatorship, I discuss the cultural status of vision within contemporary crip animation. This chapter adds the Frankfurt School's critique to the methodological intersection between disability studies and phenomenology to examine avant-garde artworks' emancipatory perception in resisting traditional forms. The connection between these theories and experimental animation about vision disabilities can be found in their shared hypothesis, according to which the possibility for change begins with a shift in perception. The four avant-garde animated films discussed here offer a political critique of the social order defining the sensual hierarchy. By doing so, they carry on the tradition of Frankfurt School scholars, especially Walter Benjamin's articulation of the optical unconsciousness and his phenomenological articulation of intoxication.

Walter Benjamin argued that acts such as experimentation with drugs, flaneurist walking, surrealist séances, and psychoanalytical sessions share parallels with effects made possible thanks to allegorical devices such as framing and montage. Such effects have a similar therapeutic role—activating unconscious memory layers in the depths of subjectivity.[20] This suggests that contemporary avant-garde animation might have similar therapeutic functions. New technologies allow animators to create abstract artistic texts, evoking various layers of the spectators' senses and therefore offering multilayered responses.

In the case of experimental animation about experiences with vision disabilities and blindness, filmmakers often present abstract and obscure images to evoke haptic senses. Avant-garde animation depicting vision disabilities creates experiences that are akin to daydreaming. Their focus is not a mere glimpse into a crip perspective but rather a sensual alternative for the sighted spectators throughout the entire film. Simultaneously, the contents of these films also deviate from "prosthetic" narratives, which operate as responses to something or someone needing to be fixed.[21] Although it has been argued that emphasizing the sense of touch is part of ableist and stereotypical representations of vision disability and blindness experiences, I highlight subversive uses of the same. Hing Tsang argues that the film *Herman Slobbe / Blind Child 2* (Johan van der Keuken, 1996) undermines stereotypes about blind people represented in film through their sense of touch and instead represents their bodies as a whole.[22] However, I argue that some experimental animated films offer subjective senses as a substitute for indexical representation of the body. Through the analysis of experimental animated films about vision disabilities, this chapter argues that while some films offer disorientation and reflexivity regarding the way they are oriented toward objects in the world, others affect their spectators' perception by "pulling" them into a dreamlike/intoxicated state. In this way, touch is presented as an ethical alternative to the spectatorship experience privileging sight.

CHALLENGING VISION-CENTRIC SPECTATORSHIP

The animated films *Ishihara* and *An Eyeful of Sound*, which address color blindness and synesthesia, offer an aesthetic and political critique of social conventions concerning "healthy" and ordinary sight. The aesthetics of *Ishihara* rely on the visual language of the color perception test and use it to criticize this diagnostic tool. At the same time, the film's narrative contributes to this effect by raising questions about the way we evaluate what we see and what is worthy of being seen. The animated documentary *An Eyeful of Sound* uses the medical diagnosis of synesthesia, and the people diagnosed with it, to subvert the value given to normative perceptions about sensual experiences. Both animated films offer a critique of the individual/medical model of disability by presenting this difference as valuable and as a source for pride.

Ishihara tells the story of a person diagnosed as color-blind. The visual language of the animation is made up of the colorful dots characterizing the color perception test. The tables in the dining room, the food trays, the people, and the whole surrounding world are animated using colorful dots (see figure 3.1). The construction of the world depicted through the dots separates them from their diagnostic purpose, thus giving them the ability to create multilayered universes. This animated film artistically emphasizes the fact that what is "visible" is constructed and that objective vision is, in fact, a falsehood. Brill

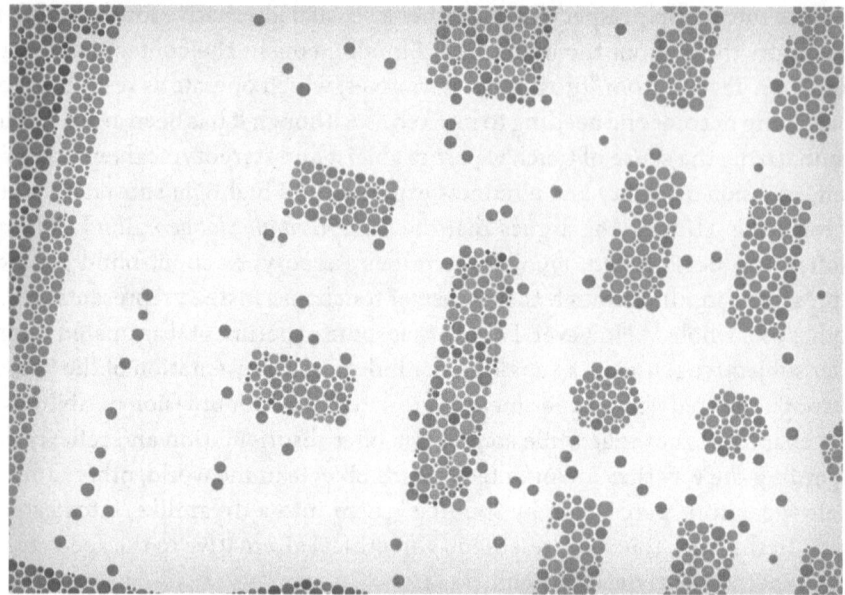

Fig. 3.1. The kibbutz's dining room © Yoav Brill, *Ishihara*, 2010

reverses the role of the dots using an artistic representation of the ways they can be used. The dots, which served as a tool to diagnose the protagonist as colorblind, become a flexible tool in exposing ableism and enjoying the creative pleasure of its deconstruction.

The animation opens with five brief shots of numbers made up of circles inside circles of different shades. The following animated scene, which seems as if it was filmed with a high-angle long shot, presents six-sided rectangular shapes made up of small circles. Circles in shades of blue, green, and brown move around the rectangles. To this scene is added a soundtrack and a voice-over, directing the spectators to interpret these shapes as tables and people.

Alongside gray dots moving from side to side, the narrator talks about the color perception test, intended to determine whether a person has color blindness: "It's kind of strange as a kid, to suddenly find yourself as an entry inside an encyclopedia, alongside all sorts of charts and strange-sounding words. I don't remember exactly when I first heard the term, first or second grade. But I could already read well enough to have all the statistics memorized. One in twelve, less for girls, a hereditary gene passed on through the mother. Chances of recovery? Not so great." The image of his childhood in the kibbutz is presented using a backward dolly shot, colorful dots making up green fields, gray

Fig. 3.2. The kibbutz and the poppies © Yoav Brill, *Ishihara*, 2010

fields, and uniformly-shaped structures (see figure 3.2). The tipping point in the protagonist's life is described when he encounters the external gaze on his condition:

> We were a small group of kids in a kibbutz surrounded by fields that for a few weeks each winter were covered with poppies. Great excuse for leaving the classroom on a field trip. When the teacher would call: "Who can find a white poppy amongst all the red ones?" I'd raise my hand and ask: "What poppies?" Then everyone would gather around me, asking all sorts of questions, and I kind of enjoyed the attention. Until one day someone asked: "So hang on, what exactly do you see?" And before I could answer, someone else said: "Nothing. I guess he sees see-through."

Following this scene, the circles representing the children and the teacher disappear, and one gray circle remains alone in the center of the frame. After a while, blue circles join the frame, and with them the sound of sea waves.

Again, the external gaze allows the protagonist a shift in perception: "This answer left me confused. Of course I didn't see see-through. And even if my red wasn't the same as theirs, who decided that it was any less red? And anyway, trying to explain to someone else what it is you don't see makes about as much

Fig. 3.3. Protagonist with his back to the camera looking at the red sea
© Yoav Brill, *Ishihara*, 2010

sense as feeling your own forehead for a temperature. And maybe it was all in my head, and I just needed to try a little harder." After he finishes this argument, the wave of blue dots wraps around the protagonist, represented by the gray point.

The color-blind protagonist's point of view is kept through the entire film as the dominant point of view, with which the spectator is meant to identify. This perspective challenges ableist norms by responding to them in questions of apparatus. The normative gaze breaks into the protagonist's world again and again, demanding him to orient toward the objects dictated by society around him—as expressed through his perception of the white poppy or the red sea. By refusing to gaze in the way he is directed to, the protagonist criticizes the normative gaze and reappropriates the language he uses by creating new syntax.

The last scene of *Ishihara* takes place in Sinai, Egypt, many years after the events in the film take place, and is reminiscent of the opening scene in the kibbutz dining room. From a high angle, square shapes appear, representing huts or canopy shades, alongside blue circles in the lower part of the frame with a soundtrack of speech, paddleball, music, and the sound of waves. The protagonist, represented through the gray dot, moves away from the noise and walks along the beach and describes an encounter similar to his experience in the kibbutz fields as a child: "Some guy was walking toward me from the opposite direction and saw me sitting on the sand. He came over and stopped in front of me." For the first time in this film, alongside the two gray dots representing the protagonist and the person in front of him, we can see a figure. The figure is made up of colorful dots, which, for a change, present a clear human form, including hair, a beard, and red pants. The protagonist's voice can be heard in the background: "'The sea really does become red at this hour,' he said. And I looked and thought to myself—what sea?" At this point, the dot clearly looks like a human figure filling up the frame (see figure 3.3). The frame becomes black, and the voice of the narrator concludes the film—"and I think I saw see-through."

This scene deepens the critique brought forth by subverting normative social perceptions about vision. The figure's fluidity and its boundary crossing are created both by the transformation from color to color and by the change from dot to human and from a sighted character to a "color-blind" character. Brill permits his protagonist to move between different social situations, thereby enhancing the dominance of his perception. For all these reasons, *Ishihara* confronts the diagnostic gaze with the protagonist's perspective. This confrontation is created using visual means, as well as through the narrative and narration, which challenge the position of the medical gaze. However, the animated film ends with what may also be interpreted as a form of internalized ableism: the protagonist grows to embody the normative notion of color blindness.

While Brill uses the diagnostic tool of "color blindness" to subvert traditional perceptions of vision, in her film *An Eyeful of Sound*, Samantha Moore uses the diagnosis of synesthesia. Synesthesia is a phenomenon in which various senses cross over cognitively.[23] Thus, for example, words may be perceived as having taste, or a certain scent might be perceived as having color. From the visual aspect, Moore's film is a classical drawn (cel) animation, as well as having documentary characteristics in terms of its soundtrack—that is, indexical voice-overs. The film crosses between testimonies of women with synesthesia and an animation of the way they perceive their environment. The soundtrack is made up of the interviewees' voices, alongside diegetic sounds to which they respond. The animation presents a variety of sounds experienced by the interviewees as colors, shapes, and movement. Moore defines her aesthetic approach as part of an attempt to use animation for describing unique mental experiences. Chris Landreth, director of the film *Ryan* (2004), defined such experiences as psychorealism.[24]

The opening sequence of *An Eyeful of Sound* consists of a blue screen slowly filling up with white words and a soundtrack composed of the indexical feminine voices. These all appear alongside the sounds of writing and erasing, hinting at the presence of the animator and director. In this way, the sequence offers a peek into the film's production process. Moreover, the audible sounds all concern direction instructions for the animation before us, similar to the opening of Avni's *Tying Your Own Shoes*. The direction is replaced with voices describing experiences of various sensual perceptions: "From the top . . . just . . . it's sort of like . . . then. Oh. Can't think of the right word. It starts like that . . . it's like they're . . . almost only much thicker than that. . . . There's more than one color there, more than one sound." This opening sequence refers to the double challenge faced by the animator. Similar to what was defined by *Ishihara*'s protagonist as feeling your own forehead for a temperature, Moore describes the difficulty of representing a subjective sensual experience. Moreover, this sequence presents the challenge of animating this mediated experience as faithfully as possible to the source.

The animation presents daily situations and the synesthetic way they are experienced by the film's protagonists. One of the interviewees describes the phenomenon of synesthesia as follows: "Hearing colors, seeing sounds, tasting smells, tasting and feeling sounds and colors." Some of the women featured in the film describe their inability to determine whether this feeling is subjective or shared by everyone. All women speak about how synesthesia is intensified while listening to live music. Thus, for example, one woman describes the experience of listenership as a colored quilt and another describes it as waves of chocolate. One of the women even wonders if the colors she sees only exist in her mind or whether they exist in objective reality, which other people cannot see.

Alongside the descriptions of synesthesia, Moore includes a medical point of view about the phenomenon of synesthesia. In contrast to the documentary tradition, which adopted the medical gaze while examining physical difference, Moore's animation offers a point of view that mixes between the medical and social models. Moore animates the colorless office of Dr. Jaime Ward from the University of Sussex in the UK and brings it to life using colors and shapes from the descriptions of people who experience synesthesia. Ward provides a scientific explanation of the phenomenon: "Synesthesia is a fascinating condition where people experience the ordinary world in very extraordinary ways. . . . When they're listening to me speaking, their tongue might feel the different taste in kind of an aberrant flow. So we think of it as an extra sensation, but to them it feels completely normal. Sort of like our experiences have something absent from them. They don't necessarily think of it as being adverse. They get used to the sensations being there, and to some extent they can filter them out." Ward's testimony is cut off by the voice of a woman saying she could not imagine the world without synesthesia and once more by another woman saying she cannot imagine how a person without synesthesia would experience classical music. Moore combines these testimonies as a sort of dialogue with scientific definitions. Thus, for example, when Ward states that synesthetic experiences might be controlled, it is confirmed in the voice of a woman saying she can tune them out.

In addition, and like the protagonist of *Ishihara*, Ward presents statistical data concerning the prevalence of this phenomenon but adds that there are people who do not tell others about their similar sensations. One of the reasons for this is that people with synesthesia are not aware of their difference because they have always experienced it. One of the peak moments of the interview is when Ward tries to imagine himself as capable of experiencing synesthesia: "If I would have synesthesia I think I would have the colored music variety.... They don't just experience colors with music, they experience shapes and movements and textures. And they're all appearing and disappearing. To actually experience it this way would be wonderful." This testimony is also cut off by the women's voices, reinforcing the idea that this experience is rich, exciting, and preferable.

As opposed to the medical model described in critical disability studies, Ward adds the social aspect of disability and emphasizes both the prevalence of synesthesia and its invisibility. As an expert, who in most cases represents the traditional medical point of view, Ward expresses appreciation and even envy toward people who experience synesthesia. The inclusion of Ward within the animation offers both a critique of the medical model and a critique of the social model. Ward's character helps the animation expose this hidden perceptual difference, although subjectively, as it is experienced as preferable to normative experience.

Both these animated films focus on a visual perception that is extraordinary and depict it by foregrounding both the social and the physical aspects of being "intensely visual." While *Ishihara* focuses on presenting social restrictions, *An Eyeful of Sound* challenges the binary between the social and medical models by presenting both perspectives while privileging the first. By so doing, they continue the work of contemporary disability scholars, who offer a corporeal ontology as a renewed starting point for disability studies.[25]

Corporeal ontology connects disability studies and scholarship about the phenomenological-political spectatorship and listenership experiences. Walter Benjamin also studied the experience of spectatorship and the sensual possibilities it allows. Benjamin examined art response patterns and focused on marginalized types of viewing, thus defining the optical unconscious: "[It is] another nature which speaks to the camera rather than to the eye: 'other' above all in the sense that a space informed by human consciousness gives way to a space informed by the unconscious.... Photography, with its devices of slow motion and enlargement, reveals the secret. It is through photography that we first discover the existence of this optical unconscious, just as we discover the instinctual unconscious through psychoanalysis."[26] Benjamin's optical unconscious provides an additional perspective about nonnormative forms of spectatorship. This type of spectatorship allows audiences to recognize people and objects they tend to oversee.[27] This argument is reminiscent of the repeated questions of *Ishihara*'s protagonist, who challenges traditional vision by attempting to present a different perception.

What was defined by Benjamin as the optical unconscious, which allows the discovery of the world's hidden aspects, becomes the subject of Sharon L. Snyder and David T. Mitchell's critique. They argue that Benjamin's position reinforces the ableist gaze on the human body: "What can 'normally be seen' or 'what is normally veiled or hidden from sight' secures a privileged position for disabled bodies on film because they promise an opportunity to practice a form of objectifying ethnography.... Film spectators arrive at the screen prepared to glimpse the extraordinary body displayed for moments of uninterrupted visual access—a practice shared by the clinical assessment rituals associated with the medical gaze.... To a great extent, film's seduction hinges on securing audience interest through the address of what which is constructed as 'outside' common visual parlance."[28] While mainstream cinema exposes the consciousness or perception of people with disabilities, the animated films discussed in this chapter prevent this gaze on disabled bodies as spectacles. They do so by replacing the indexical body with other animated forms offering complete concealment of the indexical body, alongside their critique of the traditional medical gaze.

The animated films *Ishihara* and *An Eyeful of Sound* prioritize the point of view of people with perceptual diversity beyond that of normative perception—both in their expression and in their narratives. *Ishihara* and *An Eyeful of Sound* offer their sighted, blind, and visually impaired spectators a shift in sensual perceptions, alongside a gaze that subverts the medical model. The films present the points of view of those who failed in being socially oriented as presenting a challenge to social order. We might say, then, that these animated films subvert the dichotomous perception of impairment/disability and invite their viewers to reflect upon the orientation of their own gaze. Simultaneously, however, *Ishihara*'s reliance on the medical diagnostic tool and the illustrative visual clarity of *An Eyeful of Sound* prevent the free flow of the visual associations offered to the spectators by the two animated films. The latter differs in allowing for a spectatorship experience that subverts cinema's ableist construction, promising its spectators the satisfaction of their scopic desires.

Ishihara and *An Eyeful of Sound* offer a rather coherent interpretation in depicting sensual experiences. Thanks to illustrative images and narration, the spectators enjoy the benefit of visual certainty: they know what they see. The next section presents two animated films portraying vision disability and blindness through a combination of computer technology and indexical cinematography, which deny the spectator the possibility of any certainty, especially the sighted spectators' reliance on the sense of sight. In this way, the films *A Shift in Perception* and *Many Happy Returns* critique not only the medical gaze but also the importance attributed to vision within the cinematic spectatorship experience.

VISION-DISABILITY ANIMATION AND HAPTIC SPECTATORSHIP

While *Ishihara* and *An Eyeful of Sound* invite spectators to adopt the subjective point of view of someone with color blindness or synesthesia as having nonapparent perceptual richness, thus subverting the ableist-medical gaze, *A Shift in Perception* and *Many Happy Returns* intensify the sense of touch, thus limiting reliance on vision alone. In addition, by moving the emphasis onto the haptic senses, they offer a spectatorship that resembles and provokes daydreaming. The claim that blindness does not visually translate into darkness but rather to a vivid daydream has been made by Hugues de Montalembert in the documentary *Black Sun* (Gary Tran, 2005), which detaches the visual from the audible and is further discussed later on. As opposed to the uniformity in the visual language of *Ishihara* and *An Eyeful of Sound*, the films *A Shift in Perception* and *Many Happy Returns* contain hybrid characteristics, combining computer technologies and cinematography of live motion. *A Shift in Perception* is an animated documentary presenting the stories of three blind women using live-action shots digitally manipulated to create a vague visual atmosphere akin to delirium or intoxication. *Many Happy Returns* is a film combining pixilation, stop-motion, and editing for the purpose of describing traumatic experiences from the past of an aging woman. The dreamlike or intoxicated visual atmosphere created in these films offers an experience that heightens the spectators' sense of touch.

Mainstream cinema's gaze on blind women has constructed them as inferior by depicting their look as unfocused and expressionless, thus dehumanizing them to reinforce stereotypes about disability. Studying the gaze on blind women in cinema, Johnson Cheu argued that they experience double marginalization.[29] Cheu discusses the gaze of blind feminine protagonists and defines

Fig. 3.4. Stop-motion moving objects © Dan Monceaux, *A Shift in Perception*, 2006

it as a tool for eliminating their agency.[30] Furthermore, many films about blind people present the visual experience of blindness through a complete lack of vision or blurred vision. Cinematic techniques such as the blank screen or dim shots serve the cinematic representation of the primacy of vision, according to Cheu.[31]

However, as opposed to mainstream representations of blind women, the animated film *A Shift in Perception* obfuscates the spectators' vision, making them dependent on the voices of those women. Also, the blurring of the spectators' vision serves to reinforce the characters' agency; the women's voices guide both the blind and sighted spectators while attempting to decipher the film (see figure 3.4). In this way, the primacy of vision is subverted, and dominant power is given to the protagonists, who convey their knowledge to the audience. *A Shift in Perception* makes use of animation techniques similar to those of *Many Happy Returns* for the purpose of creating a dreamlike visual experience. The spectator's being in this state may potentially allow the change in perception described by Benjamin.[32]

A Shift in Perception opens with a black-and-white shot of waves, with quiet music in the background while a woman's voice is audible saying that life without sight is not very different for her (see figure 3.5). Over a black-and-white shot of a sewing machine and attempts to thread a needle, the woman continues to talk about some of the difficult experiences of blindness. The face of the speaker, Rhonda, is shown for a few seconds while she describes her past in a sewing factory and meeting Edna, another interviewee. While the interview

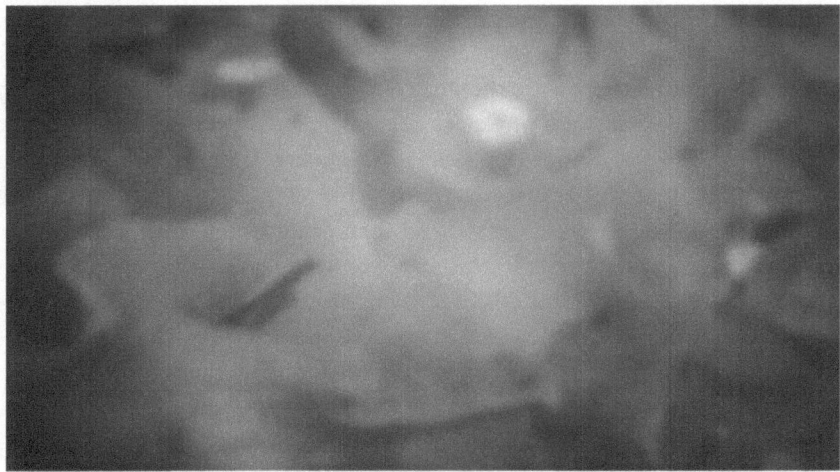

Fig. 3.5. Edna explains her blindness experience and imagination © Dan Monceaux, *A Shift in Perception*, 2006

with Edna is audible, shots of sewing, weaving, and knitting hands are juxtaposed with shots of Edna's face in a shadow on a white background. Leander, the third interviewee, is also shown through the juxtaposition of images of her playing a piano with close-ups of her face in a number of dark, high-contrast shots.

In addition to scenes describing the women's subjective viewpoints and perceptions and the ways they learned to adapt to a society accommodating sighted people, the animation focuses on the women's inner worlds and dreams in particular. The women's descriptions of the smells and sounds they enjoy are somewhat reminiscent of the descriptions of synesthesia in *An Eyeful of Sound*, especially Leander's articulation of her experiences as a musician. Leander praises Mendelssohn's work, which was played at the funeral of her father, who longed to live by the sea.[33] She talks about missing the sea, in which she could only bathe with her father's help; in his absence, she feels it is too dangerous for her, and only visits it in her dreams.

The tactile experiences invoked by the animated film were described by critics as a central source of attraction for spectators. Frank Finkelstein noted: "The best footage gives us a kinetic and tactile sense of the women's experience, how touch, sound and smells are dominant in their experience. A sequence where the camera sits behind a shopping cart, wheeling around the aisles of a supermarket, helps us to immediately understand how the weight and feel of the cart itself helps Rhonda to navigate, and a shot of jangling keys clarifies how she so easily locates the store manager for assistance."³⁴ Tactile knowledge is emphasized by the animation, especially when illustrating dreams. While images of water and the sea are shown, Edna says that she does not know why she fears dreams about water. In those dreams, she does not see herself inside the water but in a small motorboat going in circles. Rhonda talks about her dreams while visual images of water are shown: "I go through stages of dreaming. Sometimes I don't dream at all, and then other times I just can't get the dreams out of my head. And I often used to wonder because I was sighted before whether I'd dream in color.... I did dream mainly in black and white, but every now and then color would come into it." Simultaneously with the descriptions of dreams, the animation depicts the interviewees' fears. Thus, for example, the fear of running into a fire is enhanced using threatening montages of fire. These images require the spectators to rely on their auditory and tactile senses to interpret the animation.

This type of embodied knowledge plays an important role in avant-garde texts, which tend to represent the abstract, dreamlike, meditative, metaphorical. As seen through *A Shift in Perception*, as suggested in the first part of this chapter, these types of texts make it difficult for seeing spectators to solely rely on their sense of sight.

Sight, according to Merleau-Ponty, is what envelops what we see as its "flesh." Merleau-Ponty's "The Intertwining—The Chiasm" opens with an analysis of sight and vision, a position that can be read as placing vision at the top of the hierarchy of the senses and perhaps even as the most important in the perceptive process of the "objects" and "subjects" that make up the experience of being-in-the-world. Our vision of those objects/subjects seems to us to be derived from them. Therefore, vision is an issue of reaction in the sense that the seeing entity and the seen entity exist in a codependent interaction with each other. Thus, for example, seeing a color is actually seeing it in the context of its surroundings, of other colors and other shades of the same color (in ways that evoke Claude Lévi-Strauss's analysis of language), as well as in its cultural and historical context. In light of the foregoing, his conclusion is that a certain shade of the color red is a fossil composed of the depths of our imaginary worlds.³⁵

Merleau-Ponty defines the phenomenological being as carnal, the being that is part of the world's flesh. This argument was honed by the tactile example of the touching hands. Just as there is no difference between the toucher and the touched, there is also no difference between touch and sight because both of them result from the same body. The possibility of hearing and voicing sounds is also connected to the material being in the "world as flesh," but it is not given as extensive a space as that given to sight and touch. Both objects and people make sounds and have the ability to make sounds.[36] Just as there is no silence in cinema, according to Merleau-Ponty, there is no silence in the world, and there is no world in silence. But is there thought? That is, is there meaning to the sights I see, the sounds I hear and the sounds I make? In Merleau-Ponty's words, "between sound and meaning, speech and what it means to say, there is still the relation of reversibility, and no question of priority, since the exchange of words is exactly the differentiation of which the thought is the integral."[37] Merleau-Ponty returns to the subject of meaning and argues that it does not relate to language in the same way butter goes with bread or like a layer of "mental reality" that is transferred through the voice; rather, it is the totality of what is said, including the differences that exist in the verbal chain. Meaning is something given to the audible through words. Merleau-Ponty relies on Edmund Husserl in his refusal to explain meaning and compares it to the expression of an experience by means of an experience, which is impossible to do—and that is the problem of language.

The visual uncertainty emphasized by abstract animation allows the audience to experience a type of spectatorship that enhances their bodily senses. Are blind documentary subjects more vulnerable to the ableist gaze as they cannot return one, or do they already possess the antidote as they are not visually susceptible to it? *A Shift in Perception* protects its protagonists through the vague nature of the visual aspect, obfuscating spectators' vision and thus barring the sighted viewers' privilege of vision as a source of knowledge. This obfuscation of the visual convention brings attention to the neutrality of vision in the cinematic spectatorship experience. By distorting live action or documentary footage, *A Shift in Perception* and *Many Happy Returns* reverberate the idea of the optical unconscious. These films require their spectators to touch vague images by delaying and denying conventional cinematic spectatorship. This act has the potential to achieve Benjamin's aspiration of emancipatory use of new technologies.

Another example of this potential is the aforementioned feature documentary *Black Sun*. The documentary—written by Hugues de Montalembert, a French painter and filmmaker based in New York, and directed by Gary Tarn—begins with de Montalembert's assault and blinding in 1978. The film is a visually poetic documentary based on images filmed using a 16mm camera and often not synchronized with the soundtrack, which consists of de Montalembert's voice-over. The film's imagery invites the viewers to enter a spectatorship position reminiscent of daydreaming—a passage from one image to another as a chain of visual associations. This position may also be reminiscent of the visual experience of the loss of sight, as de Montalembert describes it: "Not

Fig. 3.6. Eye bandage © Marjut Rimminen, *Many Happy Returns*, 1997

receiving perception from the eye, the mind would create very strong images, vivid images. To the point I would talk to you and suddenly I would see something like a vision.... Or I would have erotic images. Very strong erotic images. Talking to somebody was very disturbing because I had very strong erotic images." The most prominent experience offered by the film is a sort of dreamlike spectatorship leading to disorientation. This experience is constructed through a chain of associative and dissociative images. In this state, spectators must rely on de Montalembert's voice, which guides them in deciphering or disregarding the multitude of tactile images. Similar to *A Shift in Perception*, the experience of disorienting daydreaming offered by the documentary *Black Sun* allows the activation of repressed memory layers of subjectivity.

The animated film *Many Happy Returns* is made up of objects and ghosts from the past returning to the protagonist's consciousness. This film combines techniques of computer-generated and manipulated images, pixilation, dolls, stop-motion, and live action. The animation presents a child doll haunting the life of an adult woman. This figure is made of a delicate and frail material emphasized as such, mostly around the eyes (see figures 3.6 and 3.7). The fragile doll-child represents the woman's childhood trauma. The animation revives the transparent and repressed child from the woman's past, thus requiring the spectator to acknowledge her.

Fig. 3.7. The doll/ghost/child looking out the window © Marjut Rimminen, *Many Happy Returns*, 1997

The animated film's opening sequence starts out with a dim shot of a dresser with a lace tablecloth and framed family photos on top. The shot changes into a live-action scene of a woman pulling a curtain aside, with her image reflected in a mirror over a white dresser bearing various artifacts. The woman stands before the mirror, looking at a photo. Her image, reflected from the mirror, transforms through animation into the image of a doll with a bandage covering her left eye. The next scene is particularly dark and shows the doll covering her eyes and stepping backward while the sound of people's voices and glass shattering increases in volume. The doll opens her eyes in front of a mirror reflecting the image of a doll with red eyes. The next shot shows a medical team from a low angle, from the doll's point of view. The following shot shows a framed photo of the doll with a bandage on her eye over a crying soundtrack. The next scene takes place in the film's present and is located in the woman protagonist's sunlit home as she leans into an armchair. The woman is replaced by the doll, which gradually shrinks with each shot, while the doctors are seen from a low angle in the window in the background. This scene transforms into a dark stop-motion montage of the apartment while objects move inside it and the sound of a crying child is audible. In the dark, the doll comes out into the apartment, walking around it and touching various objects, until the couple returns. The ending scene of the animation shows the woman opening a wrapped gift with a box inside it. Inside the box is white wrapping paper covering a face with a wounded eye. Once the wrapping is opened, the gift is revealed to be an eyelike crystal ball. The woman places the crystal ball on the white dresser, alongside the other artifacts, and looks at her reflection in the mirror. The mirror image shows the doll banging on the glass. The woman averts her eyes and leaves with the man while the doll continues to bang on the glass.

Marjut Rimminen, director of *Many Happy Returns*, was asked about this animated work in an interview for a documentary film about artists with vision disabilities.[38] Rimminen described her squint, with her for most of her life, as "terribly upsetting because you don't get that contact with people." Rimminen reported her look as not permitting contact with the other when referring to meaningful childhood memories. The animation becomes a means of processing the childhood trauma of being looked at as deformed by her mother and at the same time comments on deformation as an internalized feeling rather than a physical shape. For Rimminen, the damage to the doll's eyes was caused by her witnessing traumatic events, as well as an internalized feeling of distortion. Rimminen exposes the repressed child who failed to make contact; however, this child now subverts her oppression and demands to be seen anew.

The hybrid and obscure visual style becomes clear through the senses, mainly through invoking the spectator's tactility. The eye and the wound, the wrapping paper and the bandage, are all materials mixed together, therefore invoking sensual perception and tactile memory. This unique and uncategorizable form requires the viewers to focus on the material and texture of the animation. In a way, Rimminen's animation allows spectators to grasp what sight does not reveal—the trauma of being looked at as deformed, or worse looked through.

The experience of looking at abstract images while our haptic senses are enhanced was discussed by Benjamin in his writings about experimenting with drugs. These writings were published posthumously in the book *On Hashish*. His attempt to put the complex experience of intoxication into words did not stop with the description of the "high." In the fifth entry of March 1930, Benjamin attempts to characterize the concept of image space. He claims that while we are intoxicated, we perceive both image and sound in a way we would not have been able to in regular states of consciousness. While consuming hashish, Benjamin wrote about image perception: "There can be an absolutely blizzard-like production of images, independently of whether our attention is directed toward anyone or anything else. Whereas in our normal state free-floating images to which we pay no heed simply remain in the conscious, under the influence of hashish images present themselves to us seemingly without requiring our attention."[39] These writings allow for a reading of the spectatorship experience offered by *Many Happy Returns* and *A Shift in Perception*, including the carnal and mental state the spectator might experience. As noted by Benjamin, the result of such states might be a static gaze: "the production of images that are so extraordinary, so fleeting, and so rapidly generated that we can do nothing but gaze at them simply because of their beauty and singularity."[40] Whether watching images of delirium encourages immersion into their uncontrollable movement or creates a state of passive gazing, such films challenge the dominance of the normative gaze. Invoking the tactile experience in the spectator's bodymind offers an ideological shift in the perception of cinematic spectatorship. These tactile experiences presented through films such as *A Shift in Perception* and *Many Happy Returns* rely on the obfuscation of the gaze and an invocation of the haptic.

The abstract animation style of *Many Happy Returns* combines images of daydreaming or delirium with the presence of depression, anxiety, dysmorphia, and trauma. Such combinations invoke Jack Halberstam's queer and possibly crip use of Hall's low theory to challenge the unifying norm. In his book about the queer art of failure, Halberstam adopts the term "low theory" coined by Stuart Hall to "locate all the in-between spaces that save us from being snared by the hooks of hegemony." However, he also adds that this theory may accept the fact that alternatives to hegemony "dwell in the murky waters of a counter intuitive, often impossibly dark and negative realm of critique and refusal."[41] Offering phenomenology as an essential resource for queer studies in emphasizing the corporeal and sensual experience, Sara Ahmed argues that queer phenomenology: "emphasizes the importance of lived experience, the intentionality of consciousness, the significance of nearness or what is ready-to-hand, and the role of repeated and habitual actions in shaping bodies and worlds."[42] In this way, the lived experience includes our bodily existence or, as defined by Edmund Husserl, "lived body" (*Leib*). These insights about the body's impropriety or disorientation rely on the intersection between queer phenomenology and crip theory, art, and lived experiences.

Self-representing her own lived experiences, Rimminen uses the intoxicating atmosphere to portray the doll's transitioning into a traumatic ghost, haunting the adult through waves, a crystal ball, and, finally, a child. One of the most significant transitioning moments takes place while the doll-child's eyes alternate textures of objects and various body organs. The protagonist's lived body "touches" the spectator's body since, as described by Merleau-Ponty, "The body belongs to the order of the things as the world is universal flesh."[43]

Both animated films discussed in this section subvert the sensual hierarchy of the mainstream live-action spectatorship experience by obfuscating the sighted normative gaze and invoking all bodily senses. In this way, the animated films emphasize tactility as an ethical alternative to mainstream cinema's vision-centric gaze. Price and Shildrick's "touch ethics" emphasizes our codependency on other bodies:

> Much has been written in broadly phenomenological literature about how our sense of touch is every bit as important as, if not more important than, sight in mapping our morphology of our bodies and of the spaces in which we move. Between sentient beings, touch, unlike sight, is quintessentially an interactive sensation in which the moment of touching is indivisible from being touched. There is never a point at which we can fail to reverse the sensation, nor at which we can distinguish clearly between the active and passive mode. Again, unlike sight, touch frustrates hierarchy, and crosses boundaries rather than creates distance.[44]

Cinematic evocation of touch allows the crossing of social boundaries—the boundaries between self and other, between subject and subject, and between subject and object. This is an ethical issue since, through touch, we become "more exposed to each other, immersed in each other, opening up the possibility of facing similar experience which could arouse fear and discomfort... the thought that 'this could be me.'"[45] Moreover, by obfuscating sight and arousing touch, the boundaries between viewer and subject also collapse. The voice and the image touch the spectator, thereby complicating those boundaries. We might say, then, that these animated films offer an intersubjective spectatorship experience based on "touch ethics," in which the spectator is forced to reflect on the primacy of sight in the cinematic spectatorship experience.

The medical-normative gaze adopted by mainstream live-action cinema uses disability as the subject of what needs to be fixed, as Mitchell and Snyder suggest: "Disability does not (only) upset the social landscape because we, too, may experience the vagaries of embodiment; rather, we worry about disability's ability to elude capture by the compliances we demand of bodies, i.e. the injunction to expose their variability to the impossible conformity of standardised functionalities, capacities and appearances. Instead, we would allow disability to reference a state of being without a coherent collective of affective, aesthetic and functional experiences—a denial of the extraordinary social effort to make disability an essence only of becoming in order to be fixed."[46] Denying this gaze by blurring the spectators' vision may allow for disrupting this very social landscape.

This section suggested that the dreamlike images in the animated films *A Shift in Perception* and *Many Happy Returns* challenged their spectators' sensual perceptions and potentially subverted the basis of the classical hierarchy of the senses. This hierarchy is defined by distance, and Laura U. Marks argues that the better a certain sense overcomes physical distance, the better it is perceived as being.[47] A spectatorship that overcomes distance was defined by Sobchack as "the way in which our equally available senses have the capacity to become variously heightened and diminished, the power of culture regulating their boundaries as it arranges them into a normative hierarchy."[48] Therefore, by obfuscating sight and arousing tactility, the boundaries between spectator and subject also collapse. The voice and the image touch spectators through their bodies, thus crossing the boundaries between the text and the audience. Rather than satisfying a spectatorship experience based on staring at the disabled body, mind, or perception, these animated films offer their spectators intersubjective experiences based on touch ethics.

A spectatorship experience that arouses the haptic is created though hybrid images containing representations and animations of the world, rearranged through technological possibilities. The atmospheres in the abstract animated films *A Shift in Perception* and *Many Happy Returns* invoke a dreamlike experience. Both Benjamin and Merleau-Ponty argued that such perceptions politically emphasize the multidirectional and reversible movement of the senses. In *Phenomenology of Perception*, Merleau-Ponty writes: "A subject under mescaline finds a piece of iron, strikes the window-sill with it and exclaims: 'This is magic': the trees are growing greener. The barking of a dog is found to attract light in an indescribable way, and is re-echoed in the right foot."[49] According to his argument, this synesthetic perception is the rule, and we are only unaware of it because scientific language has made us forget how to see, hear, and generally feel, all "in order to deduce, from our bodily organization and the world as the physicist conceive it, what are to see, hear and feel."[50] Moreover, we perceive the world through our senses, but they usually remain invisible to us; art and phenomenological philosophy allow us to "remember" their existence and make them visible to us.[51] Therefore, an external shifting of our sensual perception may "remind" us how to reuse our senses. Similarly, alternative animation forms allow an exposure of ableist ideology. They do so through different spectatorship experiences, which emphasize the sensual potential of the cinematic spectatorship experience.

OVERSIGHTS

All four short experimental animated films discussed in this chapter present the point of view of people with vision-related disabilities or blindness while at the same time barring the possibility of subjecting them to the sighted, ableist gaze. *Ishihara* and *An Eyeful of Sound* offer the lived experiences of people with nonnormative vision by replacing the indexical representation of their bodies with metaphorical visual images and subjective narration. It seems that in the absence of a disabled body on-screen, the characters cannot be subjected to the ableist gaze or made into spectacles. The animated films *A Shift in Perception* and *Many Happy Returns* obfuscate the spectator's point of view by mixing obscure indexical images and abstract symbolic images. The sighted, ableist gaze is barred both by the obfuscation of the indexical body and by images that draw the spectator into the dreamlike, associative audiovisual atmosphere. The spectators' being in this state may allow them to reflect on the primacy of vision in the live-action spectatorship experience.

The four animated films present the shift in visual perception as an opportunity to animate the experience of being-in-the-world and provide an alternative spectatorship experience. *Ishihara* and *An Eyeful of Sound* animate this perceptual shift as an experience with an "ability-diverse body"; Gregor Wolbring's term is most appropriate here, which disavows the primacy of the normative experience.[52] *A Shift in Perception* and *Many Happy Returns* use vision disabilities and the alternative perceptions they offer in order to challenge the cinematic spectatorship experience, which attributes primacy to sight. Such alternative spectatorship experiences—one reflexive about vision in the represented world and the other reflexive about cinematic spectatorship—rely on the different animation styles of cel animation versus hybrid animation, which combines various techniques.

A Shift in Perception and *Many Happy Returns* replace the visual certainty of *Ishihara* and *An Eyeful of Sound* with an obfuscation that allows for sensual responses deviating from the social-medical gaze. For Adorno, the reception of artworks was a central point of interest since, according to him, the spectator is a separate subject, rather than a mass. Adorno and Horkheimer, as read by Miriam Hansen, placed an emphasis on cinema's "illegitimate" beginnings, as well as its proximity to the circus and road shows. Hansen argues that they praised marginalized genres such as the grotesque, the comedy, or certain types of musicals.[53] Talking films' repeated conflict with the output of the silent era was caused by the subversive potential that might have served as the basis for alternative cinema.[54] In his "Transparencies on Film," Adorno emphasizes the subversive potential of multilayered response patterns. According to him, this multilayeredness contains the antidote to dominant ideology: "The ideology of the culture industry contains the antidote to its own lie."[55] To borrow the same into this context, the animated films allowing their spectators to experience multilayered responses might serve to counter the construction of the ableist gaze in mainstream cinema.

Avant-garde animated films about vision disabilities offer viewers a shift in perception. However, while *Ishihara* and *An Eyeful of Sound* shift the medical-normative perception of disability, *A Shift in Perception* and *Many Happy Returns* subvert the primacy attributed to vision in the cinematic spectatorship experience. The latter films create a dreamlike atmosphere, based on abstract and ambiguous images that make the visible uncertain evoking multilayered and multisensory spectatorships. Such visual ambivalence invokes haptic connections and places the viewer in touch with the images, the sensible bodies as well as with people whose lived experiences are represented. The sensual bodies presented in these short films are exposed to the social orientation relying on compulsory able-bodiedness/able-mindedness in a culture that glorifies the visual. Therefore, analyzing the spectatorship experience in abstract animation, in the spirit of crip phenomenology, allows for a nonuniform sensual alternative to traditional spectatorship. Based on the Frankfurt School's approach, such a shift in the spectatorship experience may open up the possibility of an antidote against the social hierarchy of senses and bodies.

While considered secondary to vision in the spectatorship experience, listening to the soundtrack—dialogue, voice-over, or music—is just as, if not more integral to it in the case of portrayals of crip animation, as the next chapter shows. Furthermore, the voice, separated from the speaking body, is a central tool in enhancing critique and challenging ableist perceptions in the animated documentaries about disability. Therefore, the next chapter suggests that by disconnecting the voice from the body, these films emphasize the carnal knowledge of the subjects depicted in them, all in order to examine social limitations over the bodymind. In turn, crip animated documentary uses the disabled subject's indexical voice to anchor the lived experience of disability in social reality.

NOTES

1. An earlier version of this chapter entitled "More Than Meets the Eye: The Haptic Spectatorship Experience of Short Avant-Garde Animation about Vision Disabilities" appeared in *Frames Cinema Journal* 5, 2014 Special Issue Framing Animation Guest-edited by Bella Honess Roe, https://framescinemajournal

.com/article/more-than-meets-the-eye-the-haptic-spectatorship-experience-of-short-avant-garde-animation-about-vision-disabilities/.

2. Thirty-six million views in less than twenty-four hours. See Ian Sample, "#TheDress: Have Researchers Solved the Mystery of Its Colour?" *Guardian*, May 14, 2015.

3. A survey conducted by Buzzfeed found 71 percent of the respondents chose white and gold (1.6 million) versus only 29 percent saw blue and black. Cates Holderness. "What Colors Are This Dress?" *BuzzFeed*, February 26, 2015, https://www.buzzfeed.com/catesish/help-am-i-going-insane-its-definitely-blue?utm_source=dynamic&utm_campaign=bfsharecopy.

4. Quoted in "The Science behind the Dress Colour Illusion," *Guardian*, February 27, 2015, https://www.theguardian.com/technology/blog/2015/feb/27/science-thedress-colour-illusion-the-dress-blue-black-gold-white.

5. See: Sample, "#TheDress."

6. Norden, *The Cinema of Isolation*, 20.

7. Longmore, "Screening Stereotypes," 133, 143, and Philip DiMare, "Representations of Disability in Film," in *Movies in American History: An Encyclopedia*, vol. 1 (Santa Barbara, CA: ABC-CLIO, 2011), 1050.

8. This issue is discussed at length in chapter 1. In addition, in cases where men with vision disabilities were depicted in film as the subjects of a discussion about prejudice and injustice, the protagonists were usually veterans, serving militarist and patriarchal narratives—for example, as in the films *Pride of the Marines* (Delmer Daves, 1945) and *Bright Victory* (Mark Robson, 1951). Longmore, "Screening Stereotypes," 72, and DiMare, "Representations of Disability in Film," 1051.

9. Johnson Cheu, "Seeing Blindness On-Screen: The Blind, Female Gaze," in *The Problem Body: Projecting Disability on Film*, ed. Sally Chivers and Nicole Markotić (Columbus: Ohio State University Press, 2010), 67–81.

10. Winner of the Sundance screenplay award for 2014.

11. Plaktonrules, "Review of Blind," IMDB, September 11, 2014, https://www.imdb.com/review/rw3084973/?ref_=tt_urv.

12. As opposed to sighted actors playing blind and vision-impaired characters.

13. For example: music, digital manipulation of sound, dubbing and use of indexical sound in documentary animation, digital manipulation, pixilation, use of 8mm cameras, time and focus manipulation, classical animation, found footage, and indexical recording of live action.

14. Georgina Kleege, *Sight Unseen* (New Haven: Yale University Press, 1999), 45.

15. Kleege, *Sight Unseen*, 2–3.

16. Martin Jay, *Downcast Eyes: The Denigration of Vision in Twentieth-Century French Thought* (Berkeley: University of California Press, 1994).

17. The telescope, the microscope, and the camera obscura. Jay, 435–492.

18. For example, Henry Bergson, Claude Simon, and Jean Paul Sartre.
19. Jay, *Downcast Eyes*, 435–436.
20. Benjamin, *On Hashish*, 11.
21. David T. Mitchell and Sharon L. Snyder, *Narrative Prosthesis: Disability and the Dependencies of Discourse* (Ann Arbor: University of Michigan Press, 2001). Also, for example, reliance on the oedipal narrative defines blindness as a finite loss and enlightenment as acquired through self-harm. Michael Davidson, "Phantom Limbs: Film Noir and the Disabled Body," in *The Problem Body: Projecting Disability on Film*, ed. Sally Chivers and Nicole Markotić (Columbus: Ohio State University Press, 2010), 43–66.
22. Tsang in Catalin Brylla, "'Documentary and (Dis)ability' Symposium, University of Surrey, United Kingdom, 20 September 2013," *Studies in Documentary* 8, no. 2 (2014): 170.
23. For a comprehensive study of synesthesia, please see: Julia Simner and Edward M. Hubbard, *Oxford Handbook of Synesthesia* (Oxford: Oxford University Press, 2013).
24. See discussion in Samantha Moore, "Animating Unique Brain States," *Animation Studies Online Journal* (2011): np.
25. Shakespeare and Watson, "The Social Model of Disability," 22–28.
26. Walter Benjamin, "A Short History of Photography," *Classical Essays on Photography*, ed. Alan Trachtenberg (New Haven, CT: Leete's Island Books, 1980), 142–151.
27. Miriam Hansen, "Benjamin, Cinema and Experience: 'The Blue Flower in the Land of Technology,'" *New German Critique* no. 40 (Winter 1987): 217.
28. Snyder and Mitchell, "Body Genres," 181.
29. Cheu, "Seeing Blindness On-Screen," 67–68.
30. For example, *Dark Victory* (Edmund Goulding, 1939) and *Wait Until Dark* (Terence Young, 1967).
31. Snyder and Mitchell, "Body Genres," 71–74.
32. Benjamin, "A Short History of Photography," 142–151.
33. Wrote "Fingal's Cave" and, according to Leander, was so descriptive that "you could hear the ocean and seagulls in his musical creations."
34. Frank Finkelstein, "A Shift in Perception," Film Threat, June 2007, http://www.filmthreat.com/reviews/10793.
35. Merleau-Ponty, "The Intertwining—The Chiasm," 132.
36. Merleau-Ponty, 144–145.
37. Merleau-Ponty, editor's comment, 145.
38. *Janela da Alma* (Walter Carvalho and João Jardim, 2001).
39. Benjamin, *On Hashish*, 59–60
40. Benjamin, 60.
41. Halberstam, *The Queer Art of Failure*, 2.

42. Sara Ahmed, *Queer Phenomenology: Orientations, Objects, Others* (Durham, NC: Duke University Press, 2006), 1–2.

43. Merleau-Ponty, "The Intertwining—The Chiasm," 137.

44. Price and Shildrick, "Bodies Together," 66.

45. Price and Shildrick, 71.

46. David T. Mitchell and Sharon L. Snyder, "Minority Model: From Liberal to Neoliberal Futures of Disability," in *Routledge Handbook of Disability Studies*, 2nd ed., ed. Nick Watson and Simo Vehmas (London: Routledge, 2020), 53.

47. Marks, *The Skin of the Film*, 194–242.

48. Sobchack, "What My Fingers Knew."

49. Merleau-Ponty, "Phenomenology of Perception," in Sobchack, n/p.

50. Sobchack.

51. Baldwin, introduction to *Maurice Merleau-Ponty*, 1–11.

52. For an elaborate and thought-provoking discussion of terminologies and definitions, please see Gregor Wolbring's "Meaning of Disability, Body Image, Person and Health" at *Gregor Wolbring and the Wolbpack* (blog), accessed February 2021, https://wolbring.wordpress.com/meaning-of-disability-body-image-person-and-health/.

53. This is further discussed in my analysis of the film *My Depression*.

54. Hansen, "Introduction to Adorno," 197.

55. Theodor Adorno, "Transparencies on Film," trans. Thomas Y. Levin, *New German Critique*, no. 24–25 (Autumn 1981–Winter 1982): 199–205.

FOUR

DEAFENING THE SPECTATOR
Rethinking Sonic Pleasures and Audism

A CENTRAL ASPECT TO THE spectatorship of the discussed animated films about disability that has not been fully acknowledged in this book is the prominent means of their consumption. Even before the COVID-19 quarantine binge-streaming era,[1] short animated films have been mainly viewed on small screens—that is, computer, tablet, or smartphone—rather than at film festivals. Viewing these films on the animators' Vimeo pages or personal websites depends on if the artists chose to include closed or open captions or in some cases subtitles. Although regularly used by both hearing people and those who understand the spoken language, captions are meant for viewers who cannot hear the audio in the video, whereas subtitles are meant for viewers who can hear but do not understand the language in the video.[2] Open captions are permanently visible and the viewer does not need to actively access them, whereas closed captions are the most common and exist as a separate file, which gives the viewer the ability to switch them on or off.[3] In late October 2021, AMC announced that they would offer open captioning at 240 of their theaters. The automatic transcription of audio to text is in high demand, as the phones of many deaf and hearing social media users are muted while they are watching videos.

Examining the place of deafness within disability (studies), Jackie Leach Scully discusses "D/deaf" identities as also evolving in response to technology as evident by new modes of communication; for example, texting, email, instant messaging, and so on offer alternatives to the phonocentric dominance of communication in the hearing world as a result of shifting the experiences of both deaf and hearing people in their interaction with each other.[4] Scully argues that deafness and disability may better be investigated in terms of phenotypic variation rather than social structures or cultural identities. Having a deaf identity, in which one is a person disabled by social or attitudinal barriers, is fully compatible with the theories of disability that see physical impairments leading to disablement because of disabling social structures; however, because it does not refer to impairment at all, a model of deaf identity based on a cultural view of deafness as normative is hard to contain within existing disability theory.[5] Finally, Scully concludes that "an empirical approach that focuses on exploring the details of the mismatch between embodiment and expectation, rather than on the nature of the impairment or on the sociopolitical label of D/deaf or disabled, is also more in accord with contemporary views of identity as dynamic, contextual and intersubjective. In this way is possible to see the 'problem' of D/deaf identity as beginning to open up a theoretical space that enriches both Deaf and disability studies."[6]

The use of sound in contemporary animated documentaries about disability challenges cultural perceptions with respect to the hierarchy of the senses and offers both deaf and hearing spectators alternative sensory experiences. While it is true that phenomenological intersections between the senses are offered in every film, the use of sound in crip animation undermines social concepts of the sociocultural status of the various senses. The soundtrack of crip animation offers sensory experiences that emphasize the sense of hearing in both direct and allusive ways. The visual listenership experience offered by animated films that emphasize the auditory "deafen" the spectator and provide an experience evocative of sign languages as a non-audio-centric means of complex, elaborate, and multisensory communication.

While I explore the potentiality of animated films to offer non-vocal-centric pleasures inspired by sign language, I draw on Octavian E. Robinson and Jonathan Henner's proposal to learn from the knowledge and experiences of deaf people in research about sign languages that is generally ignored by scientists. By analyzing a book by a deaf writer, Albert Ballin, they discuss deaf people's knowledge about language and cognition in reference to disability justice. Arguing that over generations of inhabiting a different center, deaf people have developed and transmitted embodied knowledge, mainly through sign language, in developing language, cognition, and social structures, Robinson and Henner exemplify deaf people's knowledge and perspectives as crucial to the knowledge and practices of science researchers of language and the brain.[7] Robinson and Henner explain deaf epistemology as a means of affirming sign languages as not merely real—that is, having a system of phonology, syntax, and morphology, it being a lexicon, and having contact languages, creoles, and slang—but also natural to the brain.[8] This devaluation of sign language—and American Sign Language (ASL), in particular—is informed by both audism and ableism. In their earlier work, Robinson and Henner explain, "As deaf people experience the sting of audism, ableism, and inequity, they pull back and situate this discourse within the larger notions of disability justice and social justice. Even though American Sign Language (ASL) has gone vogue, deaf people continue to remain with other disabled people on the margins of U.S. society. . . . Although deaf people in the western world have historically considered themselves as sociolinguistic minority groups separate from other disabled communities, we recognize the underlying structural forces and historical, social, and cultural processes that shape deaf people's relations to society [and the academy] are tied to dis/ability and ableism."[9] It was not until the 1960s that William Stokoe, a nondeaf person, legitimized ASL by proving it to be a true language with syntax that shared many features of spoken languages.[10]

Film scholars began taking sound studies research seriously during the 1980s. Among the prominent researchers who initiated this process were Rick Altman, John Belton, Michel Chion, Mary Ann Doane, Claudia Gorbman, Kaja Silverman, Elisabeth Weis, and Alan Williams. This increased interest in sound in the early 1980s was explained by Paul Young as pertaining to technological innovations and developments from the areas of phonography, radio, and telephony that were utilized in Hollywood, such as multitrack sound recording and improvement of the synchronization between image and soundtrack.[11] Researchers such as John Belton and Michel Chion, for example, bridge the early sound period and the Dolby and multichannel stereo era in their discussions of sonic space and especially examine the ways the diegetic space is created by "sounds, dynamics, directionality, and reverberation, and how stereo processes expand diegetic space into spaces of exhibition—or better, to make exhibition space an extension of diegetic space."[12] At the end of the twentieth century, theories on sound in film were influenced by phenomenology and focused on the relationship between the soundtrack and sounds generated and heard in the auditors' physical reality. In this regard, Alan Williams, Christian Metz, and Thomas Levin focused their discussions on questions pertaining to the relationship between sound and hearing.[13] Mary Ann Doane and Kaja Silverman linked psychoanalysis to the phenomenology of listening, rather than hearing.[14] On the other hand, Michel Chion emphasized the multiple functions of the various uses of sound in films and their effects on the spectatorship-listenership experience.[15]

Studying sound in animated film, William Whittington argues that as the techniques of computer-generated animation developed at Pixar, hyperrealistic sound design became an integral aspect of this mode of storytelling and overall filmic design. Producers, directors, animators, and software engineers work "to establish an unprecedented unification of sound and computer imagery by borrowing live-action production techniques and reworking traditional animation strategies for sound use."[16] Comparing Pixar's inaugural animated short with live-action and traditional animation sound, Whittington suggests that while their "comedic outcomes remain similar between the old and the new animation forms in the *Luxo Jr.* [John Lasseter, 1986] short, the sensibilities of design and their organization have shifted to create a heightened cinematic reality that resembles live-action sound."[17] Furthermore, the sound design strategy in this animated film established an emotional vocabulary for the characters through sound effects, thereby offering an analogy to language.

Ellcessor and Kirkpatrick argue that "Captioned Films for the Deaf, for instance, was founded in 1949; for decades, it produced captions for educational and popular films and distributed them to 'Deaf clubs' around the United States. Meanwhile, Gallaudet (a university for deaf and hard-of-hearing students) has a long and possibly surprising history of radio clubs."[18] These are some examples of histories of "minority media production, postproduction, distribution, exhibition, and reception that remain so far largely unexplored. Digging into them will reveal a long and illuminating history of assistive technologies, media hacks, multitasking, repurposing, and community practice."[19] Despite not being produced by deaf animators and thus not qualifying under the first-person crip subgenre, the animated films in this chapter have deaf spectators in mind.

Deaf critique in disability studies challenges audism and the dichotomous distinctions between deaf/silent cinema and hearing/speaking cinema. The study of sound in cinema, according to Michel Friedner and Stefan Helmreich, deals with the role of listening, hearing, and sound space, with a view to undermining the traditional hierarchy of the senses.[20] In contrast to the prevailing argument that culture represses the sense of hearing and overvalues the sense of sight, deaf critique challenges the trend of excess preference for vocal language in day-to-day interactions and cultural theory. Deaf critique seeks to respond to the centrality of voice in society by indicating the visual as enabling an interactive communications space.[21]

These two areas of study—sound studies and deaf critique—are dependent upon the dichotomous distinction between hearing and sight. The distinction is reinforced by activists and deaf studies scholars, who frequently reiterate the argument that they are primarily "people of the eye."[22] In contrast to them, Friedner and Helmreich offer an objection to these dichotomies by means of a broader definition of sound. They hold that sound can be experienced as a certain frequency, which generates vibrations that can be felt through the sense of touch, rather than the sense of hearing. Thus, sound becomes an experience that challenges the perception of the deaf as "people of the eye."[23] In other words, the contrarian phrasing of sound studies, which overvalues one sense at the expense of another, does not contain the inherent relationship between the senses.

Therefore, when examining the uses of sound in animated documentary, this chapter addresses the connections between the auditory and the visual and the ways they stimulate the other senses of our bodies. As a cinematic art, animation was considered to be a genre that emphasizes the visual; present-day researchers of animation, however, actually point to the soundtrack as central to the creation of the spectatorship and listenership experience. These theoreticians claim that sound initiates, assists, and expands the forms of expression in cinema in general and animation in particular.

The sound in animation, according to Rebecca Coyle, includes music that creates motion, space, and atmosphere.[24] For Coyle, the most functional sound enables animation "to leap out of the screen" and arouse the spectator's imagination.[25] In the last fifty years, animation productions have undergone a distinct shift into the digital era as a result of the development of new technologies in sound and music, along with the computerization of animation techniques. In addition, the new possibilities of sound, for screening both in cinemas and in private homes, have increased audiences' awareness and expectations of the auditory dimension. The centrality of audio was expressed as early as the 1940s, when large studios developed stereo systems in preparation for the launch of new films.[26] From a theoretical standpoint, Coyle proposes a distinction between the terms *sound* and *soundtrack*.[27] Whereas the former refers to music and other sounds, the latter refers to all the auditory aspects that accompany the image track.[28] Therefore, the analysis of sound in crip animation and the discussion of the phenomenological aspects of the spectatorship-listenership experience in animation have to recognize all the possible sensory perceptions and not only hearing. In addition to recognizing the ways listening is alluded to in the visual text and the possibilities of feeling sound vibrations, the theater, room, or outdoor viewing area generates sounds of its own. For example, attention must be paid to other sounds that exist in the space where the film is being screened: smartphones, the sounds of popcorn being chewed, or your dog's barking if viewing at home. These "noises" affect the viewing experience of both the deaf and the hearing, while the "official" soundtrack of the film is presumed to only target the hearing.

The composer and cinematic sound researcher Michel Chion redefined silent cinema as deaf cinema because the films were not actually silent. Besides being accompanied by live music, an experience still offered to audiences on special occasions, the films presented speech and alluded to sounds, although the latter were not physically heard by the spectators but rather perceived by them with other senses. The technological development that enabled the addition of sound to the actual film and its transformation into what we know as cinema today was not welcomed by audiences, who criticized these nonessential additions.[29] Chion held that, in silent/deaf cinema, the spectators' sense of hearing is aroused by what they see on-screen.[30] In the early days of cinema, it was not necessary to portray action noises, water sounds, the sounds of footsteps, or opening and closing doors; nonetheless, spectators remembered the existence of those sounds and could hear them in their imagination. Therefore, Chion argued that cinema at times contains allusions to sound in places where no sound exists and that, at the same time, there are varied possibilities for the use of the soundtrack, thanks to sound effects.[31] Chion's perception, which focuses on the centrality of sound, whether played or alluded to, links the auditory to the visual in cinematic experience, thereby also undermining binaries of visible/audible.

The soundtracks of the animated documentaries discussed throughout this book, and especially the three films analyzed in this chapter, seek to adopt a cinesthetic address to the spectators' body.[32] This address is intensified by voices that indicate the existence of a sensory body outside the cinematic frame, music that arouses empathy, and sounds that suggest movement that transcends the limits of the human body. While the music and the sounds of movement express the detachment of the work from the disabled body off-screen, the documentary voice-over and its acousmêtric qualities suggest a reconnection. The acousmêtre, a concept proposed by Michel Chion, describes a voice entity that is, as a rule, not visible on-screen. The connection of the body is implemented by means of its visual representation in animation, photography, and drawing and by means of its representation in the indexical soundtrack. The combination of these three animated documentaries enables the process of "deafening" hearing spectators and mixing their senses in such a way as to undermine their audism. While deaf spectators may enjoy the same aspects of the films as hearing ones, they may, however, access visual pleasures deriving from their fluency in sign languages.

This chapter discusses the auditory expression of crip animation. The first part of the chapter examines the functioning of the indexical documentary voice-over, thereby challenging the centrality of the sense of sight in the spectatorship and listenership experience.[33] The voice-over functions as a semi-acousmêtre—that is, it contains the magical powers of a seeing and partially unseen voice and at the same time is linked to the bodymind of a person with a disability.[34] The second part of the chapter discusses the use of music as an empathic means of enhancing the spectator's emotional identification through an analysis of the musical animated documentary. The third part examines the sounds of motion, which are characteristic of crip animated documentary, and focuses on the nonphysical spaces in which motion is made possible. To summarize, the chapter proposes the spectatorship and listenership experience in crip animation. The combination of these techniques creates a process of "deafening" the spectator by stimulating a synesthetic experience that mingles the senses.

INDEXICAL VOICE-OVERS AND CRIP AUTHORITIES

Michel Chion prefers the sense of hearing to the sense of sight and challenges the supremacy of the latter while especially emphasizing the listening process in cinema. Chion asserts that sound is multidirectional and, unlike visual images, may be perceived from any direction: "Human vision, like that of cinema, is partial and directional. Hearing, though, is omnidirectional. We cannot see what is behind us, but we hear all around."[35] Moreover, according to Chion, hearing is apparently the first sense that develops in humans, according to the perception that infants identify their parents' voices while they are still in the womb. Sight, notwithstanding its belated appearance, undergoes significant cultural intervention in Western cultures. Chion argues that sight is the object of a much more extensive group of linguistic expressions than the limited vocabulary that describes tactile, olfactory, and even auditory phenomena. Generally speaking, spectators rely on their sense of sight because the naming and identification of forms is much more refined and precise in visual terms than in any other channel of perception.[36]

Parallel to this cinematic study, which challenged the supremacy of sight in the hierarchy of the senses, deaf studies also expose the neglect in the approach to the bodymind and its senses. During the 1980s, the Deaf Pride movement in the United States formulated its politics as a continuation of those of the civil rights movement. Friedner and Helmreich wrote that, as early as 1972, the linguist and activist James Woodward proposed to designate "the Deaf" as a cultural group by capitalizing the first letter of the word. This proposal was accepted by scholars of deaf studies and by deaf activists and is used by many to this day. Many deaf studies scholars describe a separate deaf culture that is created in communities that are connected by sign language. The transition from "hearing impaired" to "Deaf" denoted the defiant opposition to the classification of deafness as a disability and reinforced the concept of deafness as an identity ("Deafnicity").[37]

An Eyeful of Sound, the short animated documentary discussed in the previous chapter, addresses the sensory perceptions of people with synesthesia, which it presents by means of indexical voice-overs. By focusing on sound in general and the documentary voice-over in particular, the spectatorship and listenership emphasizes the sense of hearing as arousing synesthetic experiences among the viewer-listeners with varied sensory perceptions. In other words, although spectatorship is always synesthetic, as Sobchack proposes, and we tend to "listen with the eyes," as Chion proposes, viewing in a body with a different sensory organization makes it possible to examine the "viewing" and "listening" experience outside the traditional hierarchy of the senses.[38]

The animated film by Samantha Moore, *An Eyeful of Sound*, focuses on the phenomenon of synesthesia, relies on a soundtrack composed of a documentary voice-over, vocal sounds, and music. The film presents abstract forms along with realistic forms made up of a mixture of colors, movements, and textures. At the level of sound, the documentary voice-over is the most central, but it is accompanied by other sounds. The sounds flow into each other at the end of the film until they are suddenly silenced entirely and a human voice is heard saying, "I do like silence." The voice-over in *An Eyeful of Sound*, as in other crip animated films, functions as a semi-acousmêtre. The partial nature of the acousmêtre in crip animation is reflected in the fact that, on one hand, the source of the voice usually remains hidden and, on the other, it is devoid of the divine omnipotence that characterizes such an entity. When the acousmêtre, the voice entity, is a character with a disability, that character's omnipotence, which results from the authoritarian role of narration in documentary film, is challenged by a nonnormative sensory point of view.

An Eyeful of Sound opens with feminine voice-overs, sounds of drawing or erasing, and fragments of sentences projected in printed letters on a blue background. This opening alludes to the centrality of the voiced testimony and the incompleteness of the vocabulary that enables a description of sensory experiences. The women attempt to describe their sensations, and the animator attempts to portray those descriptions. Although the attempts at animation develop later in the film, the opening sequence is visually deficient and emphasizes the difficulty in describing senses through written language. The spectator is made aware of the listening process by the voice entities and the display of the written words.

In the opening sequence of *An Eyeful of Sound*, the viewer relies on the acousmêtric effect of the voice-over and does not have to invest effort in understanding the words, which are visually displayed—not as closed captions but aesthetically integrated in the visual language of the film. The voice fragments of sentences point to a self-doubt uncharacteristic of the omnipotence of the traditional acousmêtre. In this situation, the viewer-listener's awareness of the listening process is enhanced. Chion examines the viewer's awareness of the listening process and argues that films enable the spectators to hear both what the character hears and what they do not hear. Only under unique conditions does the viewer become aware of the listening process—the audience's awareness of the act of hearing in the cinema is highest when the dialogue and music are scanty, making it necessary for the listeners to exert themselves somewhat in order to understand. In addition, hearing people are used to listening to the human voice first.[39] Therefore, the opening sequence, which includes an intermingling of several voices, requires the hearing listener to maintain an enhanced awareness of the listening process.

In his book on sound in cinema, Chion describes the acousmêtre as a form of sensory phantom—in other words, perceived exclusively by a single sense in a situation in which it could have been perceived simultaneously by two senses.[40] Chion's noteworthy example of a sensory phantom in cinema is an object or person moving on-screen and making no sound.[41] Moreover, this occurs when a voice is heard but the body is not visible on-screen, playing hide-and-seek with the spectator. This voice is expressed in various ways in cinema—for example, as a character who has gone off-screen or when a film refuses to show spectators the source of a voice.[42]

An outstanding example of the use of a sensory phantom can be found in the documentary *Black Sun*, also discussed in the previous chapter. The film describes the life of the artist Hugues de Montalembert by means of his indexical voice-over. De Montalembert describes the burglary of his home, during which he was blinded, and his travels throughout the world while adjusting to his new condition. In addition to the coherent narration in his mesmerizing voice, the spectator is exposed to a series of images that refer to part of what is said in nonchronological order. For example, while de Montalembert's voice is speaking about New York, images of India are seen on the screen. The voice-over in the film is what provides the orientation to which we are accustomed on the visual level, because the images do not match the soundtrack. The undermining of the sensory hierarchy changes the spectators' traditional reliance on the sense of sight. This film features a double sensory phantom: the people and objects moving in the field of vision make no sound, and, at the same time, the visual source of the voice-over is not revealed. Therefore, the voice-over in *Black Sun*, as in *An Eyeful of Sound*, is not a complete acousmêtre because it is an extradiegetic sound.

In contrast to *Black Sun*, which relies on a sensory phantom in the form of blurred vision, the animated documentary *An Eyeful of Sound* relies on sensory excess. One of the women interviewed in the film wonders: "But I sometimes think these colors don't really exist outside our heads. I wonder if they do." In order to answer that question, the director, Samantha Moore, enlists Dr. Jamie Ward, who explains that synesthesia "is often described as a mixing of the senses, so these people have . . . an extra sensation, so when they listen to music, they might experience colored blobs of hearing and moving and swirling." Ward's testimony is juxtaposed by voice-overs of the women, who describe their sensations and perceptions in their own words; one of them says she cannot imagine how people without synesthesia enjoy listening to classical music. Ward says that there are people who, "when they're listening to speaking, their tongue might feel . . . different tastes."[43] In scans of the brains of people who experience music in the form of colors, it was found that the visual parts of their brains are activated by the sound of music. Ward describes the type of synesthesia he himself would like to have and, in fact, describes the experience offered by animated documentaries in general and by *An Eyeful of Sound* in particular: "[We] don't just experience colors with music; they experience shapes and movements and textures, and they're all appearing and disappearing." Ward indicates that synesthesia is not perceived in society as a negative phenomenon—perhaps even the opposite, and especially by comparison to deafness and blindness, which are considered by ableist perspectives as sensory deficiencies. Although an involuntary response of hearing sounds is perceived in a positive light in the case of synesthesia, this does not apply to hearing voices, which is defined as a dangerous psychosis, although both conditions share the characteristic of sensory surplus.

The experience that the animated documentary *An Eyeful of Sound* offers its spectators challenges the sensory hierarchies that define surplus or deficiency, excess or lack. The nonexposure of the indexical bodies to the spectators' eyes makes it impossible to detach the voices from the magical illusion of their omnipotent power. The de-acousmêtrization, the exposure of the body that produces the voice, shatters the solution by exposing the disabled body. According to Chion, the acousmatic is called an acousmêtre when the voice is human, especially when that voice has not yet been revealed on-screen but haunts the film like a shadow. According to him, the principle of cinema is that fact that, at any moment, the faces and bodies "behind" the voices may appear, thus making a move of de-acousmêtrization.[44] In animated documentaries in general, and in *An Eyeful of Sound* in particular, the source of the voice remains invisible and therefore becomes charged with the magic powers of the illusion of omnipotence.[45] De-acousmêtrization links the acousmêtre to a certain site and says, "Here is your body; you will be here and not in another place." In other

Fig. 4.1. Sound quilt © Samantha Moore, *An Eyeful of Sound*, 2010

words, what limits the subjects in the film to the limitations of the human body is the exposure of the source of the voice, an act from which *An Eyeful of Sound* refrains throughout its entire length.

Concealing the source of the voice undermines the possibility of stripping the voiced entity of its powers. Exposing the body is the endpoint of de-acousmêtrization, and it happens at the moment when the mouth from which the voice emerges is visually presented. According to Chion, semi-acousmêtres exist when, although we have not yet seen the mouth of the speaking character, we see other parts of the body, such as the hand, the back, the legs, or the neck. There are even quarter-acousmêtres—when the camera shows the head but the mouth is concealed. As long as the face and mouth have not yet been fully revealed, and as long as the spectator's eye has not yet confirmed the intersection between the voice and the mouth, the de-acousmêtrization has not been completed. Absent its completion, the voice remains as an aura of invulnerability with magical powers.[46] In addition to the nonexposure of the indexical body, *An Eyeful of Sound* even refrains from the symbolic representation of the body in the animation and relies exclusively on abstract images (see figure 4.1).

The body in crip animated documentary in general, and in animation that emphasizes the auditory in particular, is especially represented by means of the speaking mouth as the source of the voice. The body and its component parts are present in crip animated documentary in three principal ways.

The first way is suggested by films with indexical representation of the body, such as *A Shift in Perception, Orgesticulanismus, Petra's Poem, Tying Your Own*

Fig. 4.2. Animating a dog barking © Samantha Moore, *An Eyeful of Sound*, 2010

Shoes, and so forth.[47] Although the body is shown in its entirety and the speaking mouth is concealed in *A Shift in Perception*, in the others, the speaking mouth is emphasized in close-up shots. The de-acousmêtrization in these films shatters the omnipotence of the indexical voice-over. The second way is that of films in which the body is symbolically represented through animation—for example, the musical animated film that is discussed in the next section of this chapter, *My Depression*.[48] These films rely on symbolic de-acousmêtrization and replace the realistic human body with representations of animals or objects; they are characterized by synchronization between the voice-over and an animated human or animal character (with a speaking mouth).[49] The third way is that of films with absolutely no representation of the body; in this way, they compel the spectator to rely, attentively and with awareness, on the indexical voice-over.[50]

The nearly exclusive reliance on the voice-over and the accompanying musical sounds for orientation in the space of the film requires the hearing listener to be aware of listenership. The awareness of listening, the viewing process in *An Eyeful of Sound*, is awakened by the opening sequence of the film. This awareness increases as the spectators become exposed to the women's descriptions. The synesthetic descriptions by the women emphasizes the role of the soundtrack, which is composed of day-to-day sounds and musical sounds (see figure 4.2). The sounds are described as arousing various tastes[51] or various colors.[52] At times, colors are described as arousing the feeling of hearing certain sounds. The intermingled, intersected, and edited voice-overs create musical sounds. The repetition of a montage of the women's experiences throughout the film offers it as a sort of refrain.[53] One of the women says that she became aware of her synesthesia when she heard an orchestra playing. Another goes on to say that she did not know the orchestra produced sounds by means of separate musical instruments because she experienced them as a visual image, "some sort of colored quilt." Thus, the viewer-listener's awareness of the listening process is stimulated in *An Eyeful of Sound* by the multiplicity of abstract images, and the de-acousmêtrization of the film is prevented by the refusal to limit voice to a specific body.

At the same time, the massive reliance of the documentary voice-over on vocal means and visual images that describe and emphasize it raises questions with respect to its vococentric concept in the cinematic experience. According to Chion, vococentrism happens when, within an intermingling of sounds, the hearing listeners prefer the human voice.[54] Another kind of vococentrism appears in the film *Children of a Lesser God* (Randa Haines, 1989). James Leeds (William Hurt) reads the ASL used by Sarah Norman (Marlee Matlin) and translates it into a language that is accessible to the hearing audience but not its deaf members.[55] It could also be argued that *CODA* is vococentric in a similar way but focusing on the only hearing family member and her audio perception and more specifically focusing on music.[56] In this way, the film relies on assumptions that elevate the status of oral communication, relative to that of sign language, which is discussed in the next section of the chapter. The preference for vocalism in mainstream cinema and beyond is challenged in crip animation, which uses the range of possibilities of perception of sound in ways and by senses that are not necessarily auditory.

MUSIC AND EMOTIONS IN CRIP ANIMATION

In his book on music in cinema, David Neumeyer presents two principal arguments. The first is that the integrated soundtrack is a basic characteristic of cinema and operates hierarchically, with the human voice (speech, dialogues) at the top of the hierarchy and music and sound effects at the bottom; the second, inspired by Michel Chion, is that cinema is vococentric.[57] Neumeyer dedicates a chapter to music in vococentric cinema and argues that narrative "talkie" cinema relies on the hierarchy of sound and subordinates music to the human voice.[58] This inherent hierarchy is explained by Claudia Gorbman through psychoanalysis. Relying on Christian Metz's well-known book *The Imaginary Signifier*, Gorbman argues that, as part of the world of fiction, background music in the cinema is *meant* to be less noticed. As she puts it, music "greases the wheels of the cinematic pleasure machine by easing the spectator's passage into subjectivity." In addition, the ways of representation in narrative cinema frequently vary between genres, the style of direction, and a series of historic conditions, as do the conditions for the creation of identification or a pleasant spectacle. Furthermore, in dramatic films, music remains a "hypnotic voice bidding the spectator to believe, focus, behold, identify, consume."[59]

Similarly, Mary Ann Doane relies on psychoanalysis to describe voice in cinema as what she calls a phantasmatic body, composed of the body of the character and the body of the film. Although the visual space is restricted, the vocal space is unlimited and, in any event, comes from speakers located outside the frame. As Doane writes: "The traditional use of voice-off constitutes a denial of the frame as a limit and an affirmation of the unity and homogeneity of the depicted space."[60]

In his book *Audio-Vision: Sound on Screen*, Chion praises the connection between musical sounds and visual imagery because the principal role of music is to create an empathic effect on the spectator. There are two principal ways music creates a unique emotional relationship between the spectators and what is shown on the screen. On the one hand, music can directly express the emotions of the participants in the scene. This expression is accomplished through melody, rhythm, and tone, which produce responses of sorrow, joy, and movement—in other words, an empathic work of music, which increases the ability to feel others' emotions. On the other hand, nonempathic music can encourage indifference to an event by promoting emotional stability so that the scene takes place despite the indifference.[61]

Music in cinema, and especially in animation, is a principal means of arousing the hearing spectator's emotions. The uses of animation in music include a variety of possibilities, the most noteworthy of which are music synchronized with images of moving lips, music to emphasize a punch, and musical themes tailored to the general soundtrack. In addition, Coyle argues that music in animation may also function as a vocal effect and its sounds may create an "atmosphere" and include dialogues and vocal appearances.[62] Coyle illustrates the ways music has become a principal tool of the genre of animation and the secret of its success. Thus, for example, the cartoons produced by Warner Bros. gave a very central role to music, thereby enabling it to emphasize movement and describe the protagonists' inner world.[63] An additional example of enhanced use of music in animated films is the clay animation film *Wallace & Gromit: The Curse of the Were-Rabbit* (Steve Box and Nick Park, 2005), which includes seventy-two minutes of music out of the eighty minutes of the film.

In his analysis of Pixar's short animated film *Knick Knack* (John Lasseter, 1989), Whittington asserts that the hierarchy of image-sound relations flips the audio paradigm to resemble that of a musical. Despite the prominence of this strategy in early Warner Bros. cartoon shorts, Whittington shows that Pixar has staunchly avoided allowing music and the conventions of the musical genre to become the sole driving factor on animation in its feature films. By balancing the sound design and music in storytelling, Pixar was able to distinguish itself from two-dimensional Disney musicals like *Beauty and the Beast* (1991) and *Aladdin* (1992).[64] Animated musicals have an enhanced potential for accessible spectatorship thanks to the motion in space that accompanies the music. The animated documentary film on which this section of the chapter is focused, *My Depression*, and from which the image on the cover is taken, makes enhanced use of music by relying on the cinematic musical genre. Many books have been written on this genre, but only a few studies address the role of musicals in documentary cinema and animation.[65] Few avant-garde documentary films adopted the genre of musicals and acquired experience in its reflexive aspects. *My Depression* is a rare case of an animated documentary musical.

My Depression opens with a guitar chord. The guitar, against a white background, produces sounds that sketch the rhythm of the protagonist's speech and song in her home environment. Following the appearance of the visual aspects that fill the frame, the animated protagonist hums the guitar melody. Only after that does she address the spectators directly, introducing herself as Liz, a woman coping with depression.[66] Although the film is classified as a documentary, the animation includes narration by professional actors. This fact is exposed to the spectators upon the appearance of the opening credits, which show the title and the narrators' names.[67] In this way, the film violates the broadest consensus with respect to the definition of animated documentary as relying on the indexical nature of the voice-over.[68] *My Depression* offers, as an alternative, the documentary aspect inherent to the fact that the events described are autobiographical.[69] This section examines the cinematic role of music in musical animated documentary. Through the hybrid nature of the film genre, its musicality provides a documentary substitute for the absence of Swados's "real" voice. The autobiographical songs were written and composed by her and are sung by her illustrated image.

The music in *My Depression* mainly functions as an empathetic soundtrack. It is meant to evoke feelings of joy and sorrow for the spectator, in accordance with the scene's theme. The film's music is divided into songs intended to reflect these emotions and support the film's plot about the highs and lows of depression. Combining this empathetic music in animated documentary creates an

Fig. 4.3. A dark cloud over Liz's head © Elizabeth Swados, *My Depression: The Up and Down and Up of It*, 2014

experience that includes and alludes to all the senses of the spectator-listeners. The "musical" pieces of the animation allow for "listening" in ways that are non-vocal-centric and not audist but rather more synesthetic—conveying the audio level through visual means using images that compliment the voices or visualize them. Unintentionally, the soundtrack makes the lyrics more accessible to spectators, thus relieving them of having to experience the music through other senses.

The film's musical soundtrack enhances the drama of the scenes or balances it using upbeat rhythms. This is especially created through various uses of extradiegetic music.[70] These sounds are combined with the diegetic music, which "flows from" the musical instruments animated in the film. Alongside this, the film's most salient use of music is made through its "musical" grammar—a film genre composed of diegetic singing integrated into the plot and presented alongside dancing and movement (see figures 4.3 and 4.4).[71] These musical pieces may also be read as echoing the grammar of sign language, thus offering the spectators a multisensory experience, especially through the intersection of sight and hearing.[72] Rebecca Sanchez argues that ASL has been oversimplified and conceived of as a language of images and shows how complex the ASL grammar actually is.[73] The film's musical sequences include illustrative images of the lyrics. The film opens with the first diegetic song, empathetic music

Fig. 4.4. Liz falling into a dark hole © Elizabeth Swados, *My Depression: The Up and Down and Up of It*, 2014

evoking joy, accompanied by Liz's vocals. Similarly, the second song, through its sorrowful melody, also depicts the lyrics through illustrative animation. Thus, for example, Liz sings her apology to her dog for not feeding him while the animation shows her throwing his food bowl away. In the third musical sequence, when the narrative comes to the low point of depression, joyful and upbeat music starts playing, continuing with a song sung by a milkman. The melody of "Suicide Mobile" is joyful and upbeat, but the dark and imposing images do not convey this feeling. The last diegetic musical sequence realizes the promise of a happy ending implied by the film's subtitle: *The Up and Down and Up of It*. This joyful and calming song, which sounds almost like a lullaby, also illustratively depicts the lyrics.[74]

The music's illustrative representation in the film also raises questions about the possibilities of making cinema more accessible to deaf audiences. George Veditz, a president of the United States National Association of the Deaf, argued that the deaf community is a visual community, which communicates, conveys, and draws information and aesthetic pleasure from images, movements, bodily gestures, facial expressions, and spatial language.[75] Linguistic scholar William Stokoe has also compared ASL to the language of cinema and its use to editing as means of explaining it to the nondeaf.[76] He argued that in ASL, the narrative is neither linear nor prosaic, since the essence of sign language is cutting from

Fig. 4.5. Riding the suicide mobile © Elizabeth Swados, *My Depression: The Up and Down and Up of It*, 2014

an ordinary point of view to a close-up, long shot, and back to a close-up, even including flashbacks and flash-forwards. Not only is signing organized more like an edited film than a written narrative, but each sign is located in a way similar to a camera—the field of vision and angles are directed and shifting.[77]

My Depression is unique in its musical sequences, which are drawn from the musical film genre. Combining the genre's characteristics with animation, dancing is replaced with animated movement and images that represent the lyrics. Integrating genre aspects originating from musical and animated films, together with documentary and autobiographical aspects, creates a text evoking all the spectator-listeners' senses. Moreover, the cinematic styles of the images and singing used by Swados to represent the lyrics in the films' musical sequences echo the "cinematic" grammar of ASL (see figures 4.5 and 4.6).

The cinematic musical is one of the most popular genres among both audiences and film scholars, Bill Marshall and Robynn Jeananne Stilwell argue. Its popularity can be explained by the fact that it contains the performance of music, and pleasure from the genre's predictable structure weighed against the pleasure of its varied details. Musical film scholarship mostly relies on its connection to genre studies (for example, as in Altman's work) and focuses on narrative patterns and production histories.[78] According to Marshall and Stilwell, the musical is an art form, with its own language and history, relying on

Fig. 4.6. The joy of playing music in the end sequence © Elizabeth Swados, *My Depression: The Up and Down and Up of It*, 2014

the sense of hearing, which is culturally considered inferior to sight. Although music and sound are no less important than composition and lighting, film theory mostly fails to engage with them. Marshall and Stillwell use musical film analysis to emphasize the role that sound plays in constructing social space and time norms. They argue that the musical film provides utopian "no-place" and sometimes "no-time" moments, in which the practical and the material, as well as social and political realities, are bracketed out in favor of the fantastic, the intensification of emotion and self-expression, and displays of abundance, spontaneity, freedom, and community.[79]

In addition, the pleasure of the spectatorship listenership in musical cinema is also related to the consumer culture and its counterculture.[80] Swados's film, *My Depression*, returns to the traditional musical genre, relying on synchronization between the lyrics and lip movements, as well as other body parts. This film offers a peek into the world of the protagonist, shifting between utopia and dystopia, high and low. The transitions between these two worlds are expressed through the diegetic musical parts. Their role is to represent the character's emotions and evoke similar feelings among the spectators.

In contrast with the arguments about ASL's reliance on spatial movement, Friedner and Helmreich argue that deaf people use all their body's senses.[81] These scholars describe sound vibrations as a tool of communication that does not rely on the binaries of hearing/deaf, sound/silence. Their arguments about sound frequencies suggest that the music's artistic value—at a show, a party, a home experience, or in the context of cinema—is higher than its literal and grammatical interpretation and includes a tactile experience involving additional senses. According to Friedner and Helmreich, emphasizing vision in deaf studies might be evasive of deaf people's experiences with sound. They argue that scholars engaging with sound tend to miss the ways deaf people experience sound in general, and music in particular, due to audio-centric assumptions. Discussing various levels, types, and genres when analyzing sound perception may lead to new interpretations of "hearing with" and "being with" in a way that subverts the connection between deaf studies and the visual. Thus, for example, deaf-blind studies, as well as deaf communities, challenge the hegemony of sight and hearing. They do so by focusing on the political possibilities of tactile sign language, which emphasizes the centrality of senses not limited to sounds and visuals.[82]

And so, what part does music play in disability cinema? El-Ad Cohen and Iris Ben Moshe's live-action documentary film *The Sign for Love* (2017) revolves around the life of El-Ad, a deaf gay artist, and follows his relationships with the deaf community and his hearing family. At the DocAviv International Documentary Film Festival of the same year, Ben Moshe, a hearing person, described the experience of co-directing the film.[83] She first attempted to edit the film without sound to ensure it was appealing to deaf viewers. In an advanced stage of editing, she realized that, as a hearing spectator, she felt music was still necessary to produce meaning and create emotional effect. Eventually, to make the film more accessible to hearing viewers, it was decided, by both directors, to add music, while recognizing that not all viewers are affected by the extradiegetic sound. Hearing viewers need empathetic music. But what about deaf viewers?

Deaf studies and disability studies scholar, Octavian Robinson, explains that "Deaf people have a relationship with music. Deaf people create music. Deaf people enjoy music. Deaf people hate music. Deafness is a spectrum. Deafness is also historically, socially, and culturally contingent. Deafness is fluid and dynamic, changing throughout our lives with and without technologies. So our relationships with music vary."[84] This suggests that film has creative potential that has not yet been developed for conveying music in non-vocal-centric ways. Until then, it seems, counterintuitively, that musical animation—which includes animated motion and simulates the grammar of sign language—is not only quite accessible but may provide its own pleasures to viewers, evoking synesthetic spectatorship among both hearing and deaf audience members.

SOUND AND MOVEMENT IN CRIP ANIMATION

As indicated by animation scholarship, animated images artistic intervention is in creating motion where there was none before. The most inclusive definition of animation, according to Coyle, is a way of representing motion.[85] The intersection between music and motion creates a feeling of omnipotence among the spectators, Michael O'Pray suggests, since its motion provides spectators with the movement they wish to experience themselves.[86] The pleasure of spectatorship attained through animation exists where we identify with its virtuosity, which is an integral part of the way it affects us emotionally. The greatest pleasure is attained when the form and content reach perfection. This is because we are confronted with control through the fantasy of that control in the animated figures.[87] In animation, satisfaction is not only dependent on the ability to represent different and impossible worlds but rather its ability to remind us of the skill and virtuosity involved in form. In this way, animation is at its best when we marvel not only at the subject matter but at its means of production. We are conscious of technique in a way we are often not in live-action narrative film.[88]

Although most discussions about the exposure of the cinematic apparatus revolve around images, adding the aspect of sound to research contributes to the analysis of concepts of motion in space and time. Just as images are composed of light waves, so does sound come into our ears in the form of waves in motion. The sound fills the space through time and is not easily contained. Therefore, it can be conceived as constant movement. Animator and researcher Norman McLaren noted the role of animation in creating action that is: "outside the vocabulary offered by its mainstream counterpart."[89] Sound also moves around stereo space and transitions across scenes, frames, and juxtapositions. The title of the introduction to Coyle's book about sound in animation is *Audio Motion*, encapsulating a recognition of the fact that sound provides horizontal movement that touches the narrative and atmosphere as well as highlights the animator's hand and "personality."[90]

Animation is unique in its ability to represent the impossible and surpass the physical laws that govern reality. Animated documentary films about disability tend to surpass these laws even further. By doing so, they expose the social context of physical limitations and instead offer spaces that allow for freer movement. By focusing on the inner world of people with disabilities, crip animation reframes the bodymind's movements.[91] This framing is done by producing motion through imagination, as well as through visual and sound art.[92]

This section analyzes the soundtrack of the animated documentary *Orgesticulanismus*, briefly discussed in the introduction, and the ways it produces movement. The film revolves around physical, social, and imagined limitations of the body and its movement through space by using indexical, realistic, and symbolic sequences. *Orgesticulanismus* begins with a sequence of still photos of the film's protagonist before and after he began using a wheelchair. This is presented alongside his voice-over narration, in which he discusses movement in his life. The second sequence is made up of mechanical animation presenting the voice and image of monotonous movements of realistic bodies over an unchanging pattern. The third sequence is the most abstract, using the creative freedom of animation to produce movement in the world. This world is not subject to physical conditions or realistic body structures. This transgressive movement is enabled through animation and enhanced through upbeat music and sounds that continue even when the film's narrative is concluded.

All three sequences of this film challenge the depictions of body movements in indexical still photography and realistic representations in live-action and animated films. They offer the alternative of observing movement beyond the bounds of the human bodymind. The first sequence is made up of still photos and a documentary voice-over directly addressing movement. This emphasizes the lack of movement and sound in the still photos and highlights live action's subjection to physical laws. The second sequence is made up of black-and-white drawings and the sounds of realistic daily movement. This exposes the social policing of bodily movement. The third sequence, which is made up of abstract images and sounds, is released from the bounds of physical and social limitations, instead offering the movement of the imagination. Therefore, even after the protagonist has died and his indexical voice-over is silenced, abstract images and sounds continue to move alongside the film's credits. In this way, this film offers movement that does not rely on the body, subject to the narrative's framework.

The film's first sequence focuses on still photos alongside a documentary voice-over discussing movement (see figure 4.7). The documentary soundtrack begins with the appearance of the name of the film. The voice of a man who is speaking in French is audible, and a subtitles visible on screen reads: "I think that, when moving, you take over your own life." At this stage, the spectators cannot identify the source of the sound. Later, during the same sentence, still photos of a man in various ages and settings is visible, and accompanied by his narration: "When you're free to come and go, to have gestures of . . .

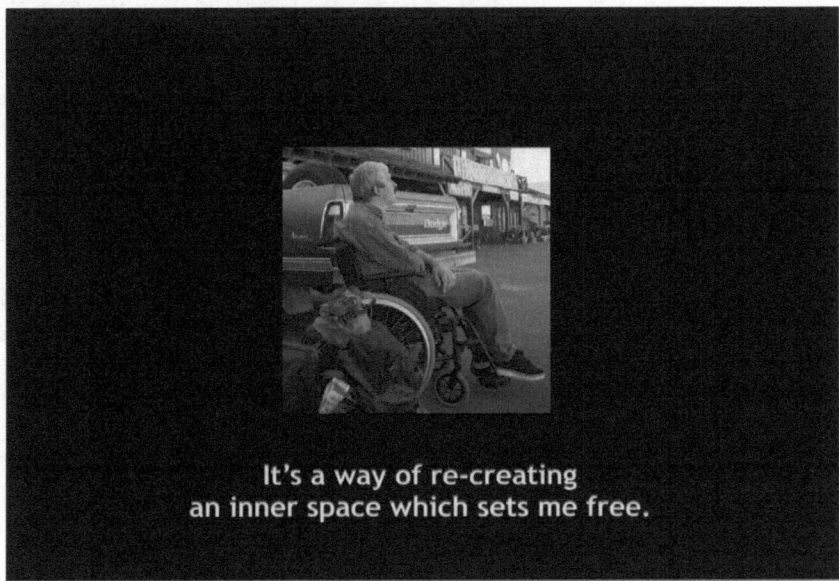

Fig. 4.7. Still photograph of Benoît Labaye in the indexical part of the film
© Mathieu Labaye, *Orgesticulanismus*, Camera-etc, 2008

love, tenderness, anger, not matter. So when you are deprived of the ability to move, as I am, as many others are . . . in order to survive you need to reinvent movement." As this sentence is spoken, the photo of a man in a wheelchair is shown on the screen. This photograph changes into a variety of images displaying different settings and places. The sequence ends as the narrator says: "What goes on in my mind is not just intellectual. It's a way of re-creating an inner space which sets me free."

The second sequence focuses on black-and-white drawings and sounds of daily movements. Using tilt and pan shots, the camera reveals repetitive movements of various bodies performing daily tasks. Alongside this, brief animated repetitive human movements are shown. Each movement is accompanied by the diegetic sounds created by that activity.[93] The sequence opens with a drawing of a three-dimensional grid tracking points of movement in the body. At its center is a person in a wheelchair. The camera tilts down, exposing "movement tracking" drawings of characters performing other tasks.[94] The camera then pans right, exposing the cyclical movement of a man with a mustache throwing a heavy sack and a woman spreading a tablecloth. The camera tilts down and shows an elderly woman flipping an omelet over a pan; a man starting up a lawn mower; a woman hanging laundry; a man urinating, pulling on his pants, and

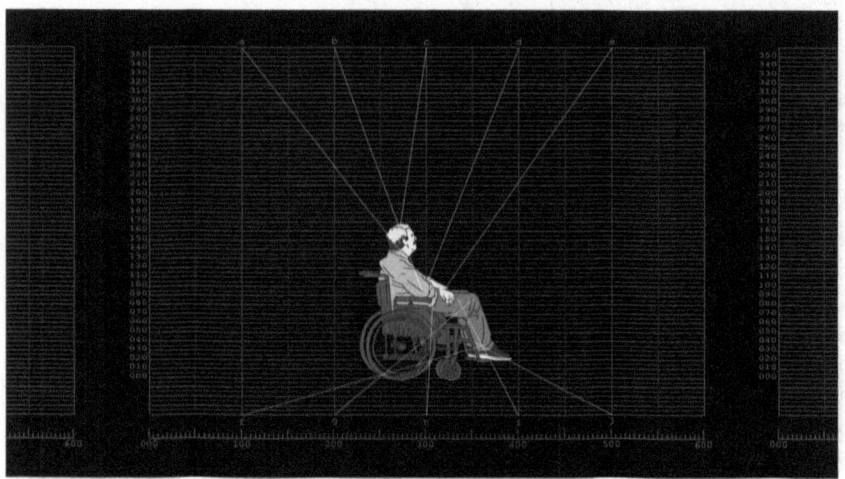

Fig. 4.8. Realistic animation of Benoît Labaye © Mathieu Labaye, *Orgesticulanismus*, Camera-etc, 2008

flushing the toilet; a woman sweeping; and a woman getting into a bath and opening the water tap.

The automatic and repetitive movements are accompanied by monotonous sounds that emphasize their banality. However, all sounds, including the voice-over, are accompanied by the extradiegetic sound used in the film's opening. At the same time, the more the images revolve around movement in more intimate spaces, the more the voice-over increases: "One who is severely handicapped, totally motionless and dependent, can neither share this, nor express it clearly. When two persons talking, want to understand each other, they need to have at least a common experience, to talk about something they both have experienced." The sequence ends as the camera stops to show one single movement of a person sitting in different chairs as well as a wheelchair (see figure 4.8), although the person changes with each shot—showing different bodies creating various movements and sounds in the space.

The third sequence is different from the previous two in that it transgresses the carnal/bodily and aesthetic rules on which the first two relied. The changing characters on the chair are painted with various colors and are cut loose from the bounds of the drawing, that is, they are not confined by the wheel/chair but rather the page or screen itself. At the film's conclusion, they burst into a "new screen" where their movement is unlimited. Simultaneously, the sound starts becoming layered with vocal music accompanied by musical instruments. The changing characters dance a continuous dance that takes place all over the space of the frame.

Fig. 4.9. Symbolic movement animation © Mathieu Labaye, *Orgesticulanismus*, Camera-etc, 2008

The more bass tones are added to the music, the more the characters become liberated from the limitations of the indexical human body, expanding the possibilities of the body beyond the flesh and outside the frame. This body grows, stretches, and extends in conjunction with the music. As the music quiets down, the body is shown taking off its clothes, skin, and inner organs until only a dancing skeleton remains, in continuous movement to the sound of drums. The skeleton turns into unidentifiable animated shapes, dust, or colorful crumbs, which change their shape until they finally turn into a beating colorful circle. This circle also changes, in turn, transforming into various shapes (see figure 4.9).

The voice-over is spoken without corresponding visual images while the sound from the beginning of the film is still playing in the background: "Of course . . . immobility and handicap lead one to gradually accept that a lot of things are now out of reach." The image of the abstract shape moving through space returns, and the supernarrator continues to speak: "Conversely, I think, it gives you other opportunities: in your inner freedom, in your inner space, but also in the way you make contact with the others. To me handicap and disease offer huge potentiality. Human beings have endless supplies of desire, energy—inner strength. These things you realize more urgently and forcefully when you cannot move." At the end of this narration, the movement of the animated image, alongside the sound, continues to accompany the spectator-listeners on the background of the film's closing credits.

The movement sounds continue to be audible even after the protagonist has died, creating an anempathetic musical expression, as defined by Chion in his book *Audio-Vision*. The anempathetic impulse in cinema produces musical bits meant to reinforce the emotion of the character and the spectator, even as the music pretends not to notice them.[95] In a certain sense, all films create a feeling of impartiality about the film presented on the screen and the sounds played through amplifiers. As an extreme form of cinematic abilities, animation produces a simulacrum of movement and life, a process intended to be hidden and unconscious. Therefore, anempathetic music connects the mechanical textures of feelings and senses.[96] The anempathetic effect is mostly produced through music but might also be created through noise or vibration—for example, in violent scenes where some sonic process continues after the death of a character, as if nothing had happened.[97] The same could potentially be achieved by any form of four-dimensional screenings, such as adding vibrations to chairs or scents to outdoors screenings.

In this way, by replacing the indexical voice-over, anempathetic music seeks to emphasize the movement of cinematic sound, which only stops when the projector and amplifier are turned off. Sound in animation is in constant movement, Coyle shows that it moves around stereo space and transitions across scenes, frames, and juxtapositions. It functions in this way because, in contrast with visual images, it cannot be frozen (freeze-frame) and in this way creates movement.[98] The sound provides its own narrative, foreshadowing, or "gag points."[99]

While sound in mainstream animated films marketed to children is recognized for its centrality and contribution to the projects' success, film scholarship tends to focus on the visual aspects of avant-garde animation.[100] Examining the sounds that make up the soundtrack and that exist between the music and the narration tracks allows for engagement with an additional layer of cinematic movement, evoked through listenership. In this way, we might think about the awareness of movement, evoked synesthesia, as an inherent component of all cinemas. The use of the soundtrack in crip animation adds a level of political critique against social limitations on the sonic bodymind.

RETHINKING SONIC PLEASURES AND AUDISM THROUGH CRIP ANIMATED DOCUMENTARY

This chapter discussed the soundtrack of crip animated documentary, as reflected in three animated films. These films' synesthetic uses of sound arouse the spectators by using indexical voice-over, empathetic music, and movement sounds that surpass the limitation of the human body. The first section of this chapter discussed the documentary voice-over, as presented in the film *An Eyeful of Sound*. Alongside the film's spectatorship listenership experience based in an alternative sensory order, its voice-over forces a massive dependency on the human voice. This subverts the glorification of the visual but, at the same time, also reinforces the centrality of vocal-centrism and oral communication. The second section examined the empathetic use of music, as presented in the musical animated documentary *My Depression*, and argued that the film allows for "listening" in ways that are non-vocal-centric and not audist. Moreover, by using abstract images edited in ways that resemble the grammar of ASL, musical animation becomes more deaf accessible, more informed by Deaf culture, thus creating a synesthetic spectatorship experience among both hearing and deaf audiences.

The third section discussed the movement sounds offered by the soundtrack of the animated documentary *Orgesticulanismus* and the ways they create movement. The transgressive movement of animation about physical disability is enabled through different animation techniques and enhanced through upbeat music and sounds that continue even after the visual images disappear. In this way, the anempathetic music replacing the indexical voice-over emphasizes the movement of cinematic sound, which only stops once the film's closing credits stop rolling. The movement sounds, existing between the music track and the voice-over track, allow for engagement with an additional level of cinematic movement aroused through listenership. This synesthetically arouses awareness of movement, criticizing social limitations over the bodymind. Therefore, this chapter argues that crip animated documentary "deafens" the spectator. This is done through a synesthetic listenership that transgresses the boundaries of dichotomous views of sight/hearing and voice/silence. This experience offers sensory perceptions that lie outside socially acceptable hierarchies.

Since hearing the voice-over in crip animated documentary is aroused through synesthesia, its visualization through a speaking mouth, highlighting the source of the voice in the disabled human body. Since the film *Orgesticulanismus* represents the speaker's indexical body in still photographs, drawings, and animation, it creates a sort of de-acousmêtrization. In doing so, it breaches the omnipotence of the vocal entity. In contrast, *My Depression* belongs to a category of films containing a symbolic representation of the body through animation. This representation includes synchronization between the voice-over and a human figure with a speaking mouth. The animated film *An Eyeful of Sound* belongs to the third, and most rare, category of crip animated documentary that eschews any representation of the corporeal body. These films force the spectators to significantly rely on the indexical voice-over and therefore can be described as vocal-centric.

Crip animation's synesthetic use of listenership challenges our perceptions about cinematic sound, as well as the status of hearing in the hierarchy of senses. Film spectatorship is similarly naturalized as an experience relying on image and sound, similar to vocal and oral communication. In contrast with the study of images, the cinematic sources of the audio-construction process have gained less attention within film history.

Chion described the introduction of sound into film in terms of intrusion or redundancy. According to him, when talkies introduced diegetic sound into cinema, they made spectators realize that film had gotten along perfectly well without it.[101] When sound entered film, it invoked criticism for its redundancy compared with the sounds dreamed about by the audience. These voices were richer and more malleable, according to each person's mental construct. For this reason, cinematic sound failed the audience's expectations: "It is comparison with that virtual sound that the arrival of real sound could seem like an intrusion, a rather vulgar appeal to hyperrealism."[102] Similar to experimental film, crip animated documentary resists the primacy of sight in the hierarchy of the senses. It does so by emphasizing sound and disrupting automatic spectatorship.

In her study of the phenomenology of intercultural cinema, Laura U. Marks suggests that when language is insufficient for experimental filmmakers to represent memories, they turn to other senses.[103] However, they avoid an exotic representation of the phantom senses and focus on the ambivalence of traditional sensory representation. Although the senses are a source of social knowledge, as with deaf epistemology, their hierarchical order is cultural and personal and therefore varies between different cultures and people. Each person's cortex is unique, and, similar to other mental capacities, sensory perception is a subjective matter. The more one makes use of a certain sense, the more developed it becomes.[104]

Animated films arouse all the senses because audiovisual images evoke the memory of our other senses. According to Marks, the narrative arouses sensory identification when the characters on the screen perform actions with which the spectator is personally familiar.[105] In this way, the sensory experience is synesthetic, as hearing sounds may arouse the feeling of a texture, seeing images may arouse a certain scent, and so on. Experimental cinema, like crip animation, stretches the boundaries of the cinematic apparatus, exploring the relationships between various bodies and various sensory perceptions.

Moreover, avant-garde animated film, which offers alternative experiences, challenges the limitations of the cinematic apparatus in creating truthful representations of sensory experiences. Critiques concerning the biases of the cinematic apparatus raise questions about our ability to make space, represent, and mediate the experience of non-"average" or hegemonic people.[106]

The experimental intercultural cinema discussed in Marks's study shares many characteristics with crip animated documentary. Both these avant-garde forms of film not only seek to represent sensory memories but also arouse the audience to experience them. This alternative sensory experience is an integral part of the spectatorship experience itself. This is in contrast with sensory representations in mainstream cinema, which use them as an "addition" for the purpose of representing "other" cultures or experiences. Similar to crip animation, intercultural avant-garde films resist the hierarchical sensory order of their cultures.[107] Marks argues that "intercultural filmmakers and videomakers know that it would be false to attempt to reproduce the sensory experience of their culture of origin. Yet they resist the sensory order of the society in which they find themselves, and they are critical of the cinematic apparatus that tends to reflect this order. Thus we can look to these works to push the cinematic apparatus in order to represent the memory of home in its multisensory fullness—and when that fails, to represent the emerging sensorium that is a product of both memory and change."[108] One main characteristic shared by diasporic film and crip animation is their critique of the cinematic apparatus, which tends to reiterate hegemonic hierarchical order.

In conclusion, crip animated documentary offers nonaudist listenership that arouse all other bodymind senses. By focusing on the soundtrack, this animation offers a spectatorship experience that reorganizes the senses, thus exposing the spectators to the construction thereof, both in film and culture. Together with the vision-disability films discussed in the previous chapter, crip animation subverts the primacy of sight through all means at its disposal. This subversion is in response to the ableist gaze, which limits the body through the cinematic apparatus.

This new cinematic form, which offers sensory alternatives and shifts in perception, may function as a sort of "inoculation" against the policing of social and sensual hierarchies. Crip animation replaces the indexical body's representation with a multitude of realistic and symbolic possibilities. Without a traditional representation of the body, the spectators are barred from enacting the ableist gaze over the characters—a gaze that constructs the body as spectacle and the audist audit that constructs vocalism as superior. Obfuscating the ableist point of view, through visual and vocal means, creates sensory phantoms among the spectators, thus evoking reflexivity with regards to the hegemonic bodily and sensory order.

NOTES

1. See: Neta Alexander, "Editor's Introduction: Rethinking Binge-Watching," in "Special Focus: Rethinking Binge-Watching in the Age of COVID-19," special issue, *Film Quarterly* 75, no. 1 (2021): 33–34.
2. Mark Cersosimpo, "The Difference between Subtitles and Captions," *Vimeo* (blog), September 2019, https://vimeo.com/blog/post/the-difference-between-subtitles-and-captions/.
3. "The Difference between Open and Closed Captions," Ai Media, accessed February 2021, https://www.ai-media.tv/the-difference-between-open-and-closed-captions-2/.
4. Jackie Leach Scully, "Deaf Identities in Disability Studies," in *Routledge Handbook of Disability Studies*, 2nd ed., ed. Nick Watson and Simo Vehmas (New York: Routledge, 2020), 50.
5. Scully, "Deaf Identities in Disability Studies," 154.
6. Scully, 155.
7. Octavian E. Robinson and Jonathan Henner, "The Personal Is Political in *The Deaf Mute Howls*: Deaf Epistemology Seeks Disability Justice," *Disability and Society* 32, no. 9 (2017): 1416–1436.
8. Robinson and Henner "The Personal Is Political," 1428.
9. Octavian Robinson and Jonathan Henner, "Authentic Voices, Authentic Encounters: Cripping the University through American Sign Language," *Disability Studies Quarterly* 38, no. 4 (2018): 1–2.
10. Robinson and Henner, "The Personal Is Political," 1428.
11. Paul Young, "Film Sound," *Oxford Bibliographies*, June 26, 2012, http://dx.doi.org/10.1093/obo/9780199791286-0100.
12. Young, "Film Sound."
13. Alan Williams, "Is Sound Recording Like a Language?" *Yale French Studies*, no. 60 (1980): 51–66; Christian Metz and Georgia Gurrieri, "Aural Objects," *Yale French Studies*, no. 60 (1980): 24–32; and Thomas Y. Levin, "The Acoustic Dimension: Notes on Film Sound," *Screen* 25, no. 3 (1984): 55–68, and "For the Record: Adorno on Music in the Age of Its Technological Reproducibility," *October* 55 (Winter 1990): 23–47.
14. Mary Ann Doane, "Ideology and the Practice of Sound Editing and Mixing," in *Film Sound*, ed. Elisabeth Weis and John Belton (New York: Columbia University Press, 1985), 54–62, and Kaja Silverman, *The Acoustic Mirror: The Female Voice in Psychoanalysis and Cinema* (Bloomington: Indiana University Press, 1988).

15. Michel Chion, *Audio-Vision*, ed. and trans. Claudia Gorbman (New York: Columbia University Press, 1994).

16. William Whittington, "The Sonic Playpen: Sound Design and Technology in Pixar's Animated Shorts," in *The Oxford Handbook of Sound Studies*, ed. Trevor Pinch and Karin Bijsterveld (Oxford: Oxford University Press, 2012), 368.

17. Whittington, "The Sonic Playpen," 370.

18. Ellcessor and Kirkpatrick, "Studying Disability," 142.

19. Ellcessor and Kirkpatrick, 142–143.

20. Michel Friedner and Stefan Helmreich, "Sound Studies Meets Deaf Studies," *The Senses and Society* 7, no. 1 (2012): 72–88.

21. Friedner and Helmreich, "Sound Studies Meets Deaf Studies," 73.

22. A phrase coined by George Veditz, a president of the United States National Association of the Deaf, in 1920.

23. Friedner and Helmreich, "Sound Studies Meets Deaf Studies," 77–78.

24. Rebecca Coyle, "Audio Motion: Animating (Film) Sound," in *Drawn to Sound: Animation Film Music and Sonicity* (London: Equinox, 2010), 1–23.

25. Coyle, "Audio Motion: Animating (Film) Sound," 1.

26. A central example of this are the stereo systems developed by Disney Studios for the showing of *Fantasia* (1940). Coyle, 2–3.

27. See also the distinctions drawn by Christian Metz and Georgia Gurrieri in "Aural Objects" with respect to the auditory channel (which is related to the visual channel), including noises, dialogue, and music. According to them, the epistemology of *sound* results from the fact that it is an adjective, in contrast to the *soundtrack*, which is a noun.

28. Coyle, "Audio Motion: Animating (Film) Sound," 3.

29. Michel Chion, *Film, a Sound Art*, trans. Claudia Gorbman (New York: Columbia University Press, 2009), 16.

30. Chion, *Film, a Sound Art*, 5.

31. Chion, 6–7.

32. Sobchack, "What My Fingers Knew."

33. The centrality of the sense of sight was discussed in the previous chapter.

34. The terms *acousmêtre* and *semi-acousmêtre* were defined by Michel Chion and are central concepts in this chapter.

35. Michel Chion, *The Voice in Cinema*, trans. Claudia Gorbman (New York: Columbia University Press, 1999), 17.

36. See the discussion on the supremacy of sight in the previous chapter, especially Jay, *Downcast Eyes*, 124–125.

37. Friedner and Helmreich, "Sound Studies Meets Deaf Studies," 74.

38. For example, a blind or deaf spectator.

39. Chion, *Film, a Sound Art*, 299–301.

40. Chion.

41. Chion, 490.

42. Chion, *The Voice in Cinema*, 18.

43. Ward argues that even though "we" think of it as an extra sensation, the sensation is entirely normal for "them," and it appears to them that our experiences are deficient. Ward adds that although the phenomenon is not talked about, it is experienced by slightly less than 5 percent of the population, and that, while the gene has not yet been found, synesthesia is known to be hereditary.

44. Chion, *The Voice in Cinema*, 21–22.

45. Chion, 23.

46. Chion, 28.

47. *A Shift in Perception* (Dan Monceaux, 2006), *Orgesticulanismus* (Mathieu Labaye, 2008), *Petra's Poem* (Shira Avni, 2012), and *Tying Your Own Shoes* (Shira Avni, 2009).

48. And also in Adam Elliot's films (especially the trilogy *Uncle*, 1996; *Cousin*, 1999; and *Brother*, 2000), *John and Michael* (Shira Avni, 2004), *Ryan* (Chris Landreth, 2004), and the films in the *Animated Minds* series (Andy Glynne, 2003–2008).

49. For example, the *Creature Discomforts* series (Leonard Cheshire Disability and Aardman Animations, 2007), discussed in chapter 1.

50. For example, the films *An Eyeful of Sound* and *Black Sun*.

51. Woman 1: "I feel it in my mouth and I taste it."

52. Woman 2: "All sounds have color."

53. Woman 1: "All sounds have color; the alphabet has color . . ." / Woman 2: "Words, numbers, things like that" / Woman 1: ". . . the days of the week have color, and each day has a color and a certain shape . . ." / Woman 2: "Hearing colors, seeing sounds, tasting smells, tasting and feeling sounds and colors . . ."

54. Chion, *Film, a Sound Art*, 499.

55. Marlee Matlin is the deaf actress who won an Oscar for her role in the film and the youngest woman to win the award to this day. Chion, 315.

56. Deaf studies and disability studies scholar Octavian Robinson explains "why this music storyline needs permanent retirement" in "Hollywood Starry-Eyed Over the Same Old Deaf Stories," April 13, 2022, https://notanangrydeafperson.medium.com/hollywood-starry-eyed-over-the-same-old-deaf-stories-3f37f8f05aa2.

57. David Neumeyer, *Meaning and Interpretation of Music in Cinema* (Bloomington: Indiana University Press, 2015).

58. Neumeyer, *Meaning and Interpretation of Music in Cinema*, 3–4.

59. Claudia Gorbman, *Unheard Melodies: Narrative Film Music* (London: British Film Institute, 1987), 68–69.

60. Mary Ann Doane, "The Voice in the Cinema: The Articulation of Body and Space," *Yale French Studies*, no. 60 (1980): 37.

61. Michel Chion, *Audio-Vision: Sound on Screen*, trans. Claudia Gorbman (New York: Columbia University Press, 1990).
62. Coyle, "Audio Motion: Animating (Film) Sound," 2.
63. Coyle, 8.
64. Whittington, "The Sonic Playpen," 382.
65. Rick Altman devoted two books to the study of musicals in cinema: *Genre, the Musical: A Reader* (London: Routledge and Kegan Paul, 1982), and *The American Film Musical* (Bloomington: Indiana University Press, 1987). A noteworthy example of the genre of documentary musicals is Brian Hill's film *Songbirds* (2007), which describes the life of women in prison in England. The film is accompanied by original songs performed by the inmates interviewed in the documentary.
66. It is important to note that the representation of Liz is drawn to look like the author of the graphic novel on which the film is based.
67. Sigourney Weaver, Steve Buscemi, Fred Armisen, and Dan Fogler.
68. See the definitions of animated documentary in the introduction and chapters 2 and 3.
69. Chapter 2, on the subject of crip subjectivity, discussed the autobiographical aspects of the work, as well as the central role of music in Swados's life.
70. The transitions between the utopian and the dystopian world were discussed in depth in chapter 2, concerning disabled subjectivity.
71. For an analysis of the film's visual metaphors, please see chapter 2.
72. Four diegetic and two extradiegetic.
73. Rebecca Sanchez, "The Image: Cinematic Poetics and Deaf Vision," in *Deafening Modernism: Embodied Language and Visual Poetics in American Literature* (New York: New York University Press, 2015), 121–122.
74. For example, a "green world" (trees), "flowers," "birds," "hands that hold me," and "I am loved" (heart) are illustrated accordingly.
75. Sanchez, *Deafening Modernism*, 121–122.
76. 1965 in Sanchez.
77. Sanchez, 122.
78. Bill Marshall and Robynn Jeananne Stilwell, *Musicals: Hollywood and Beyond* (Exeter, UK: Intellect, 2000).
79. Marshall and Stilwell, *Musicals: Hollywood and Beyond*, 1–2.
80. One example of this is the film *Golden Eighties* by Chantal Akerman (1986), which takes place in a Paris mall in the 1980s. This film subverts the boundaries of the genre and is part of a postmodern representation of a world of fragments, pastiche, and decentered identities out of which we can neither step nor dance. Marshall and Stilwell, 4.
81. Please see the discussion of the tactile spectatorship experience in chapter 3.
82. Friedner and Helmreich, "Sound Studies Meets Deaf Studies," 81.

83. This was told at a screening I attended at Docaviv, in which the film won the audience award.
84. Robinson, "Hollywood Starry-Eyed Over the Same Old Deaf Stories."
85. For example, Cholodenko, "The Animation of Cinema" in Coyle, "Audio Motion: Animating (Film) Sound," 3.
86. O'Pray, "Eisenstein and Stokes on Disney," 197.
87. O'Pray, 200.
88. O'Pray, 102.
89. "Paraphrased by Wells, 2002: 6," in Coyle, "Audio Motion: Animating (Film) Sound," 4.
90. Coyle, 4.
91. For example, psychorealism, as suggested by Moore, "Animating Unique Brain States."
92. Buchan, "The Animated Spectator," 27.
93. For example, wearing pants or flushing the toilet.
94. For example, a bearded man cutting with a knife and fork (the sound of the fork scraping the plate), closing a book, and returning it back to the shelf.
95. Chion, *Audio-Vision: Sound on Screen*, 8.
96. Please see my discussion of these terms in the previous section of this chapter.
97. For example, the noise of a machine, the hum of a fan, or a shower running (*Psycho*). See: Chion, *Audio-Vision: Sound on Screen*, 9.
98. For example, presenting it on paper or a slide.
99. Coyle, "Audio Motion: Animating (Film) Sound," 4.
100. Beauchamp, *Designing Sound for Animation*, 17, in Coyle "Audio Motion: Animating (Film) Sound," 7.
101. Except for speech.
102. Chion, *Film, a Sound Art*, 16.
103. Laura U. Marks, "The Memory of the Senses," in *The Skin of the Film: Intercultural Cinema, Embodiment, and the Senses* (Durham, NC: Duke University Press, 2000), 194–242.
104. For example, a cook's sense of smell, a photographer's sight, or a community of hunters in a dense forest relying on their sense of smell.
105. For more about identification processes in film, please also see: Baudry and Williams, "Ideological Effects of the Basic Cinematographic Apparatus," as mentioned in the introduction of this book, and especially the discussion of Linda Williams's "Film Bodies" in chapter 1.
106. Described as tools invented, engineered, and used by cis white men with average bodies. For more about this subject, please see the conclusion of this book.
107. Marks, "The Memory of the Senses," 194–242.
108. Marks, 141–142.

FIVE

TOWARD ACCESSIBLE SPECTATORSHIPS

CRIP ANIMATION USES A VARIETY of genres (documentary, film noir, autobiography, musical, and more) and techniques (cel, clay animation, puppets, pixilation, and computer-generated animation) to represent the inner worlds—feelings, thoughts, perceptions, states of mind, and so on—of people with disabilities. Crip animation contributes to the development of alternative forms of film that deviate from the traditional conventions of the cinematic medium and apparatus, thus subverting the spectators' embodied presumptions and perceptions.

Animated Film and Disability only examines a few of the available varieties of animated films offering alternatives in form and content to social perceptions that constrain the bodymind and its senses within dichotomies of abled/disabled, sane/mad, sighted/blind, and hearing/deaf. Crip animation avoids representing disabled bodies as spectacular and sensational by replacing the indexical body with abstract and metaphorical images. Alongside its avantgarde expression, this subgenre offers cinematic productions made by and for disabled people (*crip for crip*, inspired by the trans equivalent T_4T), as well as through creative collaborations between filmmakers with different disabilities, and nondisabled filmmakers. The call for "nothing without us" continues to be relevant in the world of film and television so long as the dominant norm is to cast able-bodied/able-minded/neurotypical actors to play the roles of people with disabilities. While the norms that allowed for white actors to be cast as Black people (blackface) are now finally being perceived as illegitimate, ableist perceptions still allow for the exclusion of actors with disabilities by replacing them with able-bodied/able-minded/neurotypical actors (cripface). A recent campaign sponsored by the Ruderman Family Foundation and featuring

Academy Award–winning actress Octavia Spencer is "calling on the entertainment industry to increase the casting of people with disabilities, including in on-screen roles that portray characters with disabilities." In the PSA, Spencer talks about the days of men portraying women, white actors portraying Black characters, and the overall exclusion of Asian, Native American, and LGBTQ characters.[1] Crip animation goes further than the demand of on-screen representation and relies on the subjectivity of people with disabilities, on all levels of the production process, and offers avant-garde expressions that arouse the spectator's senses.

The first chapter of this volume, "Resisting the Ableist Gaze," examines the construction of the ableist gaze as part of the cinematic apparatus and its utilization by mainstream live-action films, mainstream films with occasional experimental scenes, and short animated films that combine avant-garde with marketable expression. Mainstream live-action films use conventional means of expression to represent physical difference as a spectacle. While the spectacular representation of disabled bodies in the horror genre allows the able-bodied/able-minded spectators to alleviate their anxieties, in melodrama, such representation serves the construction of lives worth living. Mainstream films with occasional experimental scenes represent disability without using disabled bodies as a spectacle and include scenes that make use of avant-garde expression to offer the subjective perceptions of people with disabilities. The third type of film, short animated films relying on avant-garde expressions, is grounded in the subjective sensory experiences of people with disabilities. The animation of the perceptions of the world through points of view of people with disabilities challenges both the ableist gaze of mainstream cinema and that of narrative films containing subjective avant-garde scenes.

The second chapter, "Embodying Spectatorship," suggests categories for animated films about disability according to their treatment of disabled subjects within the narrative, the production process, and the film theater. The first category, first-person crip, consists of autobiographical films about disability, describing a process of self-exploration resisting the medical/psychiatric gaze. The second category, intersubjective encounters, describes films produced by able-bodied/able-minded filmmakers in intimate intersubjective relationships with their subjects, thus blurring the boundaries between disabled and nondisabled subjects. The third category, collaborative encounters, is composed of animated documentaries produced through intentional collaboration between disabled and nondisabled artists.

The third chapter, "Blinding the Spectator," discusses animated documentaries engaging with vision-related disabilities and conditions or blindness. Many animated films about sight and vision impairments subvert the construction of the ableist gaze in mainstream cinema. Such animated films offer spectators a shift in sensory perception by undermining the primacy of vision. The visual ambivalence of these films arouses the tactile senses and puts the spectators in touch with sensory images and bodies, as well as people with sight disabilities. Spectators' failure to see "straight" allows for a sensory alternative to traditional spectatorship. Such a shift may function as an alternative to the traditional hierarchy of senses and bodies.

The fourth chapter, "Deafening the Spectator," examines the soundtrack of crip animated documentary. The centrality of documentary voice-over, alongside abstract animated images, forces the spectator-listener to massively rely on the human voice. In this way, such films subvert the glorification of the visual while, at the same time, reinforcing audio-centrism and vocal communication. The empathetic use of music in documentary musical animation may seem irrelevant to deaf spectators; however, these films allow their spectators or listeners to enjoy art in both non-audio-centric and non-vocal-centric ways. Moreover, musical animation—animated in motion and simulating the grammar of sign language—may accommodate deaf spectators and invoke a synesthetic spectatorship among hearing and deaf people alike. The motion sounds, placed between the music track and the supernarrator track, allow engagement with an additional level of cinematic motion, aroused through the sense of hearing. Awareness of motion is synesthetically invoked, bringing forth a critique of social limitations over the body. Therefore, such films offer a listenership mixed with other senses, thus deviating from the boundaries of dichotomous perceptions of hearing/listening and voice/silence.

This book discusses the intersubjective relationship between spectators and films invoking a corporeal experience subverting the senses: listening without seeing, seeing without hearing, feeling textures and frequencies, understanding through memories of scents and flavors—in other words, being in touch with others. As an alternative to the limitations and constructions of the ableist gaze, crip animation offers a subversion of the traditional hierarchy of senses. The crip animated films discussed here replace the indexical body's representation with a myriad of realistic and symbolic possibilities. In the lack of a traditional representation of the bodymind through live action, spectators are barred from the option of applying the ableist gaze over the characters and making their bodies into spectacles. This obfuscation of the ableist gaze creates various sensory phantoms among the spectators, potentially invoking a demand for reflexivity concerning the hegemonic physical and sensory order. In light of the social oppression of people with disabilities, addressing temporarily able-bodied/

able-minded/neurotypical spectators and listeners is necessary for the political attempt to change social oppression and educate the oppressors. This creates an empathetic spectatorship experience that relies on cinematic aspects and narratives that offer crip subjectivity as an alternative way of being-in-the-world.

THE ASSUMPTION OF THE TEMPORARILY ABLE-BODIED SPECTATOR

As evident in the analysis of Hollywood films in the first chapter, conventional spectatorship assumes an able-bodied/able-minded/neurotypical spectator. These assumptions are apparent in the physical aspects of film projection—the projector and sound devices—and in other physical aspects of cinema theaters that are adapted to that bodymind. Thus, for example, the size of the screen, the size of the seats, and the sound system are "tailored" to the dimensions, sight, hearing, mobility, and so on of the "standard" spectator. These choices, which are based on statistical data, tend to reflect the average, at the expense of recognizing spectators' different and varied needs and desires. Furthermore, dichotomous social concepts of deaf/hearing and blind/sighted do not consider the lived experiences of people whose sensory organization is nonaverage, nonbinary, or multisensory.

Despite the involvement of people with disabilities in the production process, first-person crip animated films and films *about* crip subjectivity in the third person mostly address able-bodied/able-minded spectators. Teaching temporarily able-bodied spectators is an attempt to change the power relations in society. Accordingly, an empathetic spectatorship is created that relies on cinematic and didactic narrative aspects to present crip subjectivity as an alternative way of being-in-the-world.

Centering the desires and pleasures of nondisabled viewers (whether created by disabled or nondisabled filmmakers) is not merely prejudice but also denies what Elizabeth Ellcessor defines as "cultural accessibility." Carrie Sandahl wrote about the envisioning of disabled spectators while cowriting *Code of the Freaks*: "Our interviewees not only school the audience on their own perspectives and experiences of the movies; they also include detail that speaks directly to other disabled people by using cultural references and insider language, which is often politically incorrect. Unlike, Hollywood, then, we assume our 'general audience' includes people with disabilities."[2] Presuming an able-bodied spectator contributes in and of itself to the exclusion of people with disabilities in the public sphere.

Furthermore, people with disabilities—like trans people—are often perceived as consumers of medical care and not of movies, art, and culture. Elizabeth Ellcessor and Bill Kirkpatrick encourage scholars to write about access to film and media addressing all its mundane aspects, including "sitting, standing, punching tiny buttons on a remote, or remembering passwords for a streaming service. In such mundanities, it is impossible to miss variations of access. Disability is one such variation, and in its stark differences from 'normal' viewing positions, it illuminates the possibilities of many other viewing positions and ways of access."[3] The necessity to explore "cultural accessibility" was offered by Ellcessor in her contribution to the volume *Disability Media Studies*. The term captures the interrelationships among technological and economic access, access to representation and production, and access to the public sphere. She analyzes a crowdfunded web-series and shows how new technologies and funding platforms allow new forms of access and participation in ways that have particular relevance for the study of disability.[4] In general, attending to people with disabilities' consumption of popular culture has become more common in media studies than in film and television studies.[5]

The assumption of the able-bodied spectator creates narratives and means of expression that presume a "universal" body and do not take into account viewers with a range of diverse bodyminds and desires. Assuming an "average" spectator narrows and limits various audiences' access to a film. Following the phenomenological writings of the film, feminist, and disability studies scholars who were mentioned in this book, it can be argued that screening these films invites varied and diverse intersubjective encounters among the bodies in the movie theater and between them and the participant-subjects in the film during the production process.

Similar to the assumption of white spectators originating in live-action cinematography's apparatuses, the desired able-bodied spectator was embedded in the cinematic apparatus as well. Estelle Caswell, producer of Earworm, a video series focused on music history for Vox, made *Color Film Was Built for White People*. Through interviews with researcher Lorna Roth, a professor from Concordia University, Montreal, the film explores the apparatus's racism.[6] According to Roth, processing of Kodak color film for photography between 1940 and 1990 was based on the skin color of white women. During these decades, chemicals intended to expose dark skin tones were not in use. The early 1970s saw a change following the demand of furniture and chocolate companies wishing to produce more accurate photos of their darker products. As the film and television industry began integrating more Black American actors, the inaccurate results began to bother professionals, and in the 1990s, a team of engineers designed a photography mechanism that used two different computer chips to balance dark and light skin tones individually. Nowadays, though cameras are able to include a wider range of colors, the default for optimal photography of light skin tones still remains. These technologies continue to be embedded with inherent cultural assumptions that prioritize lighter skin tone.

Laura U. Marks examines the work of the cinematographer Arthur Jafa, who uses a shoulder camcorder while depicting the sensory experiences of diasporic Africans. According to Jafa, the shoulder camcorder allows him to simulate their unique movements, defined (similar to Black music) as subverting the stable and standard structure. Jafa affirms the findings of many film historians who studied film colors, lighting, and screening conditions: that there is a "technical" difficulty in filming people of color. This difficulty is created by the fact that the cinematic apparatus is based on capturing light-colored people or objects on dark backgrounds. Therefore, Jafa subverts analogue relationships and makes use of slow motion and freeze-frames to enhance the bodily experience and overcome the limits of the apparatus.

Similarly, the able-bodied/able-minded/neurotypical spectator assumption is embedded in the mainstream and avant-garde cinema apparatus, even including most experimental animation films about disability. Despite the change in the social treatment of people with disabilities in society and the Oscar nominations and awards to disabled filmmakers and actors, disabled people are still not perceived as a possible audience. The lack of accessibility to physically and mentally diverse audiences continues to exclude some viewers from film theaters. Experimental animation about crip experiences resists the ableist order of the sensory hierarchy embedded in the cinematic apparatus.[7] However, this resistance cannot be complete due to the lack of alternative bodily and perceptive experiences. Therefore, in order to offer a comprehensive alternative to the ableist gaze, common assumptions about the audience members and their desires must also be subverted. Similar to the white, cishet, masculine spectator assumption, the able-bodied spectator assumption manufactures narratives and ways of expression that assume a "universal" body, not taking the actual spectators into account. Addressing films to diverse audiences in terms of gender, race, body, psychology, cognition, and so on could potentially subvert ableist perceptions and allow for alternative discussion. In any case, this would likely allow diverse intersubjective interactions between disabled and nondisabled spectators in film theaters and between them and the films' participants and creators.

Defying traditional perceptions of physical hierarchies is a declared intention of many live-action and animated films; this book focused on the prominence of these endeavors in short avant-garde animated films about disability. Animated films, according to Rebecca Coyle, have challenged and strengthened institutional structures, addressing race, ethnicity, and sexuality, and have reached into spaces that were censored in mainstream cinema. The spectatorship listenership offered by animation is anchored in the intermingling of ear and eye in such a way that animation can be evaluated as an integral part of the audiovisual forms of communication.[8] Crip animation is a form of communication that undermines the traditional sensory hierarchies and enables spectators to see in places where they were supposed to hear and to hear in times where they were supposed to see, or rather evoke a sensual memory through depriving either or both.

ACCOMMODATING BODILY AND SENSORY DIVERSITY AT THE MOVIE THEATER

It was my intention to conclude this book by showing how there has been improvement in the representation of people with disabilities and by proposing that we can now move on to accommodating diverse bodyminds at movie theaters. As *Code of the Freaks* and its circular narrative show, we are not quite there yet. However, as this book aims to show, casting and representation are only one aspect of the relationship between film and people with disabilities.

In February 2016, the Disney Movies Anywhere app unveiled a feature that listens and syncs automatically with their films, allowing blind and low-vision people to control their personal audio description track on their smartphones. This project, originated by Pixar Animation Studios Emeryville and developed by Disney engineers, has involved members of the blindness community and LightHouse for the Blind and Visually Impaired, a San Francisco–based nonprofit to contribute feedback and testing for quality assurance. LightHouse published the announcement alongside their end goal for the project: "In accomplishing this, Disney-Pixar is leading the way for accessible films; and soon, we at the LightHouse are confident that this mobile Audio Description experience will be possible for all movies, everywhere." Furthermore, after a trial screening, "The response was universal acclaim. The app's beta version worked seamlessly. People both blind and sighted left the event joyously; celebrating the idea of being able to go back to the movie theater or watch a movie in their homes exactly the way they want."[9]

In June 2017, Edgar Wright released *Baby Driver*, a film about a getaway driver with a special love of music. This film is an ode to the cinematic soundtrack and almost completely relies on the music accompanying all the protagonist's actions. The protagonist's father, a deaf man, communicates with him through ASL. In contrast with what spectators have become accustomed to, the father teaches his son to read the world through audio frequencies that can be felt through the body. This film was praised by the deaf community for casting a deaf actor, CJ Jones, to play the deaf father, as well as for its accurate use of ASL. Moreover, the film avoided reinforcing the common convention of a tragic ending for a protagonist who has lost his hearing and has become a person with a disability. In contrast with ableist cinematic conventions, this film provides the possibility of vibrations, which undermine the binary of hearing/deaf and offer the potential of sensory memory and creativity.

Alongside its innovation in representing disability and the participation of people with disabilities in key roles in the film, it still assumes the existence of an exclusively sighted, hearing spectator. Despite its anti-ableist ways of representation, the film's screening conditions are unsuitable to deaf spectators. I do not mean merely adding open or closed captions or subtitles, although this is a fundamental requirement. It would have been possible to adapt the screening to the film's expression by playing the soundtrack through audio frequencies that could be felt through the seat. An accessible spectatorship experience of this kind might have offered a new phenomenological spectatorship.

Friedner and Helmreich describe a social-artistic experiment with sound frequencies perceived by both "hearing" and "deaf" people. They argue that, notwithstanding the fact that the participants were exposed to identical content, the manner in which it was perceived by each of them was different. Furthermore, the experience can even change with respect to the same individual and can be experienced in a variety of synesthetic ways. They therefore held that phenomenologies of frequencies are not singular.[10] The sounds and images of crip animation, like the frequencies in the experiment, invite experiences that involve and mingle various senses and, therefore, leave room for diverse bodyminds that experience the world differently.

Beyond the political undermining of dichotomies such as hearing/sight and sound/silence, crip animation seeks to challenge the social sensory organization with an alternative spectatorship and listenership. In addition to the model of phenomenological analysis, which makes it possible to examine sensory communication in the spectatorship listenership, the social model of disability studies, and especially deaf critique studies, allows us to examine sensory and physical variety at the movie theater.

While many crip animated films address able-bodied/able-minded/neurotypical audiences, there are few examples of films intentionally addressing diverse audiences. Thus, for example, Shira Avni's animated films, which were produced in collaboration with filmmakers and artists with Down syndrome, take people with Down syndrome into account as the films' audience.[11] Therefore, the films are made cognitively accessible by using animated images as well as writing some of the words. Another example is the film *A Is for Autism* (Tim Webb, 1992), which uses editing that improves the film's accessibility to neurodivergent and neurotypical people by weaving in repetitive images and organizing statements as well as the framing of the narrative with a clear announcement of its beginning and end.[12] This film aims to provide aesthetic pleasure for both these audiences. Elizabeth Swados's musical animation *My Depression* (2014) also imagines spectators living with depression as a desired audience and addresses them as well. Many of the creators of these films hope for an audience of people with disabilities and are aware of the need to accommodate diverse modes of spectatorship and listenership. However, it is impossible to make the films fully accessible due to the various needs of diverse people, and, in the lack of any adjustments, the films still assume a "universal" spectator.[13]

One unique example of accessibility offered to spectators with disabilities, while not standing at the center of the film, is an unintentional inclusion of deaf audiences in an animated work about depression. In *My Depression*, all music featured in the film can be interpreted through the sense of sight. Moreover, the "cinematic" ways Swados has animated the music's lyrics echo the grammar of ASL. In this way, without necessarily intending the film is made accessible to deaf spectators, as well as expanding the spectatorship listenership of hearing viewers. This type of analysis of the animation might lead to the conclusion that films hold yet-underdeveloped creative possibilities for conveying music in more synesthetic and non-vocal-centric ways. Animated musicals that echo the grammar of sign language are one possible route to accessibility in film that allows for transformative spectatorship experiences.

Although we cannot expect films to make their contents, expression, and screening conditions accessible to all bodies and sensory experiences, partially accessible spectatorship listenership might still subvert ableist perceptions based on the able-bodied audience assumption. Making films accessible to diverse audiences offers an intersubjective experience between different bodyminds in the world. This calls for a reexamination of film theaters designed for the "average" body. Although there are a few more wheelchair-accessible film theaters than in prior decades, they often provide no other type of accommodation and are lacking the required aids to make screenings accessible to deaf and hard-of-hearing people, sight-impaired people, and other groups within the disability community.[14]

Although not screened in movie theaters because of the pandemic, *Crip Camp* (James LeBrecht and Nicole Newnham, 2020) became an interesting case study to examine accessibility. The documentary focuses on the evolution of the disability rights movement from the activists' first encounter at a crip summer camp in the 1960s and 1970s to the current time. The film is available on Netflix and has been widely watched and praised by spectators and critics. It has so far won the audience award for best documentary at the Sundance Film Festival in 2020 and the best feature at the International Documentary Association in 2021, among others, and was shortlisted for best documentary by the Academy Awards.

Mobilizing the attention the film is receiving, Documentary Filmmakers with Disabilities, in association with the UK's DocSociety and supported by Netflix, with consultation from communications agency, WDW Entertainment, launched a *Toolkit for Inclusion and Accessibility: Changing the Narrative of Disability in Documentary Film*. This document contains a chapter with instructions on "How to Make Films More Accessible for Audiences." The most prominent tools it discusses are professional captions and audio descriptions: "The quality of these accessible versions is a significant factor in the economic and creative success of a film. The creation of high-quality audio description and captions for all films should be seen as a critical component of media development for majority audiences, rather than a post-production element for a niche audience."[15] The most compelling argument in the toolkit fostering accessibility immersion, experience, and experimentation derives from an analysis of artist and TED Fellow Christine Sun Kim's short film about the creative potential for closed captioning.[16] Kim's film suggests creative opportunities for filmmakers to not only make accessible films but also offer "immersion in the imaginative process of interrogating how other people engage with sound and visuals; surely one of the principal concerns of cinema."[17]

A reexamination of accessibility in film theaters and screening methods intended for diverse audiences may bring forth creative solutions. These, in turn, could improve the spectatorship experience of a variety of audiences. Insofar as such reexaminations would take the audience's physical and sensory diversity into account, this might create enhanced multisensory cinematic experiences for all audiences. Such a shift in perception encapsulates opportunities for new experience, such as sending vibrations through seats, designing seats in various sizes and heights, using scents to accompany certain lighting, and countless other possibilities. In this way, film may, as Vivian Sobchack suggested, "Open[s] our eyes far beyond their discrete capacity for vision, open[s] the film far beyond its visible containment by the screen, and open[s] language to a reflective knowledge of its specific carnal origins and limits."[18]

However, making the screening conditions accessible is still separate from a film's cinematic and narrative approach toward people with disabilities. Thus, for example, in screenings for neurodiverse audiences the lights remain dim, the volume is lowered, and no one is forced to sit still and quietly in their seats, and no one is denied the right to stim. Movie theaters providing minimal accessibility accommodations for blind, hearing-impaired, and deaf spectators is rare to nonexistent.

As the fruit of intersubjective collaborations between disabled and nondisabled filmmakers, animated films are expressly addressed to both audiences. This is in contrast with the physical accessibility of screening conditions. By addressing issues concerning people with disabilities and being produced through collaborations between disabled and nondisabled filmmakers, such films invite viewing by diversely embodied spectators. They do not assume the existence of a monolithic "universal" or "average" viewer. Rather, they assume the existence of varied and diverse bodyminds.

Collaborative animation projects utilize a cinematic language that makes the content of a film accessible. For example, a film about autism provides aesthetic pleasure for a neurodivergent audience, while a film about the deaf community is made so that a deaf audience can experience the film fully without relying solely on the open captions. Public screenings of such films in festivals, cinematheques, and art house theaters invite a broad variety of intersubjective viewing experiences. Within such screenings, audience members with different bodyminds and disabilities can sit together in the theater and view the film as a subjective experience—described by various communities. The diverse audiences offer a variety of connections with the subjectivity presented on-screen, as well as with other spectators in the audience. Addressing a film to differently able-bodied spectators, taking diverse sensual communication with the world into account, invites a tangible physical closeness within the movie theater and overall allows additional and unexpected interactions.

The assumption of an able-bodied/able-minded/neurotypical spectator is embedded within the ableist approach. Animated films produced through cooperation and collaboration between disabled and temporarily able-bodied artists reflexively shed light on the power relations between these two audiences. Moreover, such films reflexively expand their canvas by imagining an intersubjective spectatorship listenership and welcoming the diverse needs and passions of a variety of spectators in the audience. In other words, making spectatorship accessible to diverse audiences is not only a question of the physical screening conditions but derives from taking into consideration diverse viewers and recognizing their differences of experience from the very beginning of the creative process.

This book suggests a methodology for cripping spectatorship through an analysis of anti-ableism in animation, particularly experiences that include a variety of sensory perceptions in diverse bodies. Disability-focused animation evokes the intersubjective relationship between viewer-listeners and films that offer new perspectives of daily experiences through the senses. The senses are aroused by listening to voices whose source is hidden, viewing without hearing the voice coming from the body, the sensation of textures evoking the sense of touch, and understanding through memories of tastes and scents. All these techniques allow for intersubjective relationships between diverse bodies and senses.

In addition to the theoretical aspects of the intersection between the spectatorship experience and people with disabilities as film consumers, there are also practical aspects related to the physical structure of film theaters. While there is some attention to wheelchair accessibility in public places (especially where enshrined by law), other groups are rarely taken into account when imagining the "general audience." Moreover, current solutions for improving accessibility in film theaters for deaf or blind people offer individual experiences focused on the sensory phantom. However, a practical examination of the possibilities of arousing all our senses as part of the cinematic spectatorship experience could offer groundbreaking ways of screening. If four-dimensional innovations build on the screening accommodations of people with disabilities, cinema would be able to offer a new form of immersive and synesthetic crip spectatorship.

NOTES

1. Ruderman Family Foundation, "On the 30th Anniversary of the ADA, Oscar-Winning Actress Octavia Spencer Joins the Ruderman Family Foundation for an Important Message on Authentic Representation," July 22, 2020, https://rudermanfoundation.org/press_releases/psa/.
2. Sandahl, "It's All the Same Movie," 148.
3. Ellcessor and Kirkpatrick, "Studying Disability," 142.
4. Elizabeth Ellcessor, "Kickstarting Community: Disability, Access, and Participation in *My Gimpy Life*," in *Disability Media Studies*, ed. Elizabeth Ellcessor and Bill Kirkpatrick (New York: New York University Press, 2017), 31–51.

5. See, for example, Katie Ellis's analysis of social- and cultural-model approaches to disability in popular culture, emphasizing the role of consumption and critical involvement as a way to engage with the pleasure of popular culture. "Producerly Disability Popular Culture: The Collision of Critical and Receptive Attitudes," in *The Routledge Companion to Disability Studies*, ed. Katie Ellis, Gerard Goggin, Beth Haller, and Rosemary Curtis (New York: Routledge, 2020), 149–157.

6. Estelle Caswell, *Color Film Was Built for White People*, VOX, September 15, 2015, https://www.vox.com/2015/9/18/9348821/photography-race-bias.

7. Marks, *The Skin of the Film*, 194–242.

8. Coyle, "Audio Motion: Animating (Film) Sound," 17.

9. LightHouse for the Blind and Visually Impaired, "Every Pixar Film Is Now Accessible with Mobile Audio Description from Disney," February 23, 2016, https://lighthouse-sf.org/2016/02/23/every-pixar-film-is-now-accessible-with-mobile-audio-description-from-disney/#.

10. Friedner and Helmreich, "Sound Studies Meets Deaf Studies," 77.

11. *John and Michael* (2005), *Tying Your Own Shoes* (2009), and *Petra's Poem* (2012). For a discussion of Avni's films, please see chapter 2.

12. Please see discussion in chapter 2.

13. Such needs may even contradict each other. For example, while a person with sensory overload would prefer dim lighting, people with sight impairments would find it difficult to watch a film in a theater that is not completely dark.

14. Among the most prominent examples are FM devices, subtitles, audio frequencies that can be felt through the seats for deaf and hard of hearing audience members, and audio narration through earphones for blind and visually impaired spectators..

15. Lindsey Dryden, Samantha Steele, Day Al-Mohamed, Kyla Harris, Alysa Nahmias, and Emrys Mordin, *Toolkit for Inclusion and Accessibility: Changing the Narrative of Disability in Documentary Film*, FWD-Doc, BFI Press Reset Campaign, Higher Ground Productions, Netflix, and WDW, February 2021, https://static1.squarespace.com/static/5dd1c2b5a0f7a568485cbedd/t/602d4708d39c1d1154d0902a/1613581716771/FWD-Doc+Toolkit+small.pdf, 34–35.

16. Christine Sun Kim, "Artist Christine Sun Kim Rewrites Closed Captions," *Pop-up Magazine*, October 2020, https://www.youtube.com/watch?v=tfe479qL8hg&ab_channel=Pop-UpMagazine.

17. Lindsey Dryden, Samantha Steele, Day Al-Mohamed, Kyla Harris, Alysa Nahmias, and Emrys Mordin, *Toolkit for Inclusion and Accessibility: Changing the Narrative of Disability in Documentary Film*, FWD-Doc, BFI Press Reset Campaign, Higher Ground Productions, Netflix, and WDW, February 2021, https://static1.squarespace.com/static/5dd1c2b5a0f7a568485cbedd/t/602d4708d39c1d1154d0902a/1613581716771/FWD-Doc+Toolkit+small.pdf, 34–35.

18. Sobchack, "What My Fingers Knew."

BIBLIOGRAPHY

ABC7. "Pixar's 'Loop' Gives an Autistic Lead Character a Powerful Voice." January 10, 2020. https://abc7.com/5837089/.

Adorno, Theodor. "Transparencies on Film." Translated by Thomas Y. Levin. *New German Critique*, no. 24–25 (Autumn 1981–Winter 1982): 199–205.

Ahmed, Sara. *Queer Phenomenology: Orientations, Objects, Others*. Durham, NC: Duke University Press, 2006.

Ai Media. "The Difference between Open and Closed Captions." Accessed February 2021. https://www.ai-media.tv/the-difference-between-open-and-closed-captions-2/.

Alexander, Neta. "Editor's Introduction: Rethinking Binge-Watching." In "Special Focus: Rethinking Binge-Watching in the Age of COVID-19," special issue, *Film Quarterly* 75, no. 1 (2021): 33–34.

Allmer, Açalya. "The Poetics of the Real in Julian Schnabel's The Diving-Bell and the Butterfly." Paper presented at Design Cinema: International Design and Cinema Conference, Istanbul, Turkey, 2008.

Altman, Rick. *The American Film Musical*. Bloomington: Indiana University Press, 1987.

Altman, Rick. *Genre, the Musical: A Reader*. British Film Institute Readers in Film Studies. London: Routledge and Kegan Paul, 1982.

American Cinematheque. "Julie Delpy Presents Freaks." October 24, 2021. https://www.americancinematheque.com/now-showing/julie-delpy-presents-freaks/.

Baldwin, Thomas. Introduction to *The World of Perception*, by Maurice Merleau-Ponty, 1–11. Translated by Oliver Davis. New York: Routledge Classics, 2009.

Baril, Alexandre. "Transness as Debility: Rethinking Intersections between Trans and Disabled Embodiments." *Feminist Review* 111 (2015): 59–74.

Barker, Jennifer M. *The Tactile Eye*. Berkeley: University of California Press, 2009.

Baudry, Jean-Louis, and Alan Williams. "Ideological Effects of the Basic Cinematographic Apparatus." *Film Quarterly* 28, no. 2 (1974): 39–47.

Behlil, Melis. "Ravenous Cinephiles: Cinephilia, Internet, and Online Film Communities." In *Cinephilia: Movies, Love and Memory*, edited by Marijke de Valck and Malte Hagener, 111–123. Amsterdam: Amsterdam University Press, 2005.

Bendazzi, Giannalberto. *Animation: A World History*. Vol. 3, *Contemporary Times*. New York: Routledge, 2017.

Benjamin, Walter. *On Hashish*. Cambridge, MA: Harvard University Press, 2006.

Benjamin, Walter. "A Short History of Photography." In *Classical Essays on Photography*, edited by Alan Trachtenberg, 142–151. New Haven, CT: Leete's Island Books, 1980.

Benjamin, Walter. "The Work of Art in the Age of Mechanical Reproduction." Translated by Harry Zohn. In *Illuminations*, edited by Hannah Arendt, 217–251. New York: Schocken Books.

Ben-Moshe, Liat. *Decarcerating Disability: Deinstitutionalization and Prison Abolition*. Minneapolis: University of Minnesota Press, 2020.

Ben-Moshe, Liat, Chris Chapman, and Allison C. Carey. *Disability Incarcerated: Imprisonment and Disability in the United States and Canada*. New York: Palgrave MacMillan, 2014.

Biderman, Shai, and Assaf Tabeka. "The Monster Within: Alienation and Social Conformity in *The Elephant Man*." In *The Philosophy of David Lynch*, edited by William J. Devlin and Shai Biderman, 207–223. Lexington: University Press of Kentucky, 2011.

Blair, Jeremy Michael. "Animated Autoethnographies: Stop Motion Animation as a Tool for Self-Inquiry and Personal Evolution." *Art Education* 67, no. 2 (2014): 6–7.

Brooke, Michael. "Creature Comforts (1989)." BFI ScreenOnline. Accessed December 28, 2018. http://www.screenonline.org.uk/film/id/588459/index.html.

Brylla, Catalin. "'Documentary and (Dis)ability' Symposium, University of Surrey, United Kingdom, 20 September 2013." *Studies in Documentary* 8, no. 2 (2014): 169–171.

Buchan, Suzanne. "The Animated Spectator: Watching Quay Brothers' Worlds." In *Animated Worlds*, edited by Suzanne Buchan, 17–40. London: John Libbey, 2006.

Burt, Jonathan. *Animals in Film*. London: Reaktion Books, 2002.

Butler, Judith. *Gender Trouble: Feminism and the Subversion of Identity*. New York: Routledge, 1990.

Campbell, Fiona Kumari. "Refusing Able(ness): A Preliminary Conversation about Ableism." *M/C Journal* 11, no. 3 (2008): 46–55.

Canby, Vincent. "Film: Mask, Bogdanovich Tale of a Rare Disease." *New York Times*, March 1985. https://www.nytimes.com/1985/03/08/movies/film-mask-bogdanovich-tale-of-a-rare-disease.html.

Carroll, Noël. "Why Horror? The Paradox of Horror." In *The Philosophy of Horror: Or, Paradoxes of the Heart*, 159–195. London: Routledge, 1990.
Carter-Long, Lawrence. "A Manifesto: Where Have You Gone, Stephen Dworkin? On Disability Film." *Film Quarterly* 72, no. 3 (2019): 26–29.
Caswell, Estelle. "How Sign Language Innovators Are Bringing Music to the Deaf." *VOX*, March 27, 2017. http://www.vox.com/videos/2017/3/27/15072526/asl-music-interpreter.
Cersosimpo, Mark. "The Difference between Subtitles and Captions." *Vimeo* (blog), September 2019. https://vimeo.com/blog/post/the-difference-between-subtitles-and-captions/.
Chen, Mel Y. *Animacies: Biopolitics, Racial Mattering, and Queer Affect*. Durham, NC: Duke University Press, 2012.
Cherney, James L. "Sexy Cyborgs: Disability and Erotic Politics in Cronenberg's *Crash*." In *Screening Disability: Essays on Cinema and Disability*, edited by Christopher R. Smit and Anthony Enns, 164–180. Lanham, MD: University Press of America, 2001.
Cheu, Johnson. "Seeing Blindness On-Screen: The Blind, Female Gaze." In *The Problem Body: Projecting Disability on Film*, edited by Sally Chivers and Nicole Markotić, 67–81. Columbus: Ohio State University Press, 2010.
Chion, Michel. *Audio-Vision: Sound on Screen*. Translated by Claudia Gorbman. New York: Columbia University Press, 1994.
Chion, Michel. *Film, a Sound Art*. Translated by Claudia Gorbman. New York: Columbia University Press, 2009.
Chion, Michel. *The Voice in Cinema*. Translated by Claudia Gorbman. New York: Columbia University Press, 1999.
Chivers, Sally. "The Horror of Becoming 'One of Us': Tod Browning's Freaks and Disability." In *Screening Disability: Essays on Cinema and Disability*, edited by Christopher R. Smit and Anthony Enns, 57–64. Lanham, MD: University Press of America, 2001.
Cholodenko, Alan. "The Animation of Cinema." *Semiotic Review of Books* 18, no. 2 (2008): 1–10.
Concordia University Faculty of Fine Arts. "Shira Avni, MFA." Accessed September 18, 2018. http://www.concordia.ca/finearts/cinema/faculty.html?fpid=shira-avni.
Coyle, Rebecca. "Audio Motion: Animating (Film) Sound." In *Drawn to Sound: Animation Film Music and Sonicity*, 1–22. London: Equinox, 2010.
Darke, Paul. "No Life Anyway: Pathologizing Disability on Film." In *The Problem Body: Projecting Disability on Film*, edited by Sally Chivers and Nicole Markotić, 97–108. Columbus: Ohio State University Press, 2010.
Davidson, Michael. "Phantom Limbs: Film Noir and the Disabled Body." In *The Problem Body: Projecting Disability on Film*, edited by Sally Chivers and Nicole Markotić, 43–66. Columbus: Ohio State University Press, 2010.

DiMare, Philip. "Representations of Disability in Film." In Vol. 1 of *Movies in American History: An Encyclopedia*, 1045–1051. Santa Barbara, CA: ABC-CLIO, 2011.
Doane, Mary Ann. "Ideology and the Practice of Sound Editing and Mixing." In *Film Sound*, edited by Elisabeth Weis and John Belton, 54–62. New York: Columbia University Press, 1985.
Doane, Mary Ann. "The Voice in the Cinema: The Articulation of Body and Space." *Yale French Studies*, no. 60 (1980): 33–50.
Dobson, Nichola, Annabelle Honess Roe, Amy Ratelle, and Caroline Ruddell. *The Animation Studies Reader*. New York: Bloomsbury Academic, 2018.
Dreyfus, Hubert. *Being-in-the-World: A Commentary on Heidegger's Being and Time*. Cambridge, MA: MIT Press, 1991.
Dryden, Lindsey, Samantha Steele, Day Al-Mohamed, Kyla Harris, Alysa Nahmias, and Emrys Mordin. *Toolkit for Inclusion and Accessibility: Changing the Narrative of Disability in Documentary Film*. FWD-Doc, BFI Press Reset Campaign, Higher Ground Productions, Netflix, and WDW. February 2021, 34–35.
Durham, April. "Slips, Breaks, and Tangles: Creative Collaboration and the Aesthetic Process of Trans-Subjectivity." *Camera Obscura* 31, no. 3 (2016): 35–63.
Ellcessor, Elizabeth. "Kickstarting Community: Disability, Access, and Participation in *My Gimpy Life*." In *Disability Media Studies*, edited by Elizabeth Ellcessor and Bill Kirkpatrick, 31–51. New York: New York University Press, 2017.
Ellcessor, Elizabeth, and Catalin Brylla. "Crip Camp." Docalogue. September 2020. https://docalogue.com/crip-camp/.
Ellcessor, Elizabeth, and Bill Kirkpatrick. *Disability Media Studies*. New York: New York University Press, 2017.
Ellcessor, Elizabeth, and Bill Kirkpatrick. "Studying Disability for a Better Cinema and Media Studies." In "In Focus: Cripping Cinema and Media Studies," special issue, *JCMS: Journal of Cinema and Media Studies* 58, no. 4 (2019): 139–144.
Ellis, Carolyn, and Arthur P. Bochner. "Autoethnography, Personal Narrative, Reflexivity: Researcher as Subject." In *The Handbook of Qualitative Research*. 2nd ed., edited by Norman. K. Denzin and Yvonna S. Lincoln, 733–768. Newbury Park, CA: Sage, 2000.
Ellis, Katie. "Producerly Disability Popular Culture: The Collision of Critical and Receptive Attitudes." In *The Routledge Companion to Disability Studies*, edited by Katie Ellis, Gerard Goggin, Beth Haller, and Rosemary Curtis, 149–157. New York and London: Routledge, 2020.
Finger, Anne. "Forbidden Fruit." *New Internationalist*, no. 233 (1992): 8–10.
Fink, Moritz. "People Who Look Like Things: Representations of Disability in The Simpsons." *Journal of Literary & Cultural Disability Studies* 7, no. 3 (2013): 255–270.

Finkelstein, Adi. "Estrangement and Alienation in Chronic Illness Experience: Narratives of Women Suffering from Chronic Fatigue Syndrome and Fibromyalgia Syndrome." PhD diss., The Hebrew University, 2008 [Hebrew].
Finkelstein, Frank. "A Shift in Perception." Film Threat. June 2007. http://www.filmthreat.com/reviews/10793.
Fleischer, Doris Zames, and Frieda Zames. "Compassionate Killings." *Disability Studies Quarterly* 25, no. 3 (2005): np.
Foucault, Michel. *The History of Sexuality*. Vol. 1, *An Introduction*. Translated by Robert Hurley. New York: Vintage Books, 1990.
Foucault, Michel. *The History of Sexuality*. Vol. 2, *The Use of Pleasure*. Translated by Robert Hurley. New York: Vintage Books, 1990.
Foucault, Michel. *The History of Sexuality*. Vol. 3, *The Care of the Self*. Translated by Robert Hurley. New York: Vintage Books, 1988.
Freud, Sigmund. "Mourning and Melancholia." In *The Standard Edition of the Complete Psychological Works of Sigmund Freud Volume XIV (1914–1916): On the History of the Psycho-Analytic Movement, Papers on Metapsychology and Other Works*. Translated by James Strachey. Edited by Anna Freud, Alix Strachey, and Alan Tyson, 237–258. London: Hogarth Press and the Institute of Psycho-Analysis, 1964.
Friedner, Michel, and Stefan Helmreich. "Sound Studies Meets Deaf Studies." *The Senses and Society* 7, no. 1 (2012): 72–88.
Garland-Thomson, Rosemarie. *Extraordinary Bodies: Figuring Physical Disability in American Culture and Literature*. New York: Columbia University Press, 1997.
Garland-Thomson, Rosemarie. *Staring: How We Look*. Oxford: Oxford University Press, 2009.
Ginsburg, Faye. "Foreword to the *Routledge Companion to Disability and Media* (Or: A Companion on the Ramp Less Traveled)." In *Routledge Companion to Disability and Media*, edited by Katie Ellis, Gerard Goggin, Beth Haller, and Rosemary Curtis, xxii–xxvi. London: Routledge, 2020.
Goodley, Dan. *Dis/ability Studies: Theorising Disablism and Ableism*. New York: Routledge, 2014.
Gorbman, Claudia. *Unheard Melodies: Narrative Film Music*. London: British Film Institute, 1987.
Gorney, Edna. "'If Only I Had Petals, My Situation Would Be Different': The Curious Case of Nature Reserves and Shelters for Battered Women." In *Ecofeminism in Dialogue*, edited by Douglas A. Vakoch and Sam Mickey, 77–92. New York: Lexington Books, 2018.
Greenberg, Slava. "(Dis)abling the Spectator: Embodying Disability in Animated Documentary." In *Documentary and Disability*, edited by Catalin Brylla and Helen Hughes, 129–143. London: Palgrave Macmillan, 2017.

Greenberg, Slava. "Disclosure: Toward Communal Trans Spectatorship." Docalogue, October 2020. https://docalogue.com/disclosure/.

Greenberg, Slava. "Disorienting the Past, Cripping the Future in Adam Elliot's Claymation." *Animation: An Interdisciplinary Journal* 2, no. 12 (2017): 123–137.

Greenberg, Slava. "Stories Our Bodies Tell: The Phenomenology of Anecdotes, Comings Out, and Embodied Autoethnographies." *Review of Disability Studies: International Journal* 14, no. 4 (2018): 1–16.

Grue, Jan. *Disability and Discourse Analysis*. New York: Routledge, 2016.

Hague, Helen. "Wiped Out: Activist's Anti-Charity Website Blocked." *Guardian*, May 2, 2001. https://www.theguardian.com/society/2001/may/02/guardiansocietysupplement2.

Halberstam, J. Jack. "Finding Nemo and Transgender Creatures." In *21st Century Sexualities: Contemporary Issues in Health, Education, and Rights*, edited by Gilbert Herdt and Cymene Howe, 63–66. London: Routledge, 2007.

Halberstam, J. Jack. *The Queer Art of Failure*. Durham, NC: Duke University Press, 2011.

Halberstam, J. Jack. *Trans*: A Quick and Quirky Account of Gender Variability*. Oakland: University of California Press, 2018.

Hansen, Miriam. "Benjamin, Cinema and Experience: 'The Blue Flower in the Land of Technology.'" *New German Critique*, no. 40 (Winter 1987): 179–224.

Hansen, Miriam. "Introduction to Adorno's 'Transparencies on Film' (1966)." *New German Critique*, no. 24–25 (Autumn 1981–Winter 1982): 36–56.

Hansen, Miriam Bratu. *Cinema and Experience: Siegfried Kracauer, Walter Benjamin, and Theodor W. Adorno*. Berkeley: University of California Press, 2012.

Haraway, Donna. "A Cyborg Manifesto: Science, Technology and Socialist-Feminism in the Late Twentieth Century." In *Simians, Cyborgs and Women: The Reinvention of Nature*, 149–181. New York: Routledge, 1991.

Hayes, Michael, and Rhonda Black. "Troubling Signs: Disability, Hollywood Movies and the Construction of a Discourse of Pity." *Disability Studies Quarterly* 23, no. 2 (2003). https://dsq-sds.org/article/view/419/585.

Heidegger, Martin. *Being and Time*. Translated by John Macquarrie and Edward Robinson. New York: Harper & Row, 2008.

Hernández, María Lorenzo. "The Double Sense of Animated Images: A View on the Paradoxes of Animation as a Visual Language." *Animation Studies* 2 (2007): 36–44.

Hoeksema, Thomas B., and Christopher R. Smit. "The Fusion of Film Studies and Disability Studies." In *Screening Disability: Essays on Cinema and Disability*, edited by Christopher R. Smit and Anthony Enns, 33–43. Lanham, MD: University Press of America, 2001.

Holderness, Cates. "What Colors Are This Dress?" *BuzzFeed*, February 26, 2015. https://www.buzzfeed.com/catesish/help-am-i-going-insane-its-definitely-blue?utm_source=dynamic&utm_campaign=bfsharecopy.

Honess Roe, Annabelle. *Animated Documentary.* New York: Palgrave Macmillan, 2013.
Internet Movie Database. "Cake." Accessed August 28, 2019. https://www.imdb.com/title/tt3442006/?ref_=fn_al_tt_1.
Internet Movie Database. "The Diving Bell and the Butterfly." Accessed June 16, 2018. https://www.imdb.com/title/tt0401383/?ref_=fn_al_tt_1>.
Internet Movie Database. "Mask." Accessed June 16, 2018. https://www.imdb.com/title/tt0089560.
Internet Movie Database. "Thumbsucker." Accessed June, 2018. https://www.imdb.com/title/tt0318761/?ref_=nv_sr_1.
Jamele, Dan. "What Is 4D Cinema?" *Film Journal International.* April 20, 2015. http://fj.webedia.us/columns/what-4d-cinema-and-why-you-should-care.
Jauss, Hans Robert. *Toward an Aesthetic of Reception.* Minneapolis: University of Minnesota Press, 1982.
Jay, Martin. *Downcast Eyes: The Denigration of Vision in Twentieth-Century French Thought.* Berkeley: University of California Press, 1994.
Kafer, Alison. *Feminist, Queer, Crip.* Bloomington: Indiana University Press, 2013.
Kawin, Bruce F. *Mindscreen: Bergman, Godard, and First-Person Film.* Rochester, NY: Dalkey Archive Press, 2006. Originally published 1978.
Keegan, Cáel M. "Epilogue—Event Horizon: Sense8." In *Lana and Lilly Wachowski,* 106–129. Urbana: University of Illinois Press, 2018.
Keegan, Cáel M. *Lana and Lilly Wachowski.* Urbana: University of Illinois Press, 2018.
Keith, Lois. "Punishment and Pity: Images and Representations of Disability, Illness and Cure." In *Take Up Thy Bed and Walk: Death, Disability and Cure in Classic Fiction for Girls,* 15–32. New York: Routledge, 2001.
Kim, Christine Sun. "Artist Christine Sun Kim Rewrites Closed Captions." *Pop-up Magazine,* October 2020. https://www.youtube.com/watch?v=tfe479qL8hg&ab_channel=Pop-UpMagazine.
Kim, Eunjung. "'A Man, with Same Feelings': Disability, Humanity, and Heterosexual Apparatus in Breaking the Waves, Born on the Fourth of July, Breathing Lessons, and Oasis." In *The Problem Body: Projecting Disability on Film,* edited by Sally Chivers and Nicole Markotić, 131–156. Columbus: Ohio State University Press, 2010.
Kirn, Walter. *Thumbsucker: A Novel.* New York: Anchor Books, 1999.
Kleege, Georgina. *Sight Unseen.* New Haven, CT: Yale University Press, 1999.
Koch, Gertrud. "Film as Experiment in Animation: Are Films Experiments on Human Beings?" Translated by Daniel Hendrickson. In *Animating Film Theory,* edited by Karen Beckman, 131–144. Durham, NC: Duke University Press, 2014.
Kutchins, Herb, and Stuart A. Kirk. *Making Us Crazy: DSM—The Psychiatric Bible and the Creation of Mental Disorders.* London: Constable, 1999.

LeBesco, Kathleen. "There's Something about Disabled People." *Disability Studies Quarterly* 24, no. 4 (2004): np. https://dsq-sds.org/article/view/895/1070.

Levin, Thomas Y. "The Acoustic Dimension: Notes on Film Sound." *Screen* 25, no. 3 (1984): 55–68.

Levin, Thomas Y. "For the Record: Adorno on Music in the Age of Its Technological Reproducibility." *October* 55 (Winter 1990): 23–47.

LightHouse for the Blind and Visually Impaired. "Every Pixar Film Is Now Accessible with Mobile Audio Description from Disney." February 23, 2016. https://lighthouse-sf.org/2016/02/23/every-pixar-film-is-now-accessible-with-mobile-audio-description-from-disney/#.

Longmore, Paul K. "Screening Stereotypes: Images of Disabled People in Television and Motion Pictures." In *Images of the Disabled, Disabling Images*, edited by Alan Gartner and Tom Joe, 65–78. New York: Praeger, 1987.

Mallon, Thomas. "In the Blink of an Eye." *New York Times*, June 15, 1997. https://www.nytimes.com/1997/06/15/books/in-the-blink-of-an-eye.html.

Manovich, Lev. *The Language of New Media*. Cambridge, MA: MIT Press, 2001.

Markotić, Nicole. "The Many in the One: Depression and Multiple Subjectivities in Inside Out." In "In Focus: Cripping Cinema and Media Studies," special issue, *JCMS: Journal of Cinema and Media Studies* 58, no. 4 (2019): 162–168.

Marks, Laura U. *The Skin of the Film: Intercultural Cinema, Embodiment, and the Senses*. Durham, NC: Duke University Press, 2000.

Marshall, Bill, and Robynn Jeananne Stilwell. *Musicals: Hollywood and Beyond*. Exeter, UK: Intellect, 2000.

McGlensey, Melissa. "Film Starring People with Down Syndrome Takes Aim at Misconceptions." The Mighty. September 30, 2015. https://themighty.com/2015/09/film-starring-people-with-down-syndrome-takes-aim-at-misconceptions/#/ixzz3nqadoRw3.

McMahan, Alison. *The Films of Tim Burton: Animating Live-Action in Contemporary Hollywood*. New York: Continuum, 2006.

McRuer, Robert. "Introduction: Compulsory Able-Bodiedness and Queer/Disabled Existence." In *Crip Theory: Cultural Signs of Queerness and Disability*, 1–32. New York: New York University Press, 2006.

McRuer, Robert. Introduction to "In Focus: Cripping Cinema and Media Studies," special issue, *JCMS: Journal of Cinema and Media Studies* 58, no. 4 (2019): 134–139.

McRuer, Robert. "Neoliberal Risks: Million Dollar Baby, Murderball, and Anti-National Sexual Positions." In *The Problem Body: Projecting Disability on Film*, edited by Sally Chivers and Nicole Markotić, 159–177. Columbus: Ohio State University Press, 2010.

Merleau-Ponty, Maurice. "The Intertwining—The Chiasm." In *The Visible and the Invisible*, edited by Claude Lefort, translated by Alphonso Lingis, 130–155. Evanston, IL: Northwestern University Press, 1968.

Metz, Christian, and Georgia Gurrieri. "Aural Objects." *Yale French Studies*, no. 60 (1980): 24–32.
Mills, Mara, and Jonathan Sterne. "After Word II: Dismediation—Three Proposals, Six Tactics." In *Disability Media Studies*, edited by Elizabeth Ellcessor and Bill Kirkpatrick, 365–378. New York: New York University Press, 2017.
Mitchell, David, and Sharon L. Snyder. "Minority Model: From Liberal to Neoliberal Futures of Disability." In *Routledge Handbook of Disability Studies*, 2nd ed., edited by Nick Watson and Simo Vehmas, 42–50. London: Routledge, 2020.
Mitchell, David T., and Sharon L. Snyder. *Narrative Prosthesis: Disability and the Dependencies of Discourse*. Ann Arbor: University of Michigan Press, 2001.
Mollow, Anna, and Robert McRuer. *Sex and Disability*. Durham, NC: Duke University Press, 2012.
Moore, Samantha. "Animating Unique Brain States." *Animation Studies Online Journal* (2011). https://journal.animationstudies.org/samantha-moore-animating-unique-brain-states.
Mulvey, Laura. "Visual Pleasure and Narrative Cinema." *Screen* 16, no. 3 (1975): 6–18.
Murphy, Robert F. *The Different World of the Disabled: The Body Silent*. New York: W. W. Norton, 1990.
Neale, Steve. "Questions of Genre." In *Film and Theory: An Anthology*, edited by Robert Stam and Toby Miller, 157–178. New York: New York University Press and Blackwell, 1991.
Neumeyer, David. *Meaning and Interpretation of Music in Cinema*. Bloomington: Indiana University Press, 2015.
Norden, Martin F. *The Cinema of Isolation: A History of Physical Disability in the Movies*. New Brunswick, NJ: Rutgers University Press, 1994.
Norris, Van. "Taking an Appropriate Line: Exploring Representation of Disability within British Mainstream Animation." *Animation Studies* 3 (2008): 67–76.
Oliver, Michael. *Understanding Disability: From Theory to Practice*. New York: St. Martin's, 1996.
O'Pray, Michael. *Avant-Garde Film: Forms, Themes and Passions*. London: Wallflower, 2003.
O'Pray, Michael. "Eisenstein and Stokes on Disney: Film Animation and Omnipotence." In *A Reader in Animation Studies*, edited by Jane Pilling, 195–202. London: John Libbey, 1997.
Parry, Ryan. "The True Story behind Jennifer Aniston's Cake—How Movie's Scriptwriter Was Inspired by the Brutal Murder of His Brother's Wife, Baby Daughter and Mother-in-Law." *DailyMail*, February 24, 2015. https://www.dailymail.co.uk/news/article-2962358/The-true-story-Jennifer-Aniston-s-Cake-movie-s-scriptwriter-inspired-brutal-murder-brother-s-wife-baby-daughter-mother-law.html.

Paterson, Kevin, and Bill Hughes. "Disability Studies and Phenomenology: The Carnal Politics of Everyday Life." *Disability and Society* 14, no. 5 (1999): 597–610.

Pernick, Martin S. "The Black Stork." In *The Black Stork: Eugenics and the Death of 'Defective' Babies in American Medicine and Motion Pictures since 1915*, 143–158. New York: Oxford University Press, 1996.

Pick, Anat. *Creaturly Poetics: Animality and Vulnerability in Literature and Film*. New York: Columbia University Press, 2011.

Plaktonrules. "Review of Blind." IMDB, September 11, 2014. https://www.imdb.com/review/rw3084973/?ref_=tt_urv.

Plumwood, Val. *Feminism and the Mastery of Nature*. New York: Routledge 1993.

Pointon, Ann. "Disability and Documentary." In *Framed: Interrogating Disability in the Media*, edited by Ann Pointon and Chris Davies, 84–92. London: British Film Institute/The Arts Council of England, 1997.

Price, Janet, and Margrit Shildrick. "Bodies Together: Touch, Ethics and Disability Theory." In *Disability/Postmodernity: Embodying Disability Theory*, edited by Marian Corker and Tom Shakespeare, 62–75. London: Continuum, 2002.

Price, Margaret. "The Bodymind Problem and the Possibilities of Pain." *Hypatia* 30, no. 1 (2015): 268–284.

Price, Margaret. *Mad at School: Rhetorics of Mental Disability and Academic Life*. Ann Arbor: University of Michigan Press, 2011.

Puar, Jasbir K. "Disability." *Transgender Studies Quarterly* 1, no. 1–2 (2014): 77–81.

Pyne, Jake. "Autistic Disruptions, Trans Temporalities: A Narrative 'Trap Door' in Time." *South Atlantic Quarterly* 120, no. 2 (2021): 343–361.

Quendler, Christian. "Subjective Cameras Locked-In and Out-of-Body." *Image and Narrative* 15, no. 1 (2014): 71–88.

Rangan, Pooja. "Audibilities: Voice and Listening in the Penumbra of Documentary—An Introduction." *Discourse* 39, no. 3 (2017): 279–291.

Razack, Sherene H. "From Pity to Respect: The Ableist Gaze and the Politics of Rescue." In *Looking White People in the Eye: Gender, Race, and Culture in Courtrooms and Classrooms*, 130–156. Toronto: University of Toronto Press, 1998.

Reed-Danahay, Deborah. *Auto/Ethnography: Rewriting the Self and the Social*. New York: Berg, 1997.

Reid-Hresko, John. "Deconstructing Disability: Three Episodes of South Park." *Disability Studies Quarterly* 25, no. 4 (2005): np.

Renov, Michael. "New Subjectivities: Documentary and Self-Representation in the Post-Vérité Age." In *Feminism and Documentary*. Vol. 5, *Visible Evidence*, edited by Diane Waldman and Janet Walker, 84–94. Minneapolis: University of Minnesota Press, 1999.

Richards, C. Alan, Caroline Brain, and Christian Martin Bailey. "Craniometaphyseal and Craniodiaphyseal Dysplasia, Head and Neck

Manifestations and Management." *Journal of Laryngology and Otology* 110, no. 4 (1996): 328–338.

Robinson, Octavian, and Jonathan Henner. "Authentic Voices, Authentic Encounters: Cripping the University through American Sign Language." *Disability Studies Quarterly* 38, no. 4 (2018): 1–23.

Robinson, Octavian E., and Jonathan Henner. "The Personal Is Political in *The Deaf Mute Howls*: Deaf Epistemology Seeks Disability Justice." *Disability and Society* 32, no. 9 (2017): 1416–1436.

Rohrer, Judy. "Toward a Full-Inclusion Feminism: A Feminist Deployment of Dis-ability Analysis." *Feminist Studies* 31, no. 1 (2005): 34–63.

Rotten Tomatoes. "Mask." Accessed June 2018. https://www.rottentomatoes.com/m/1013472_mask.

Ruderman Family Foundation. "On the 30th Anniversary of the ADA, Oscar-Winning Actress Octavia Spencer Joins the Ruderman Family Foundation for an Important Message on Authentic Representation." July 22, 2020. https://rudermanfoundation.org/press_releases/psa/.

Sample, Ian. "#TheDress: Have Researchers Solved the Mystery of Its Colour?" *Guardian*, May 14, 2015.

Samuels, Ellen. "Six Ways of Looking at Crip Time." *Disability Studies Quarterly* 37, no. 3 (2017): np.

Sanchez, Rebecca. "The Image: Cinematic Poetics and Deaf Vision." In *Deafening Modernism: Embodied Language and Visual Poetics in American Literature*, 121–146. New York: New York University Press, 2015.

Sandahl, Carrie. "It's All the Same Movie: Making Code of the Freaks." In "In Focus: Cripping Cinema and Media Studies," special issue, *JCMS: Journal of Cinema and Media Studies* 58, no. 4 (2019): 145–150.

Sandahl, Carrie. "Queering the Crip or Cripping the Queer: Intersections of Queer and Crip Identities in Solo Autobiographical Performance." *GLQ* 9, no. 1–2 (2003): 25–56.

Sarlin, David. "Touching Histories: Personality, Disability, and Sex in the 1930s." In *Sex and Disability*, edited by Anna Mollow and Robert McRuer, 145–162. Durham, NC: Duke University Press, 2012.

Sarto, Dan. "Signe Baumane, Mental Health and Her Brutally Frank 'Rocks in my Pockets.'" Animation World Network, March 26, 2015. http://awn.com/animationworld/signe-baumane-mental-health-and-her-brutally-frank-rocks-my-pockets.

Schalk, Sami. *Bodyminds Reimagined: (Dis)ability, Race, and Gender in Black Women's Speculative Fiction*. Durham, NC: Duke University Press, 2018.

Schalk, Sami. "Disability: Keywords for Gender and Sexuality Studies." New York University Press. Accessed October 22, 2021. https://keywords.nyupress.org/gender-and-sexuality-studies/essay/disability/.

Schalk, Sami. "Resisting Erasure: Reading (Dis)Ability and Race in Speculative Media." In *The Routledge Companion to Disability Studies*, edited by Katie Ellis, Gerard Goggin, Beth Haller, and Rosemary Curtis, 137–146. New York: Routledge, 2020.

Schormans, Ann Fudge. "Media Review: Tying Your Own Shoes—One Film, Four Perspectives." *Journal on Developmental Disabilities* 17, no. 1 (2011): 83–92.

Schwartz, Karen, Zana Marie Lutfiyya, and Nancy Hansen. "Social Imagery in the Film Million Dollar Baby: An Analysis Based on Wolf Wolfensberger's Social Role Valorization." *Disability Studies Quarterly* 25, no. 3 (2005): np.

Scully, Jackie Leach. "Deaf Identities in Disability Studies." In *Routledge Handbook of Disability Studies*, 2nd ed., edited by Nick Watson and Simo Vehmas, 145–157. New York: Routledge, 2020.

Shakespeare, Tom, and Nicholas Watson. "The Social Model of Disability: An Outdated Ideology?" *Research in Social Science and Disability* 2 (2002): 9–28.

Sheets-Johnstone, Maxine. "Fundamental and Inherently Interrelated Aspects of Animation." In *Moving Ourselves, Moving Others: Motion and Emotion in Intersubjectivity, Consciousness and Language*, edited by Ad Foolen, Ulrike M. Ludtke, Timothy P. Racine, and Jordan Zlatev, 29–55. Amsterdam: John Benjamins, 2012.

Shildrick, Margrit. "Sexuality, Subjectivity and Anxiety." In *Dangerous Discourses of Disability, Subjectivity and Sexuality*, 81–102. London: Palgrave Macmillan, 2009.

Siebers, Tobin. "Disability in Theory: From Social Constructionism to the New Realism of the Body." *American Literary History* 13, no. 4 (2001): 737–754.

Silverman, Kaja. *The Acoustic Mirror: The Female Voice in Psychoanalysis and Cinema*. Bloomington: Indiana University Press, 1988.

Simner, Julia, and Edward M. Hubbard. *Oxford Handbook of Synesthesia*. Oxford: Oxford University Press, 2013.

Smit, Christopher, and Anthony Enns. *Screening Disability: Essays on Cinema and Disability*. Lanham, MD: University Press of America, 2001.

Smith, Sidonie, and Julia Watson. *Reading Autobiography: A Guide for Interpreting Life Narratives*. London: University of Minnesota Press, 2010.

Snyder, Sharon L., and David T. Mitchell. "Body Genres: An Anatomy of Disability in Film." In *The Problem Body: Projecting Disability on Film*, edited by Sally Chivers and Nicole Markotić, 179–204. Columbus: Ohio State University Press, 2010.

Sobchack, Vivian. "Animation and Automation, or, the Incredible Effortfulness of Being." *Screen* 50, no. 4 (2009): 375–391.

Sobchack, Vivian. *Carnal Thoughts: Embodiment and Moving Image Culture*. Berkeley: University of California Press, 2004.

Sobchack, Vivian. "Film's Body." In *The Address of the Eye: A Phenomenology of Film Experience*, 203–248. Princeton, NJ: Princeton University Press, 1992.

Sobchack, Vivian. "'Surge and Splendor': A Phenomenology of the Hollywood Historical Epic." *Representation* 1, no. 29 (1990): 24–49.

Sobchack, Vivian. "What My Fingers Knew: The Cinesthetic Subject, or Vision in the Flesh." *Senses of Cinema*. 2000. https://www.sensesofcinema.com/2000/conference-special-effects-special-affects/fingers/.

Stawarska, Beata. "From the Body Proper to Flesh: Merleau-Ponty on Intersubjectivity." In *Feminist Interpretations of Maurice Merleau-Ponty*, edited by Dorothea Olkowski and Gail Weiss, 91–106. University Park, PA: Penn State University Press, 2006.

Steinbock, Eliza. *Shimmering Images: Trans Cinema, Embodiment, and the Aesthetics of Change*. Durham, NC: Duke University Press, 2019.

Straayer, Chris. "Phantom Penis: Extrapolating Neuroscience and Employing Imagination for Trans Male Sexual Embodiment." *Studies in Gender and Sexuality* 21, no. 4 (2020): 251–279.

Straayer, Chris. "Trans Men's Stealth Aesthetics: Navigating Penile Prosthetics and 'Gender Fraud.'" *Journal of Visual Culture* 19, no. 2 (2020): 254–271.

Stephens, Lindsay, Susan Ruddick, and Patricia McKeever. "Disability and Deleuze: An Exploration of Becoming and Embodiment in Children's Everyday Environments." *Body & Society* 21, no. 2 (2015): 194–220.

Stump, Madeline. "The Rambling of a Chronically Ill Mad Trans Femme." *Queer Disability Studies Network* (blog), November 3, 2021. https://queerdisabilitystudies.wordpress.com/the-ramblings-of-a-chronically-ill-mad-trans-femme/?fbclid=IwAR2MLgjSMWStAe7nshChhbowLDaMrouFolrtYhkt-1qkcm_w3NfifhoTAfw.

Symons, Stéphane. "'The Creature That Can Still Survive': Walter Benjamin on Mickey Mouse and Rhythmic Movement." *Telos*, no. 176 (2016): 165–186.

Thomas, Gareth M., and Dikaios Sakellariou. *Disability, Normalcy, and the Everyday*. New York: Routledge, 2018.

Timmons, Niamh. "My Gender Is Crip: Engaging the Experience of Being Trans and Disabled." In *TransNarratives: Scholarly and Creative Works on Transgender Experience*, edited by Kristi Carter and James Brunton, 249–261. Toronto: Women's Press, an imprint of CSP Books, 2021.

Timmons, Niamh. "Towards a Trans Feminist Disability Studies." *Journal of Feminist Scholarship* 17, no. 17 (2020): 46–63.

Transnoodle. "How the World's First Deaf Rock Band Feels Music." *Medium*, June 9, 2017. http://medium.com/dose/how-the-worlds-only-deaf-rock-band-feels-music-9508534c398f.

Waldschmidt, Anne. "Disability Goes Cultural: The Cultural Model of Disability as an Analytical Tool." In *Culture—Theory—Disability: Encounters between Disability Studies and Cultural Studies*, edited by Anne Waldschmidt, Hanjo

Berressem, and Moritz Ingwersen, 19–27. Bielefeld, Germany: Transcript Verlag, 2017.

Wark, McKenzie. "The Cis Gaze and Its Others (for Shola)." *E-Flux Journal*, no. 117 (2021): 1–12. https://www.e-flux.com/journal/117/387134/the-cis-gaze-and-its-others-for-shola/.

Warren, Karen. *Ecofeminist Philosophy: A Western Perspective on What It Is and Why It Matters*. Lanham, MD: Rowman and Littlefield, 2000.

Watson, Nick, and Simo Vehmas. "Disability Studies: Into the Multidisciplinary Future." In *Routledge Handbook of Disability Studies*, 2nd ed., 3–13. London: Routledge, 2020.

Wells, Paul. *Animation: Genre and Authorship*. London: Wallflower, 2002.

Whittington, William. "The Sonic Playpen: Sound Design and Technology in Pixar's Animated Shorts." In *The Oxford Handbook of Sound Studies*, edited by Trevor Pinch and Karin Bijsterveld, 367–386. Oxford: Oxford University Press, 2012.

Williams, Alan. "Is Sound Recording Like a Language?" *Yale French Studies*, no. 60 (1980): 51–66.

Williams, Linda. "Film Bodies: Gender, Genre and Excess." *Film Quarterly* 44, no. 4 (1991): 2–13.

Wilson, Anne, and Peter Beresford. "Madness, Distress and Postmodernity: Putting the Record Straight." In *Disability/Postmodernity: Embodying Disability Theory*, edited by Miriam Corker and Tom Shakespeare, 143–158. London: Continuum, 2002.

Wolbring, Gregor. "Meaning of Disability, Body Image, Person and Health." *Gregor Wolbring and the Wolbpack* (blog). Accessed February 15, 2021. https://wolbring.wordpress.com/meaning-of-disability-body-image-person-and-health/.

Wollen, Peter. "The Two Avant-Gardes." *Studio International* 190, no. 978 (November/December 1975): 171–175.

Young, Paul. "Film Sound." *Oxford Bibliographies*, June 26, 2012. http://dx.doi.org/10.1093/obo/9780199791286-0100.

FILMOGRAPHY

A Is for Autism. Tim Webb, UK, 1992.
Aladdin. Ron Clements and John Musker, US, 1992.
American Dad! Mike Barker, Seth MacFarlane, and Matt Weitzman, US, 2005–.
Animated Minds. Andy Glynne, UK, 2003–2008.
The Awesomes. Seth Meyers and Michael Shoemaker, US, 2013–2015.
Baby Driver. Edgar Wright, UK, US, 2017.
A Beautiful Mind. Ron Howard, US, 2001.
Beauty and the Beast. Gary Trousdale and Kirk Wise, US, 1991.
Big Mouth. Jennifer Flackett, Andrew Goldberg, and Nick Kroll, US, 2017–.
Black Sun. Gary Tarn, UK, 2005
Blind. Eskil Vogt, Norway, 2014.
The Blind Boy. S. Lubin, US, 1908.
Bojack Horseman. Raphael Bob-Waksberg, US, 2014–.
Born on the Fourth of July. Oliver Stone, US, 1989.
Breaking the Waves. Lars von Trier, Denmark, Sweden, France, Netherlands, Norway, Iceland, Spain, 1996.
Breathe. Andy Serkis, UK, 2017.
Bright Victory. Mark Robson, US, 1951.
Brother. Adam Elliot, Australia, 2000.
The Cabinet of Dr. Caligari. Robert Wiene, Germany, 1920.
Cake. Daniel Barnz, US, 2014.
Chicken Run. Peter Lord and Nick Park, UK, US, France, 2000.
Children of a Lesser God. Randa Haines, US, 1989.
City Lights. Charlie Chaplin, US, 1931.
A Close Shave [a.k.a. *Wallace and Gromit in A Close Shave*]. Nick Park, UK, 1995.
CODA. Sian Heder, US, 2021.

Code of the Freaks. Salome Chasnoff, US, 2020.
Cousin. Adam Elliot, Australia, 1999.
Crash. David Cronenberg, Canada, 1996.
Creature Comforts. Nick Park, UK, 1989.
Creature Comforts America. Merlin Crossingham, Dave Osmand, and Richard Starzak, UK, US, 2007.
Creature Discomforts. Leonard Cheshire Disability and Aardman Animations, UK, 2007.
Crip Camp. James Lebrecht and Nicole Newnham, US, 2020.
Disclosure. Sam Feder, US, 2020.
The Diving Bell and the Butterfly. Julian Schnabel, France, US, 2007.
Dr. Strangelove or: How I Learned to Stop Worrying and Love the Bomb. Stanley Kubrick, UK, 1964.
Dumb and Dumber. Peter Farrelly and Bobby Farrelly, US, 1994.
The Elephant Man. Davis Lynch, US, UK, 1980.
Even Dwarfs Started Small. Werner Herzog, West Germany, 1970.
Everything's Gonna Be Okay. Josh Thomas, US, 2020–.
An Eyeful of Sound. Samantha Moore, Canada, Netherlands, UK, 2010.
Family Guy. Seth MacFarlane and David Zuckerman, US, 1999–.
Fantasia. James Algar, Samuel Armstrong, Ford Beebe Jr., Norman Ferguson, David Hand, Jim Handley, T. Hee, Wilfred Jackson, Hamilton Luske, Bill Roberts, Paul Satterfield, and Ben Sharpsteen, US, 1941.
Ferdinand. Carlos Saldanha, US, 2017.
Finding Dory. Andrew Stanton and Angus MacLane, US, 2016.
Forbidden Maternity. Diane Maroger, France, 2002.
Forrest Gump. Robert Zemeckis, US, 1994.
Frank. Lenny Abrahamson, UK, Ireland, US, 2014.
Freaks. Tod Browning, US, 1932.
Frozen. Chris Buck and Jennifer Lee, US, 2013.
Futurama. David X. Cohen and Matt Groening, US, 1999–2013.
Golden Eighties. Chantal Akerman, France, Belgium, Switzerland, 1986.
A Grand Day Out [a.k.a. *Wallace and Gromit—Una Fantastica Gita*]. Nick Park, UK, 1989.
Herman Slobbe [*Blind Child 2*]. Johan van der Keuken, Netherlands, 1966.
Hot Pursuit. Bernard McEveety and Bernard Kowalski, US, 1984.
In My Language. Mel Baggs, US, 2007.
Inside Out. Pete Docter, US, 2015.
Invalid's Adventures. Unknown, UK, 1907.
Ishihara. Yoav Brill, Israel, 2010.
Janela da Alma [*Window to the Soul*]. Walter Carvalho and João Jardim, Brazil, 2001.

John and Michael. Shira Avni, Canada, 2004.
Knick Knack. John Lasseter, US, 1989.
Lady in the Lake. Robert Montgomery, US, 1947.
Laser Beak Man. Tim Sharp, Australia, 2011.
Learning to Drive. Roderick E. Stevens, US, 2015.
Le Labyrinthe. Mathieu Labaye, Belgium, 2013.
Loop. Erica Milsom, US, 2020.
Luxo Jr. John Lasseter, US, 1986.
Many Happy Returns. Marjut Rimminen, UK, 1996.
Mary and Max. Adam Elliot, Australia, 2009.
Mask. Peter Bogdanovich, US, 1985.
Maternity Forbidden. Diane Mroger, US, 2002.
A Matter of Loaf and Death [a.k.a. *Wallace and Gromit in Trouble at' Mill*]. Nick Park, UK, 2008.
Million Dollar Baby. Clint Eastwood, US, 2004.
My Depression: The Up and Down and Up of It. Elizabeth Swados, US, 2014.
My Left Foot. Jim Sheridan, Ireland, UK, 1989.
The Near-Sighted Cyclist. Unknown, France, 1907.
Near-Sighted Mary. Unknown, US, 1909.
New Mindset. Danny Capozzi, UK, 2018.
Oasis. Lee Chang-dong, South Korea, 2002.
Orgesticulanismus. Mathieu Labay, Belgium, 2008.
Orphans of the Storm. D.W. Griffith, US, 1921.
The Other Side of the Mountain. Larry Peerce, US, 1975.
The Other Side of the Mountain, Part 2. Larry Peerce, US, 1978.
Out of Sight. Daniel Syrkin, Israel, 2006.
Passion Fish. John Sayles, US, 1992.
A Patch of Blue. Guy Green, US, 1965.
Petra's Poem. Shira Avni, Canada, 2012.
The Boys. Eric Kripke, US, 2009.
The Piano. Jane Campion, New Zealand, Australia, France, 1993.
Pride of the Marines. Delmer Davies, US, 1945.
Psycho. Alfred Hitchcock, US, 1960.
Rick and Morty. Dan Harmon and Justin Roiland, US, 2013–.
Rocks in My Pockets. Signe Baumane, US, Latvia, 2014.
Ryan. Chris Landreth, Canada, 2004.
Say No to Leonard Cheshire. Paul Darke, UK, 2001.
Sense8. J. Michael Straczynski, Lana Wachowski, and Lilly Wachowski, US, 2015–2018.
Shaun the Sheep Movie. Mark Burton and Richard Starzak, UK, France, US, 2015.
A Shift in Perception. Dan Monceaux, Australia, 2006.
Shutter Island. Martin Scorsese, US, 2010.

The Sign for Love. Iris Ben Moshe and El-Ad Cohen, Israel, 2017.
The Simpsons. James L. Brooks, Matt Groening, and Sam Simon, US, 1989–.
Some Protection. Marjut Rimminen, UK, 1987.
Something Special. Allan Johnston, UK, 2003–2005.
Songbirds. Brian Hill, UK, 2007.
South Park. Trey Parker, Matt Stone, and Brian Graden, US, 1997–.
Special. Ryan O'Connell, US, 2019–.
Still Alice. Richard Glatzer and Wash Westmoreland, US, France, 2014.
Stuck on You. Peter Farrelly and Bobby Farrelly, US, 2003.
There's Something About Mary. Peter Farrelly and Bobby Farrelly, US, 1998.
Third Body. Zohar Melinek-Ezra and Roey Victoria Heifetz, Israel, Germany, 2020.
Thumbsucker. Mike Mills, US, 2005.
Tying Your Own Shoes. Shira Avni, Canada, 2009.
Uncle. Adam Elliot, Australia, 1996.
V for Vendetta. James McTeigue, US, UK, and Germany, 2005.
Vital Signs: Crip Culture Talks Back. David E. Mitchell and Sharon L. Snyder, US, 1996.
Wait Until Dark. Terence Young, US, 1967.
Wallace & Gromit: The Curse of the Were-Rabbit [a.k.a *Wallace and Gromit: The Great Vegetable Plot*]. Steve Box and Nick Park, UK, 2005.
The Waterdance. Neal Jimenez and Michael Steinberg, US, 1992.
When Billy Broke His Head. Billy Golfus, US, 1995.
Whose Life Is It Anyway? John Badham, US, 1981.
The Wolf of Wall Street. Martin Scorsese, US, 2013.
Wonderstruck. Todd Haynes, US, 2017.
X-Men. Bryan Singer, US, 2000.
Zootopia. Bryon Howard, Rich Moore, and Jared Bush, US, 2016.

INDEX

Page locators in italics refer to figures

Aardman Animations, 10, 31, 55, 56
ableism: compulsory able-bodiedness, 82–83, 121; internalized, ix, 105, 116; paternalistic attitude of pity, 40, 42. *See also* death; eugenics; medical/individual model of disability; social model of disability
ableist gaze, 25n21, 30–67, 160; able-bodied/able-minded audience assumed, 162–65; death as redemption from disability, 39–43; happy endings for able-bodied spectators, 44–51; horror of becoming disabled, 35–39; in live-action films, 21, 32–35; subversion of, 31–35, 51, 59, 101, 113, 153, 161, 164–65. *See also* gaze; horror genre; mainstream genres; medical gaze; melodrama; spectatorship
abstract animation style, 44, 100, 137, 146, 149, 151, 161; in *Many Happy Returns*, 98, 112–13, 117, 119, 121
accessibility of spectatorship, 15, 23, 159–60, 171n5; accommodating bodily and sensory diversity at the movie theater, 165–70, 171nn13, 14; assumption of spectator as temporarily able-bodied, 162–65; captions and subtitles, 125, 128, 166, 168; four-dimensional screenings, 150; mundane aspects, 163; unintentional, 167; vibrations, 128–29, 166

acousmêtre, 130–36, 155n34; de-acousmêtrization, 134–36; semi-acousmêtre, 130, 132, 135
actors: able-bodied replacements (cripface), 159; with disabilities, xi, 3, 35, 81, 137, 156n55, 166; voice-overs by professional, 94n17, 139
The Address of the Eye (Sobchak), 20
Adorno, Theodor, 15, 120–21
Ahmed, Sara, 117
A Is for Autism (*AIFA*, Tim Webb, 1992), 70, 87–90, 92, 167
Aladdin (Disney, 1992), 139
AMC theaters, 125
American Sign Language (ASL), 126–27, 151, 166; grammar of, 140–42, 161
Americans with Disabilities Act (ADA), ix, 13–14, 39
anempathetic music, 150–51
animals, disabled, used to explain human behavior, 8, 58–60
Animals in Film (Burt), 57
animaphilia, 55–56
Animated Minds (Andy Glynne, 2003–2018), xi, 2, 87
animation, 7; all levels of life represented, 91; alternative worlds created by, xii, 1, 10–11, 23, 35, 83, 161–62; animated musical documentary, 136, 139, 142–43, 151, 167;

INDEX

for children, 7–9, 150; definitions of, 5–6, 145; live-action techniques used in, 109, 127–28; move toward crip animation, 55–61; production processes foregrounded, 89–90; subversive nature of, 7, 10, 31, 59, 61, 101; therapeutic functions, 100–101. *See also* avant-garde and experimental animation; crip animation; soundtrack

animation studies, 5–6, 10, 23n2, 145. *See also* film and television studies

antagonists, as disabled, 15–16, 27–28n67, 34, 36

antipathological narratives, 71, 75–76, 79

anxiety: about being disabled, 36–37, 160; about genders, 33; as disability category, 45–48

Audio Motion (Coyle), 145

Audio-Vision: Sound on Screen (Chion), 138

audism, 22, 126–28, 144; reinforcement of in soundtrack, 161; rethinking through crip animated documentary, 150–54; undermined by acousmêtre, 130

autism, 2, 8, 26n36, 87–88, 95n37, 96n44; autibiography, 88, 96n45; autistic-trans stories, 88–89. *See also A is for Autism* (Tim Webb, 1992); *Loop* (Erica Milsom, 2020)

"Autistic Disruptions, Trans Temporalities" (Pyne), 88–89

autobiographical films, xi, 21, 37, 44, 53, 70–80; alternative genres, 75; ethnography integrated with, 71, 75, 77

autoethnographic films, 13, 21–22, 71, 75, 77

autosomatography, 71

avant-garde and experimental animation, 7, 30–31, 98; aimed at cinephiles, 9–10; dreamlike/intoxicated states in, 21, 101–2, 109–14, 116–17, 119–21; therapeutic role of, 100–101. *See also* animation; hybrid style

avant-garde and experimental films, non-animated, 9–11, 30. *See also* abstract animation style; animation; avant-garde animation; hybrid style; independent films

Avni, Shira, 80–86, 90–92

Baby Driver (Edgar Wright, 2017), 166
Ballin, Albert, 126

Baril, Alexandre, 13
Barry, Kevin M., 13
Bauby, Jean-Dominique, 44, 51–55
Baumane, Signe, 11, 71–74, 78
A Beautiful Mind (Ron Howard, 2001), 2
Beauty and the Beast (Disney, 1991), 139
Behlil, Melis, 55–56
being-in-the-world, xi, 11, 21, 50, 112; "middle," sense of, 85, 85, 86
being-in-the-world with others, 50, 85–86, 92
Belton, John, 127
Benjamin, Walter, 6, 7, 100, 107, 110; *On Hashish*, 116–17
Ben-Moshe, Liat, 57–58, 59–60
Biderman, Shai, 38
Big Mouth (Netflix), 9
Black Sun (Gary Tarn, 2005), 89, 109, 113–14, 133
Blind (Eskil Vogt, 2014), 98
The Blind Boy (S. Lubin, 1908), 97–98
blindness. *See* vision disabilities and blindness
Blue Sky, 8
body: ability-diverse, 120; cinematic, 19–20; cinesthetic address to, 130; disabled as excessive, 4, 19, 31, 34, 39–40; genres of, 19, 34, 42; hidden phenomena uncovered by disabled, 17; indexical, 1, 135, 151, 153, 159, 161, 55108; instability of, 69; nonexposure/replacement of indexical, 134–36, 151; normative, subversion of, 120; outside cinematic frame, 22, 130; reflexive nature of, 91–92; sensible/sentient, 18–20, 121. *See also* embodying spectatorship
bodymind, xii, xviii12, 4–5, 48, 117; movements of reframed, 145–46; social limitations over, 121, 161
Bojack Horseman (Netflix), 9, 26n43
Born on the Fourth of July (Oliver Stone, 1989), 82
Bouldin, Joanna, 6
Breaking the Waves (Lars von Trier, 1996), 82
Brill, Yoav. *See Ishihara* (Yoav Brill, 2010)
Brooke, Michael, 56
Browning, Tod, 3, 35, 36
Buchan, Susan, 6
Buñuel, Luis, 52

INDEX

Burt, Jonathan, 57
Burton, Joanna, 88–89

The Cabinet of Dr. Caligari (Robert Wiene, 1920), 2
Cake (Daniel Barnz, 2014), 31, 32, 44, 48–51, 54
camera: as active presence, 52; bodily analogy, 19–20; subjective, 21, 31–32, 43, 44, 51–53, 55
Capitol Crawl (March 12, 1990), 39
captions and subtitles, 125, 128, 166, 168
Carey, Allison C., 57–58
Carnal Thoughts (Sobchak), 20
Carroll, Noël, 38
Carter-Long, Lawrence, 40
Caswell, Estelle, 163
Chaplin, Charlie, 97
Chapman, Chris, 57–58
charities, 31, 58–59
Chen, Mel Y., 59
Cher, 39
Cherney, James L., 82
Cheu, Johnson, 109–10
chiasm of senses, 19, 69
Chicken Run (2000), 8, 56
children, animated films targeting, 7–9, 150
Children of a Lesser God (Randa Haines, 1989), 137
Chion, Michel, 127, 129–35, 137, 150
Chivers, Sally, 36, 37
Cholodenko, Alan, 5
Chrisley, Ron, 97
chronic pain, 48–51
cinema: deaf/silent and hearing/speaking cinema, 128; diasporic/intercultural cinema, 20–21, 152–53, 164; as form of animation, 5–6; "illegitimate" beginnings of, 120; indexical nature of, 1, 55; musical genre conventions, 139, 142; silent film, 16, 97, 120, 128, 152
cinema studies, 15–16
cinematic apparatus, 5–6, 16, 90, 92, 145, 159–60, 163–64; bodily analogy, 19–20; critique of, 152–53. *See also* production processes
cinematic body, 19–20

cinephilia, 55–56
cine-zoo animaphilia, 60, 66n90
circular narrative, 3, 44, 165
City Lights (Charlie Chaplin, 1931), 97
CODA (Siân Heder, 2021), x–xi, 89, 137
Code of the Freaks (Salome Chasnoff, 2020), 3, 36, 162, 165
collaboration: and accessible spectatorships, 160, 169; between disabled and temporarily able-bodied filmmakers, 21–22, 70, 86–93; intersubjective encounters and touch ethics, 80–86; reflexive, 22, 70, 86–93; and self-representation, 22, 80, 87, 90, 92. *See also* filmmakers, able-bodied/able-minded
color blindness, 98, 101–5. See also *Ishihara* (Yoav Brill, 2010)
Color Film Was Built for White People (Caswell), 163
coming-of-age films, 39–40, 44–48
community of people with disabilities: inner-community solidarity, 35, 36, 38; possibility of joining negated in films, 44–45, 47–48, 51
"compensation," criticism of, 19
composite model of disability, 13
consciousness, 116–17; optical unconscious, 100, 107–8, 113
Couser, G. Thomas, 71, 88
Coyle, Rebecca, 129, 138, 145, 150, 165
Crash (David Cronenberg, 1996), 2
Creature Comforts (Aardman Animations, 1989), 55–60, 94n21
Creature Comforts America, 56
Creature Discomforts (Aardman Animations, 2007–2008), 31, 32, 55–60, 87
crip, as term, 4
crip animation, 4–5, 70; auditory expression of, 130; deaf audience, films aimed at, 89, 125, 128, 166, 168; dreamlike/intoxicated states in, 21, 101–2, 109–14, 116–17, 119–21; genres of, 159; move toward, 55–61; rethinking audism through, 150–54; sound and movement in, 145–50; vococentrism challenged in, 137. *See also* abstract animation style; animation; documentaries, animated; soundtrack; synesthesia; *specific films*

Crip Camp (James LeBrecht and Nicole Newnham, 2020), 39, 70–71, 168
cripping, as term, 66–67n91
crip theory. *See* critical disability studies/crip theory
Crip Theory (McRuer), 82
critical disability studies/crip theory, x, 2–3, 11, 15, 17, 107, 117. *See also* crip theory

Darke, Paul, 42, 60
Davis, Brian, 81
D/deaf people, 125–26; all senses used by, 143–44; Deaf Pride movement, 131; "people of the eye"/visual community, 128–29, 141; sociolinguistic minority groups, 127. *See also* hearing; sound
deaf audience, films aimed at, 89; captions and subtitles, 125, 128, 166, 168
deaf studies, 128, 131, 144, 156n56, 167
death, 44; medical negligence as reason to die, 41, 42, 54; as narrative relief, 34–35; as only alternative for disabled people, 38; as redemption from disability, 39–43
Dennis, Roy L. "Rocky," 98
Descartes, René, 18
developmental disabilities, 80–81; ADHD, 45–48; autism, 2, 8, 26n36, 87–88, 95n37, 96n44; Down syndrome, 80–86, 90–93. *See also* mental disability
Diagnostic and Statistical Manual (*DSM*), viii, 13–14
diasporic/intercultural cinema, 20–21, 152–53, 164
diegetic sound, 105, 127, 143–44, 147–48, 152; musical sound, 140–41; non-or extra-diegetic phenomena, 92, 133, 140, 144, 148
Digital Disability: The Social Construction of Disability in New Media (Goggin and Newelll, 2003), 14
disability: being-in-the-world with, xi, 11, 21, 50; composite model of, 13; cultural model of, 12; death as redemption from, 39–43; decarcerating, 60; lives worth living, social construction of, 34, 41, 42, 53, 160; medical/individual model of, 7–8, 11–12, 34–35, 48, 101, 106–9; pharmaceutical treatment of, 45–49, 76–77, 79; social aspects of, 145–46; social model of, 8, 11–12, 76, 92, 106–7, 126, 166–67; as spectacle, 19, 23, 30–31, 39, 54, 108, 160, 161. *See also* identity category of disability
Disability and New Media (Ellis and Kent, 2013), 14
Disability and Social Media: Global Perspectives (Ellis and Goggin, 2017), 14–15
Disability Incarcerated: Imprisonment and Disability in the United States and Canada (Ben-Moshe, Chapman, and Carey), 57–58
disability media studies, 14–18, 163
Disability Media Studies (ed. Ellcessor and Kirkpatrick), 15, 17, 163
disability rights movement, viii, 2, 40–41, 70, 126–27, 168; Nothing about us without us/Nothing Without Us, 40–41, 70, 90, 159–60. *See also* Mad Pride movement
disability studies: of D/deaf identities, 125–26; deaf critique studies, 128, 131, 144, 156n56, 167; as dis/ability studies, 12–13; embodiment model of, 20; feminist, 11; intersectionality with film studies, 15–18, 34, 40; intersectionality with phenomenology, 23, 69, 70, 100, 117; third-phase scholarship, 15–18, 34, 42–43; touch ethics of, 80, 86; writing models, 11–12. *See also* medical/individual model of disability; social model of disability
Disclosure (Sam Feder, 2020), 3
Disney, 7, 8, 139, 165
The Diving Bell and the Butterfly (Julian Schnabel, 2004), 31, 32, 44, 51–55
Doane, Mary Ann, 127, 138
DocSociety, 168
documentaries, animated, 71–72, 77, 161; about loss of sight, 113–14; animated musical documentary, 136, 139, 142–43, 151, 167; authoritarian role of narration in, 132, 133; new wave of about, 92; rethinking sonic pleasures and audism through, 150–54. *See also My Depression: The Up and Down and Up of It* (Elizabeth Swados, 2014); *Rocks in My Pockets* (Signe Baumane, 2014)

documentary film, mainstream: ableist and medical gaze reproduced in, 34; filmmaker's point of view, 77–78
Documentary Filmmakers with Disabilities, 168
Downcast Eyes: The Denigration of Vision in Twentieth-Century French Thought, (Jay) 100
Down syndrome, collaborative films about, 80–86, 90–93
dreamlike/intoxicated states in avant-garde animation, 21, 101–2, 109–14, 116–17, 119–21; animation techniques used for, 98–99, 122n13
Durham, April, 87

Earworm video series, 163
Edna (protagonist, *A Shift in Perception*), 110–11
Eisenstein, Sergey, xi, 6, 23n19
The Elephant Man (David Lynch, 1980), 2, 16, 30, 32, 34, 37–39, 42; bodily excess in, 40; erasure of options for living with disability, 54
Ellcessor, Elizabeth, 14, 15, 17, 128, 162–63
Elliott, Adam, 11, 90, 156n48
Ellis, Katie, 14–15
embodying spectatorship, xi, 13, 18–23, 68–96, 169; disabled body at center of inquiry, 69; embodied intelligence of spectators, 20; expectation, mismatch with, 126; intersubjective encounters and touch ethics, 80–86; "lived body," 117; and production processes, 90–91. See also autobiographical films; body; first-person crip films; intersubjective relations; spectatorship; touch
emotions, 22, 31, 53, 78–79, 81, 83; emotional and physical pain linked, 48–51, 54; and melodrama, 42–43; and music, 131, 137–45, 140–42; and sound design, 128
ethnography, 71, 75, 77, 108
eugenics, 33, 34, 62n17, 81, 92; "lives worth living," 34, 41, 42, 53, 81, 160
Everything's Gonna Be Okay (Josh Thomas), 96n44
excess, bodily, 4, 19, 31, 34, 39–40, 133–34

expressionist cinematic style, 35, 38–39
Extraordinary Bodies: Figuring Physical Disability in American Culture and Literature (Garland-Thomson), 32–33
An Eyeful of Sound (Samantha Moore, 2010), 98, 101, 105–9, 112, 135, 136; indexical body not represented in, 134–36, 151; indexical voice in, 132–37; sensory excess in, 133–34

Ferdinand (Blue Sky), 8
film and television studies, 5, 15–18, 34, 40, 55, 163. See also animation studies; media studies
filmmakers, able-bodied/able-minded, 160; ally position, problematics of addressed, 80, 84. See also collaboration; intersubjective relations; mainstream genres
filmmakers with disabilities, 21–22, 80; collaboration between disabled and temporarily able-bodied, 21–22, 70, 86–93; involvement level of, 61, 70, 80, 87
Finding Dory (2016), 8
Finding Nemo (2003), 8
Finger, Anne, 82
Finkelstein, Adi, 49
Finkelstein, Frank, 111
first-person crip films, 21–22, 70–80; films by non-disabled filmmakers disguised as, 22, 80, 87, 88, 92, 160; visual metaphors in, 79–80. See also *My Depression: The Up and Down and Up of It* (Elizabeth Swados, 2014); *Rocks in My Pockets* (Signe Baumane, 2014)
Fleischer, Doris Zames, 41
Forbidden Maternity (Diane Maroger, 2002), 92
Frankfurt School, 100, 121
Freaks (Tod Browning, 1932), 2, 3, 30, 32, 34–36, 42
"freak shows," 9, 16, 39
Freud, Sigmund, 51
Friedner, Michel, 128–29, 131, 143–44, 166
Frozen (Disney), 8

Gallaudet University, 128
Garland-Thomson, Rosemarie, 11, 32–33

gaze: on blind women, 109–10; cissexist, 33; erotic, 32–33; human, at animals, 57–60; male, 33; stare distinguished from, 4–5, 11, 17, 33; and vision disabilities, 99, 104; voyeuristic, 57–58; zoo gaze, 57. *See also* ableist gaze; medical gaze
gender dysphoria, viii, 13
"gender identity disorder" (GID), viii, x, xvn2, 13–14
genres: "animation film," 6; bodily, 19, 34, 42; hybrid style, 10, 31, 55, 139, 160; musical genre conventions, 139, 142–43. *See also* autobiographical films; documentaries; horror; hybrid style; mainstream genres; melodrama
Ginsburg, Faye, 14–15
Goggin, Gerard, 14–15
Gorbman, Claudia, 137–38
Gorney, Edna, 58
Gossett, Reina, 88–89
grotesque imagery, 9, 10, 120

Halberstam, Jack, x, xi, 6–8, 117
Hall, Stuart, 117
Haller, Beth, 14
Hansen, Miriam, 120
Hansen, Nancy, 42
"happy endings," 44–51, 54
haptic spectatorship, 22, 109–19, 121
hearing, 22–23, 121; and listening, 127, 129, 133, 140; and sensory phantom, 133, 170; and sight as dichotomous, 128–29, 151; and synesthesia, 131–32, 134, 136–37, 140; and tactile sense, 144; vision, connection with, 129, 131, 140. *See also* D/deaf people; hierarchy of senses; music; sound; soundtrack; voice; voice-overs
Helmreich, Stefan, 128–29, 131, 143–44, 166
Henner, Jonathan, 126–27
Herman Slobbe / Blind Child 2 (Johan van der Keuken, 1996), 101
heterosexuality, compulsory, 82
hierarchy of senses, 5, 98–100, 126, 131–34, 151–54, 161, 164–65; hearing and sight as dichotomous, 128–29, 151; and physical distance, 119; privileging of vision, 21–22, 101, 112–13, 142; sound, 137–39; subversion of, 20–21, 118–19, 121, 128, 161, 165
Hoeksema, Thomas B, 43
"Hollywood Shaming Documentaries," 3
Honess Roe, Annabelle, 2, 71, 87
horizon of expectations, 35, 37, 62n19
Horkheimer, Max, 120
horror, 19, 32, 42, 160; fantasy of sadomasochism in, 34; horror of becoming disabled, 35–39; monsters, attractiveness of, 38. *See also Freaks* (Tod Browning, 1932)
Husserl, Edmund, 18, 113, 117
hybrid style, 10, 31, 51, 55, 84–85, 139, 160; and haptic spectator experience, 109, 116, 119–20. *See also Cake* (Daniel Barnz, 2014); *Thumbsucker* (Mike Mills, 2005)

identity category of disability, 12, 44–45, 51, 126; denial/repudiation of, 44, 47–48, 54
"I," disabled, 70
The Imaginary Signifier (Metz), 137
imagination, 1, 21, 44, 52–56, 129–30, 146
incarceration, 56–60
independent films, 9, 11, 30, 31, 44, 55
indexical material: voice-overs, 105, 130–37, 139, 146, 150–52
indexical/realistic representations: of body, 1, 135, 151, 153, 159, 161, 55108; as limited, 1, 55; subjective senses as substitute for, 101; of voice, 4, 22, 87, 105–6, 121
Inside Out (Pete Docter, 2015), 18
insider language, 3, 162
institutions, 57–60, 94n21
internalized ableism, ix, 105, 116
International Documentary Association, 71, 168
intersubjective relations, 4, 21–22; films by able-bodied/able-minded filmmakers disguised as first-person films, 80, 87, 88, 92, 160; and physical closeness, 22, 80, 91; reversibility of, 68–69, 91–92; and touch ethics, 80–86. *See also* embodying spectatorship
"The Intertwining-The Chiasm" (Merleau-Ponty), 19, 112–13
Invalid's Adventures (1907), 16

Ishihara (Yoav Brill, 2010), 98, 101–5, 106, 107, 108; visual certainty in, 109, 120
"It's All the Same Movie" (Sandahl), 3, 41

Jafa, Arthur, 164
Jauss, Hans Robert, 61
Jay, Martin, 100
John and Michael (Shira Avni, 2005), 70, 80–84, 83, 84, 95n24
Jones, CJ, 166

Kafer, Alison, ix, 4, 11
Kant, Immanuel, 18
Kawin, Bruce, 52
Keegan, Cáel M., 33
Kent, Mike, 14
Kim, Christine Sun, 168
Kim, Eunjung, 82
Kirk, Stuart, 76
Kirkpatrick, Bill, 14, 17, 128, 163
Kirn, Walter, 45
Kleege, Georgina, 99
Knick Knack (John Lasseter, 1989), 139
Koch, Gertrud, 6
Kutchins, Herb, 76

Labaye, Benoît, 1, *147*, *148*
Labaye, Mathieu, xi, 1, 135, 146–50, 151
Landreth, Chris, 105
language: American Sign Language, 126–27, 140–42, 151, 161; carnal origins of, 169; and meaning, 113
Leonard Cheshire Disability, 58–60
Levin, Thomas, 127
Lévi-Strauss, Claude, 112
LightHouse for the Blind and Visually Impaired, 165
linearity, challenges to, 3, 48, 141
live-action films, 6–7, 18, 23n2, 160; ableist gaze in, 21, 32–35; about vision impaired or blind people, 98; limitations of, 1–2, 6; move toward animation-like points of view, 21; rejection of, 55. *See also* mainstream genres
live-action techniques used in animation, 109, 127–28
lives worth living, 34, 41, 42, 53, 81, 160

Liz (protagonist, *My Depression*), 139
Longmore, Paul K., 15–16, 36, 40
Loop (Erica Milsom, 2020), 2, 8
Lord, Peter, 56
Lorenzo Hernández, María, 89
low theory, 19, 117, 120
Lutfiyya, Zana Mary, 42
Luxo Jr. (John Lasseter, 1986), 127
Lynch, David, 38, 62n30

Mad Pride movement, viii, 76. *See also* disability rights movement
magical powers, xii, 7, 130, 134–35, 199
mainstream genres, 164; adopting disabled subjectivities in, 51–55; antagonists as disabled, 15–16, 27–28n67, 34, 36; documentary film, 34, 77–78; happy endings for able-bodied spectators, 44–51; subjective points of view and experimental cinematography in, 44; subversion of conventions of, 43–45, 61, 118. *See also* genres; horror; live-action films; melodrama
Manovich, Lev, 5, 89
Many Happy Returns (Marjut Rimminen, 1996), 98, 109, 114, 114–21, *115*; abstract animation style in, 98, 112–13, 119
"The Many in the One: Depression and Multiple Subjectivities in Inside Out" (Markotić), 18
Marianetti, Robert, 77
Marks, Laura U., 6, 20, 119, 152–53, 164
Marshall, Bill, 142–43
Mary and Max (Adam Elliot, 2009), 11
Mask (Peter Bogdanovich, 1985), 2, 30, 32, 34, 39–40, 42, 63n39; erasure of options for living with disability, 54
Matlin, Marlee, xi, 137, 156n55
McLaren, Norman, 145
McRuer, Robert, 4, 11, 17, 40, 82
media studies, 150, 163; cripping the screen, 11–18. *See also* animation studies; film and television studies
medical gaze, 34, 38–39, 43, 45–46; clinical assessment rituals, 108; "fixing" as focus of, 11–12, 118–19; replaced with disabled subjectivity, 31, 52, 55, 79–80

medical/individual model of disability, 7–8, 11–12, 34–35, 48, 101; subversion of, 106–9

melancholia, 51

melodrama, 19, 32, 42, 160; arguments for use of, 43; fantasy of masochism in, 34; paternalistic attitude of pity, 40, 42; soul, disfigurement of, 16, 36

mental disability: antipathological narratives, 71, 75–76, 79; depression, 72–74, 78–80; as narrative prosthesis, 48; psychiatric categorization, challenges to, 73, 76–77; psychiatric diagnostic process, viii, 79; schizophrenia, 75–76, 79. *See also* developmental disabilities

mental space, 53, 65n69

Merleau-Ponty, Maurice, 4, 32, 69–70, 91; sensible body, concept of, 18–19; Works: "The Intertwining-The Chiasm," 19, 112–13; *Phenomenology of Perception*, 18, 119. *See also* phenomenology

Metz, Christian, 127, 137

"middle," sense of, 85, *85*, 86

millennial concerns, 7–9

Million Dollar Baby (Clint Eastwood, 2004), 30, 32, 34, 40–42; disability activist protests against, 40; erasure of options for living with a disability, 47, 54

mimicry, bodily, 19

Mitchell, David T., 17, 31, 34, 42, 68, 92, 108, 118

Monceaux, Dan. See *A Shift in Perception* (Dan Monceaux, 2006)

monstrosity, 34, 42

Montalembert, Hugues de, 113–14, 133

Moore, Samantha, 105–6. *See also An Eyeful of Sound* (Samantha Moore, 2010)

mourning, depathologization of, 51

"Mourning and Melancholia" (Freud), 51

movement: limited by indexical/realistic representation, 1, 55; music used to emphasize, 138; in nonphysical spaces, 131; repetitive, 147–48; social policing of, 146; and sound, 22, 131, 145–50, 151, 161; symbolic, 148–49, *149*; and synesthetic experience for spectator, 144–45, 150–52, 161

Mulvey, Laura, 33

Murphy, Robert F., 82

music, 22, 129, 131, 137–45, 161, 167; anempathetic, 150–51; diegetic, 140–41; and emotions, 131, 137–45, *140–42*; as empathetic tool, 22, 130–31, 138–41, 144, 151, 161–62; as vocal effect, 138. *See also* sound; soundtrack

musical, genre of, 139, 142–43, 167

My Depression: The Up and Down and Up of It (Elizabeth Swados, 2014), 70–72, 77–80; as animated musical documentary, 136, 139, 142–43, 151, 167; graphic novel, 77; music in, 136, 139–43, *140–43*

My Left Foot (Jim Sheridan, 1989), 16, 43

The Near-Sighted Cyclist (1907), 2, 16, 97

Near-Sighted Mary (1909), 97

negligence, medical, 41, 42, 54

neoliberal values, 7–8, 40, 42, 45, 55

Netflix, 9, 168

Neumeyer, David, 137

neurodivergent and neurotypical spectators, 2, 88–90, 92–93. *See also* autism; Down syndrome, collaborative films about

neurotypical, as term, 95n37

Newell, Chris, 14

New Mindset (Danny Capozzi, 2018), 58

nonapparent disabilities, 13, 48–51, 64n53, 69, 78, 80, 109

Norden, Martin F., 16

Nothing about us without us/Nothing Without Us, 40–41, 70, 90, 159–60

Oasis (Lee Chang-dong, 2002), 82

objective-coherent view-perception, 98

object/subject binary, 18, 69, 80

omnipotence, 4, 24n19, 132–36, 145, 151

On Hashish (Benjamin), 116–17

O'Pray, Michael, 24n19, 145

optical unconscious, 100, 107–8, 113

Orgesticulanismus (Mathieu Labaye, 2008), xi, 1, 135, 146–50, *147–49*, 151; closing credits, 149, 151

Orphans of the Storm (D.W. Griffith, 1921), 98

othering, 7, 13, 58, 60

The Other Side of the Mountain, Parts 1 and 2 (Larry Peerce, 1975, 1978), 16

paralysis, films about, 51–55; move from excess able-bodiedness to disability, 41, 54
Park, Nick, 56
Passion Fish (John Sayles, 1992), 16
A Patch of Blue (Guy Green, 1965), 98
paternalistic attitude of pity, 40, 42
patriarchy, 14, 33, 58, 122n8
people with disabilities: alternative values of, 40; bitterness attributed to, 36; "I," disabled, 70; inner-community solidarity, 35, 36, 38; involvement in production process, 60–61; sexuality of, 81–84, *83, 84*; spectators forced into identification with, 37, 51–55
perception, 18; dress debate on Internet, 97, 122n3; organization of senses, 18, 20–21, 119, 128, 132, 153, 166; shift in visual, x–xi, 22, 61, 100, 103–4, 108, 120–21. *See also* synesthesia; visual perception
Petra's Poem (Shira Avni, 2012), 70, 80, 84–86, *85*, 135
phantasmatic body, 138
phantom, sensory, 133, 152, 153–54, 161, 170
pharmaceutical treatment of disability, 45–49, 76–77, 79
phenomenology, xi, 4, 18, 32, 68–70, 91, 166; being as carnal, 112; intersectionality with disability studies, 23, 69, 70, 100, 117; intersubjectivity, approach to, 69, 70; of living with a disability, 20; queer, 117. *See also* Merleau-Ponty, Maurice
Phenomenology of Perception (Merleau-Ponty), 18, 119
philosophy, 1–2; ecofeminist, 58; French thought, 100; postmodern approaches, 11, 157n80. *See also* phenomenology
photography, 107–8, 146; racism in processes of, 163–64
physical ontology, 12, 107
Pilling, Jane, 5
Pixar, 8, 127–28, 139, 165
point-of-view scenes, 31, 32, 43, 48–51. *See also* subjective camera
"positive" life philosophy, 54–55
posthuman, the, 2, 6–7
power relations, 22, 69, 87, 162
Price, Janet, 50, 69, 80, 91, 118

Price, Margaret, xvin12, 2, 64n53
prison or penal abolition, 60
production processes, 22, 105–6; amplifiers and projectors, 150, 162; directors inscribed into films, 90–91, 105–6; embodied, 90–91; and physical interaction of bodies, 91; pleasure in virtuosity of, 145; reflexive, 1, 9, 51, 86–93. *See also* cinematic apparatus
"prosthetic" narratives, 101
psychoanalysis, 19, 100, 108, 137–38
psychorealism, 105
Puar, Jasbir, 13–14
Pyne, Jake, 88–89

queerness, and compulsory heterosexuality, 82
queer phenomenology, 117
queer theory, 11, 59
Quendler, Christian, 52, 53

racism, 41, 163–64
"The Ramblings of a Chronically Ill Mad Trans Femme," 14
A Reader in Animation Studies (ed. Pilling), 5
Reading Autobiography: A Guide for Interpreting Life Narratives (Smith and Watson), 71
reflexive production processes, 1, 9, 51, 86–93
reflexive spectatorship, 10, 43, 87
Renov, Michael, 77
Representing Disability in an Ableist World: Essays on Mass Media (Haller, 2010), 14
Restricted Access: Media, Disability and the Politics of Participation (Ellcessor, 2016), 15
reversibility, 19, 68–69, 91–92, 113
Rhonda (protagonist, *A Shift in Perception*), 110–12
Rimminen, Marjut, 116, 117. *See also Many Happy Returns* (Marjut Rimminen, 1996)
Robinson, Octavian E., 126–27, 144
Rocks in My Pockets (Signe Baumane, 2014), xi, 11, 70, 71, 73, 74; production process, 72–73
Roth, Lorna, 163
Routledge Companion to Disability and Media (2020), 14

Routledge Handbook of Disability Studies (2020), 12
Ruderman Family Foundation, 159–60

Salacia (Tourmaline, 2019), 14
Samuels, Ellen, 4, 48
Sanchez, Rebecca, 140
Sandahl, Carrie, 3, 4, 5, 41, 66–67n91, 162
Sarlin, David, 69
Schalk, Sami, xii, xvin12, 11, 64n53
Schnabel, Julian, 51
Schwartz, Karen, 42
Scully, Jackie Leach, 125–26
self-representation, 22, 80, 87, 90, 92
senses: enhanced by spectatorship, 44, 53, 113, 116, 119, 131, 133; hierarchical order of, 5, 20–21, 98–100, 112, 126, 128, 131–34, 137, 118–19; hierarchy of, 5, 20–21, 98–100, 112, 126, 128, 131–34, 137, 151–54, 161, 164–65, 118–19
sensible body, 18–20, 121
sensoriums, 20, 29n86, 153
sensory overload, portrayal of, 2, 19, 24n8, 171n13
sensual disorientation, 9–10
sentimentality, 42, 43
sexuality and intimacy of people with disabilities, 81–84, 83, 84
shame, 44, 74, 78, 80
Shaun the Sheep Movie (2015), 56
Sheets-Johnson, Maxine, 91
A Shift in Perception (Dan Monceaux, 2006), 98, 109–14, 110, 111, 135–36. See also *An Eyeful of Sound* (Samantha Moore, 2010)
shifts in perception: accessibility for spectators with disabilities, 168–69; visual, x–xi, 22, 61, 100, 103–4, 108, 120–21
Shildrick, Margrit, 50, 69, 80, 81, 91, 118
Shutter Island (Martin Scorsese, 2010), 2
Sight Unseen (Kleege), 99
The Sign for Love (El-Ad Cohen and Iris Ben Moshe, 2017), 89, 144
silence, 112–13
silent film, 16, 97, 120, 128; as deaf cinema, 129–30; introduction of sound criticized, 130, 152

Silverman, Kaja, 127
The Simpsons, 9
Smit, Christopher R., 43
Smith, Sidonie, 71, 75
Snyder, Sharon L., 17, 31, 34, 42, 68, 92, 108, 118
Sobchack, Vivian, xi, 6–7, 19–20, 119, 132, 169
social model of disability, 8, 11–12, 44, 76, 92, 106–7, 126, 166–67
Something Special (CBeebies show), 58
sound: frequencies/vibrations, 128–29, 143–44, 150, 166, 168; hierarchy of, 137–39; and movement, 22, 131, 145–50, 151, 161; as multidirectional, 131; non-vocal-centric films, 126, 140, 144, 161, 167; silent film as deaf cinema, 129–30; technological advances, 127–29; and touch, 128–29, 166. See also D/deaf people; hearing; music; soundtrack; voice; voice-overs
sound effects, 128, 130, 137
sound studies, 127–29
soundtrack, 87; as central to animation, 129; and "deafening" of spectator, 22–23, 126, 130, 151; hierarchical nature of, 137; as political critique, 150; and synesthesia, 22–23, 105, 132–33, 136–37, 140, 161; synesthetic effect on spectator, 22–23, 132, 134, 136–37, 140, 145, 150–51, 152, 161. See also music; voice-overs
South Park, 9, 47
Special (Netflix series, 2019), 95n26
spectacle, disability as, 23, 30–31, 39, 54, 108, 160, 161
spectators: as accomplices in ableism, 39; animating, 5–11; assumption of as temporarily able-bodied, 162–65; "blinding," 98–99, 110; crip subjectivity provided for, 98; "deafening" of, 22–23, 126, 130, 151; with disabilities, 3, 9, 162–67; education of, 3, 7, 10, 162; embodied intelligence of, 20; forced into identification with disabled people, 37, 51–55, 92; neurodivergent and neurotypical, 2, 88–90, 92–93; types of, 7–10
spectatorship: adopting disabled subjectivities, 51–55; alone vs. in community, 3; alternative, 4–6, 10–11,

20–23, 30–31, 43; haptic, 22, 109–19, 121; as intercorporeal, 4–5, 18–19; marginalized/nonmainstream types of viewing, 107–8; multilayered and multisensory experience, 100–101, 121, 126, 140, 152, 166, 168–69; reflexive, 10, 43, 87; senses enhanced by, 44, 53, 113, 116, 119, 131, 133; spectatorship-listenership, 22; synesthetic, 22–23, 132; "universal" or "average" viewer, 3, 90, 163, 167, 169; vision-centric, challenging, 99, 101–9. *See also* ableist gaze; embodying spectatorship

Spencer, Octavia, 159–60, 170n1
Sproxton, David, 56
Stanley, Eric, 88–89
stare, 4–5, 11, 17, 32–33. *See also* gaze
Staring: How We Look (Garland-Thomson), 32
Stawarska, Beata, 91
Sterne, Jonathan, 15
stigmatization, viii, 11, 71, 76, 77, 79–80
Stilwell, Robynn Jeananne, 142–43
Stokoe, William, 127, 141–42
"Studying Disability for a Better Cinema and Media Studies" (Ellcessor and Kirkpatrick), 17
Stump, Madeline, 14
subjective camera, 21, 31–32, 43, 44, 51–53, 55
subjectivities: medical gaze replaced with disabled, 31, 52, 55, 79–80
subjectivity, 160; adopting disabled, 51–55; animation as means of illustrating, 1–2; trans-subjectivity, 87
subversion: of ableist gaze, 31–35, 51, 59, 101, 113, 153, 161, 164–65; of body/soul and object/subject binaries, 18; of connection between deaf studies and the visual, 144; of disability/impairment binary, 12, 108; of hierarchy of senses, 20–21, 118–19, 121, 128, 161, 165; of mainstream conventions, 43–45, 61, 118; medical model critiqued, 106–9; of multilayered response patterns, 121, 166; of racist film conventions, 164; subversive nature of animation, 6–7, 9–10, 23, 31, 59, 61, 101; of trauma, 116; of visual primacy, 105, 110, 121, 151–53, 161
"Surge and Splendor" (Sobchak), 20

surrealism, 7, 39, 100
Swados, Elizabeth, 72, 77–79. *See also My Depression: The Up and Down and Up of It*
synesthesia, 32, 98, 101, 111, 132, 156n43; evoked by movement, 144–45, 150–52, 161; and sound, 132, 134, 136–37, 140, 145, 150–51, 152, 161. *See also* perception

Tabeka, Assaf, 38
Third Body (Zohar Melinek-Ezra and Roey Victoria Heifetz, 2020), 63n31
Thumbsucker (Mike Mills, 2005), 31, 32, 44–48; erasure of options for living with disability, 47, 54
Timmons, Niamh, 14
Tolley, Petra, 84–86
Toolkit for Inclusion and Accessibility: Changing the Narrative of Disability in Documentary Film (Documentary Filmmakers with Disabilities), 168
touch, 161; haptic spectatorship, 22, 109–19, 121; and production process, 92; reversibility of, 68–69, 92; and sound frequencies, 128–29, 143–44, 166; subversion of, 101; and vision disability and blindness experiences, 101
touch ethics, 80, 86, 101, 118–19
tragedy narrative, 11–12, 34, 36, 75, 166
"Transparencies on Film" (Adorno), 120–21
trans studies, 13–14, 33
trans-subjectivity, 87
Trap Door (Gossett, Stanley, and Burton), 88–89
trauma, 41–42, 109, 114, 116–17
Tsang, Hing, 101
Tying Your Own Shoes (*TYOS*, Shira Avni, 2009), 70, 87, 90–93, 106, 135–36

United States National Association of the Deaf, 141

Vehmas, Simo, 12
victimization, narratives of, 75
"villain," as disabled, 15–16
vision: challenging vision-centric spectatorship, 99, 101–9; as constructed,

100–102; hearing, connection with, 129, 131, 140; and hearing as dichotomous, 128–29, 151; privileging of, 21–22, 101, 112–13, 142; technological extensions of, 100. *See also* hierarchy of senses

vision disabilities and blindness, 97–124, 160–61; animation and haptic spectatorship, 22, 109–19, 121; "blinding the spectator," 98–99, 110; blind women used to engage with men's physical disabilities, 39–40, 63n38, 98, 122n8; color blindness, 98, 101–5; dreamlike states in avant-garde animation, 21, 98–99, 101–2, 109–14, 116–17, 119–21, 122n13; gaze of people with, 99, 104; history of films about, 97–98; oedipal narrative, 123n21; social perceptions about, 99, 109–10, 123n21; strabismus, 116

visual primacy, subversion of, 105, 110, 121, 151–53, 161

vococentrism, 137–38, 151–52, 161

voice: concealed source of, 134–35; indexical, 4, 22, 87, 105–6, 121; omnipotence of vocal entity, 132–36, 145, 151

voice-overs, 52, 87, 105–6, 114; acousmêtre, 130–35, 155n34; indexical, 22, 105, 130–37, 139, 146, 150–52; and movement, 146; narration by professional actors, 94n17, 139; as semi-acousmêtre, 130, 132, 135; supernarrator, 149, 161; vococentric, 137–38, 151–52, 161. *See also* soundtrack

voyeuristic gaze, 57–58

Wachtenheim, David, 77
Wait Until Dark (Terence Young, 1967), 98
Waldschmidt, Anna, 12–13
Wallace and Gromit (1989, 1995, 2005, and 2008), 56

Wallace & Gromit: The Curse of the Were-Rabbit (Steve Box and Nick Park, 2005), 138
Ward, Jaime, 106–7, 134, 156n43
Wark, McKenzie, 33
Warner Bros., 138, 139
The Waterdance (Neal Jimenez and Michael Steinberg, 1992), 16
Watson, Julia, 71, 75
Watson, Nick, 12
Webb, Tim, 90, 92. See also *A Is for Autism* (*AIFA*, Tim Webb, 1992)
Wells, Paul, 6
"What My Fingers Knew" (Sobchak), 20
Whittington, William, 127–28, 139
Whose Life Is It Anyway? (John Badham, 1981), 16, 41, 54
Williams, Alan, 127
Williams, Linda, 19
Wolbring, Gregor, 120
women: blind, dehumanization of, 109–10; blind, use of to engage with men's physical disabilities, 39–40, 63n38, 98, 122n8; experiences of discredited, 48; IPV survivors, shelters as institutions for, 57, 58
Wonderstruck (Todd Haynes, 2017), 2
Woodward, James, 131
"The Work of Art in the Age of Mechanical Reproduction" (Benjamin), 7
world, flesh of, 112–13, 118
Wright, Edgar, 2017
"writing back," 75

Young, Paul, 127

Zames, Frieda, 41
zoo gaze, 57
Zootopia (Bryon Howard, Rich Moore, and Jared Bush, 2016), 9, 26n34

SLAVA GREENBERG is a Casden Institute postdoctoral teaching fellow at the University of Southern California's School of Cinematic Arts and Department of Gender and Sexuality Studies. His research explores the potential of mainstream and emerging media forms to offer transformative experiences in reference to disability studies, trans studies, and gender. His articles have appeared in *Film Quarterly, TSQ, Animation, The Moving Image, Journal of Feminist Studies in Religion, Review of Disability Studies,* and *Jewish Film and New Media.* He has also contributed to anthologies on disability and documentary, accent studies, queer television studies, and new media. He is currently writing a second book focusing on the history and visual culture of gender dysphoria through the lens of trans and crip theories.

www.ingramcontent.com/pod-product-compliance
Lightning Source LLC
Chambersburg PA
CBHW031814220426
43662CB00007B/639